"The Editors take a genuinely co
autism field that is often both over
affirmative vibe and deeply embe
will be a valuable addition to an
mental well-being of autistic child

Dr Luke Beardon, *Senior Lecturer in Autism,
University of Sheffield, UK*

"For mental health professionals that are dedicated to supporting autistic children and young people, this is a must-read handbook. With meticulous insight and a compassionate approach, it serves as an invaluable guide, offering practical strategies and nuanced understanding to enhance the therapeutic journey and positive outcomes for autistic individuals. This resource is an indispensable tool for both clinicians and supervisors committed to fostering mental wellbeing within the autistic community."

Freena Tailor, *Anna Freud Clinical Associate in Applied
Psychology and Programme Director for PG Cert
Supervision/PG Dip Senior Wellbeing Practitioner (SWP)
University College London, London, UK*

"This book meets an outstanding need in improving care for autistic children, young people, and their families. It is a rare and desperately needed resource directly aimed at helping clinicians and practitioners working with autistic children and young people to move professionals away from a deficit-based therapeutic model to a partnership approach, with the voice of autistic people guiding this narrative alongside national experts. A hugely important book for all involved in children and young people's service delivery."

Dr Lesley French, *Consultant Clinical Psychologist &
Head of Clinical Help, Anna Freud Schools Division,
Honorary Lecturer, UCL, London, UK*

"A timely and invaluable publication which translates evidence-based mental health research into practical and accessible tools for parents and professionals to inclusively support the celebrated neurodiversity of mental health in autistic children and young people."

Dr Narad Mathura, *MBBS, MSc, FRCPCH, Consultant
Paediatrics & Child Health, Evelina London Children's Community
Services, Guys & St Thomas NHS Foundation Trust*

"In these times of rapid changes, it is crucial to get the best information available, so I can only encourage mental health professionals and, frankly anybody curious about autism today, to read this practical, comprehensive, neuroaffirmative and wonderfully documented book. Thank you!"

Bernadette Grosjean, *M.D. RET- Distinguished Fellow of the American Psychiatric Association Associate Professor of Psychiatry, David Geffen School of Medicine at UCLA, Los Angeles, USA*

"This is an important book written truly in the spirit of co-production that it advocates, with valuable contributions from autistic and neurodiverse professionals and self-advocates. Although the book is written for therapists and other mental health professionals, I found it highly pertinent to my work in paediatric diagnostic services – which is perhaps where autistic and children and young people with other neurodivergencies first encounter health and mental health professionals. Applying the principles covered in this book to the diagnostic process is a valuable opportunity to start these young people and their caregivers on an affirming journey of their diversity. The chapters are highly readable and full of pragmatic ideas that one could use to further enhance the diagnostic and post diagnostic process as a humane, holistic, therapeutic and affirming encounter. This includes ways to improve organizational culture and attitude, clinician competence, communication approaches, setting up the sensory environment and considering the experiences of the extended family (e.g. siblings and caregivers) with all their diversity (neurodiversity, cultural diversity, gender and sexual identify diversity etc.). A deeper understanding of these experiences allows diagnostic clinicians to advise, refer and signpost children, young people and their caregivers effectively."

Dr Ramzi Nasir, *MD MPH Consultant Neurodevelopmental Paediatrician, Imperial College Healthcare NHS Trust, London, UK*

"I thoroughly recommend this excellent book which brings together the perspectives of autistic and non-autistic experts in a highly readable and constructive way in considering the needs of autistic children, young people, and their families. It discounts the deficit model of autism and insists on a collaborative approach to all aspects of the relationships between autistic and non-autistic people. It also provides highly practical, clear advice about the day-to-day experiences of autistic children and their families so that the reader can see how theory translates into very helpful practice."

Dr Peter Fuggle, *AMBIT Consultant and Clinical Director of Clinical Services, Anna Freud, London, UK*

"This magnificently written, breathtakingly comprehensive book is a milestone, offering solid theoretical grounding and practical approaches for making mental health care more accessible to autistic children and young people, while encouraging their autonomy and learning from their insights. The authors are on the front lines of a compassionate transformation in society's understanding of neurodivergent people that is both long overdue and desperately needed."

Steve Silberman, *author of* NeuroTribes: The Legacy of Autism and the Future of Neurodiversity

"There is a growing recognition that in order to be effective therapeutic interventions need to be adapted to meet the specific needs of autistic people. What is currently lacking is guidance for clinicians on how to achieve this in practice. Finally, we have a book that fills this gap. It offers both rich theoretical underpinnings that explain why adaptations are required and practical advice on what changes are needed across different settings and therapeutic modalities. Voice of autistic people can be heard loud and clear throughout the text to ensure that authenticity and respect towards the autistic community remain central to any therapeutic work."

Dr Anna Rebowska, *Consultant Child and Adolescent Psychiatrist*

"There is an urgent need to develop mental health work with autistic children and young people and their families: to make it more empowering, accessible, and effective. This treasure trove of insights, understandings, and practical guidance is a wonderful means of addressing that gap: developing evidence based practices that put the client – in all their complexity, agency, and humanity – at the heart of the work."

Mick Cooper, *Professor of Counselling Psychology, University of Roehampton*

Improving Mental Health Therapies for Autistic Children and Young People

This unique, collaborative book, featuring contributions from autistic and non-autistic experts, presents cutting-edge thinking on mental health and service transformation in relation to autistic children and young people (CYP) and their families.

Investigating how to implement collaborative approaches to supporting autistic CYP's mental health, this book considers ways for professionals to share power and co-design models of support, promoting self-agency and supportive environments for autistic acceptance and well-being. Each chapter includes reflections and vignettes from autistic CYP and allies, key questions, and thinking points for readers to consider. The book also includes a link for an e-library with multimedia material with the top take aways for clinicians such as animations, flyers, and recorded interviews.

The book will be of immense interest to individuals working with autistic CYP and their families in mental health at any level.

Georgia Pavlopoulou is Associate Professor at University College London, psychotherapist, Director and Co-strategic Lead of the NHS-funded National Autism Trainer Programme at Anna Freud and founder of UCL's Group for Research in Relationships And Neurodiversity-GRRAND.

Laura Crane is Professor of Autism Studies at the University of Birmingham, where she is Director of the Autism Centre for Education and Research (ACER).

Russell Hurn is a Chartered Counselling Psychologist and Programme Director for the CYP IAPT Programme at Anna Freud. He specialises in trauma and is an EMDR consultant/supervisor.

Damian Milton works part-time for the University of Kent as Senior Lecturer in Intellectual and Developmental Disabilities.

Anna Freud: Key Ideas and Best Practice
Series Editors: Chloe Campbell & Elizabeth Allison

The Anna Freud centre has long been a centre of both research and clinical innovation. Each book in the Routledge/AFC series explores a different area of cutting-edge thinking in mental health and its treatment, with a strong but not exclusive focus on children and families. Accessible and clearly written, these books will range from clinical practice through to research and implementation issues, and will be of interest to a wide audience of those concerned with mental health and the latest thinking on prevention and treatment as well understanding more about the experience of psychological difficulties and their development.

Titles in the series:

High-Conflict Parenting Post-Separation
The Making and Breaking of Family Ties
By Eia Asen, Emma Morris

Improving Mental Health Therapies for Autistic Children and Young People
Promoting Self-agency, Curiosity and Collaboration
Edited by Georgia Pavlopoulou, Laura Crane, Russell Hurn and Damian Milton

For more information about this series please visit: https://www.routledge.com/The-Anna-Freud-National-Centre-for-Children-and-Families/book-series/AFNCCFBP

Improving Mental Health Therapies for Autistic Children and Young People

Promoting Self-agency, Curiosity and Collaboration

Edited by Georgia Pavlopoulou

With Laura Crane, Russell Hurn and Damian Milton
Foreword by Peter Fonagy

Routledge
Taylor & Francis Group

LONDON AND NEW YORK

Designed cover image: Getty Images

First published 2025
by Routledge
4 Park Square, Milton Park, Abingdon, Oxon OX14 4RN

and by Routledge
605 Third Avenue, New York, NY 10158

Routledge is an imprint of the Taylor & Francis Group, an informa business

British Library Cataloguing-in-Publication Data
A catalogue record for this book is available from the British Library

Library of Congress Cataloging-in-Publication Data
Names: Pavlopoulou, Georgia, editor. | Crane, Laura (Laura May), editor. | Hurn, Russell, editor. | Milton, Damian, editor. | Anna Freud National Centre for Children and Families. Best practice.
Title: Improving mental health therapies for autistic children and young people: promoting self-agency, curiosity and collaboration / edited by Dr Georgia Pavlopoulou; with Dr Laura Crane, Dr Russell Hurn, Dr Damian Milton; foreword by Peter Fonagy.
Description: Abingdon, Oxon; New York, NY: Routledge, 2025. | Series: Anna Freud: key ideas and best practice | Includes bibliographical references and index. |
LCCN 2024028248 (print) | LCCN 2024028249 (ebook) | ISBN 9781032402840 (hardback) | ISBN 9781032372525 (paperback) | ISBN 9781003352327 (ebook)
Subjects: MESH: Autism Spectrum Disorder—therapy | Child | Adolescent
Classification: LCC RJ506.A9 (print) | LCC RJ506.A9 (ebook) | NLM WS 350.8.P4 | DDC 618.92/85882—dc23/eng/20240723
LC record available at https://lccn.loc.gov/2024028248
LC ebook record available at https://lccn.loc.gov/2024028249

ISBN: 978-1-032-40284-0 (hbk)
ISBN: 978-1-032-37252-5 (pbk)
ISBN: 978-1-003-35232-7 (ebk)

DOI: 10.4324/9781003352327

Typeset in Times New Roman
by codeMantra

Printed and bound in Great Britain by Bell and Bain ltd, Glasgow

For my parents – Ευγενία Καραβοκύρη και Κωνσταντίνο Παυλόπουλο who infused me with the ideas of agency, curiosity, and collaboration. I love you.

Για τους γονείς μου- Ευγενία Καραβοκύρη και Κωνσταντίνο Παυλόπουλο που με εμφύσησαν με τις ιδέες της αυτενέργειας, της περιέργειας και της συνεργασίας. Σας αγαπώ.

In memory of Freideriki K., an autistic young woman with learning disability, who suffered a premature and preventable death at the age of 17 with very limited access to timely and sensitive community support. She should be here with us.

To Stefan, a 15 year old autistic young man who left this world as he didn't know how to stay in a world which didn't accept him.

Contents

Foreword

by **Peter Fonagy** OBE, FBA, FAcSS, FMedSci
Head of the Division of Psychology and
Language Sciences at University College London;
Chief Executive of the Anna Freud

This book represents extraordinary progress in the evolution of mental health support tailored for autistic children and young people. The Anna Freud Centre has long been renowned for its integration of thorough academic research with clinical expertise to advance best practices. By adding to our continuous effort to reshape mental health care, this volume introduces a collaborative, sensitive-to-experience, and values-oriented approach. This approach moves practitioners to pay attention to the individual's experiences and needs in the context of their own lives. Therefore, it can improve the poor experiences of autistic people accessing mental health care, something which is an urgent need given the disproportionately high incidence of mental health difficulties and suicidality (McGreevy et al., 2024). It offers a broad and inventive array of ideas, experiences, recommendations and insights, encouraging professionals to reflect on their approach to working with neurodivergent individuals. Some sections of the material are profoundly moving and challenging to confront. The frankness with which some contributors share their personal or their children's neurodivergent experiences, particularly the shortcomings encountered by those expected to offer support, is startling. It's a stark reminder that, too often, we look back on the past as a time of harsh, careless and uninformed practices – for instance, the harshly judgemental "refrigerator mother" theory that was widespread in the 1950s. It's a sobering realisation that today, autistic children and young people still face harmful and counterproductive mental health support.

A central theme revisited in this book is the concept of the double empathy problem – the powerful idea that interactions between autistic and neurotypical individuals are marked by mutual, two-way challenges in understanding (Milton, 2012). This perspective challenges the conventional focus on the autistic individual's difficulties in empathising with others, highlighting that neurotypical people also struggle to understand their autistic counterparts. Such a dynamic can lead to a detrimental cycle of miscommunication and estrangement. Escaping the pain of being misunderstood through isolation is not just understandable; it is also likely to be an effective strategy.

It has been previously discussed that trauma can emerge when a distressing or adverse event is coupled with the sensation of isolation. The ability to share perspectives with another person can help to mitigate and reframe an otherwise intimidating experience (Fonagy et al., 2017). The double empathy problem almost guarantees that autistic individuals experience a profound sense of isolation. The autistic individual is made vulnerable to the traumatogenic potential of even mild adversity by their isolation. Many of the behaviours and responses labelled as "challenging behaviour" could be reinterpreted as characteristics of an individual who has experienced severe trauma such as the necessity for stability and predictability to counterbalance the disarray caused by a deep-seated fear of being alone and/or othered.

One of the book's major contributions is its effective dismantling of the misconception that autistic individuals lack interest in forming relationships. On the contrary, the authors vividly illustrate how autistic people often seek connection with others but are hindered by the barriers imposed by the double empathy problem. The recounting of these painful experiences is a recurring theme, presenting a challenge for mental health professionals who might find it uncomfortable to confront the shortcomings or lack of understanding in their practice. I strongly encourage all those involved in child and adolescent mental health care to engage with this content. It is crucial for anyone working with autistic individuals, offering profound insights that can transform our approach and enhance our empathy and effectiveness. As psychological clinicians, we are committed to understand and respect other minds even if they seem to work differently from ours. Reading this book forces reflection and a realisation that sometimes our appreciation of difference falls far short of what is required and our self-delusion and the pretence of understanding can force our communication partner to draw a veil over their experience at some cost to themselves.

There is much for most of us to learn about the autistic experience and important learning leading to real systemic change CAN start here, with this excellent book.

References

Fonagy, P., & Campbell, C. J. P. H. (2017). Mentalizing, attachment and epistemic trust: how psychotherapy can promote resilience. *Psychiatria Hungarica*, *32*(3), 283–287.

Milton, D. E. (2012). On the ontological status of autism: The 'double empathy problem'. *Disability & Society*, *27*(6), 883–887.

Preface

Autistic individuals receiving mental health care for anxiety, depression, and/ or trauma must be supported by people who understand sensory and communication differences, legislation, and the duty to make reasonable adjustments. However, hundreds of autistic people are currently in mental health hospitals in England, often subject to seclusion, over-medication, and unnecessary restraint.

Despite the best intentions of staff, there is often a lack of collaborative, experience-sensitive, and value-based work. Services may rely on behavioural narratives that focus on deficits and impose rules and systems made by non-autistic people. In many cases, staff are not aware of environmental triggers that might impact autistic people's mental health such as sensory differences. This is a key contributor to the premature and preventable deaths of autistic people.

There is a need to encourage understanding of non-autistic people and cultures rather than teaching how to poorly mimic non-autistic ways of being. This is a key strategy to reduce stress in autistic individuals.

Teams often misinterpret autism-friendly strategies or make assumptions about which strategies or techniques might be useful for an autistic person without directly asking them to use multimodal communication. Behaviours of distress are often characterised as challenging, leading to reactive, restrictive management, which is dangerous for all. In many cases, this can be traumatic or re-trigger trauma responses for autistic individuals such as masking.

This book has been inspired by the training efforts I co-lead at Anna Freud with autistic individuals. I began testing out ideas that would eventually evolve into the National Autism Trainer Programme back in 2018. While it may not always be easy, synergies with autistic people have been necessary if we truly want to rewrite the narrative that sees autism as a set of deficits. In 2018, I began working at Anna Freud, co-designing, and co-delivering the Children and Young People's Psychological Trainings curricula with teams of autistic individuals of all ages and clinicians. Through this experience, I witnessed the barriers, opportunities, and benefits of placing autistic individuals at the heart of planning and implementation. The mental health experiences of autistic individuals must be shared with our trainees if we aim to improve local mental health services. Trainees must be aware of stressors, autistic burnout, alexithymia, factors that contribute to autistic happiness, and how to collaborate with autistic individuals in therapy rather than working on or for them. By working together, we maximise the chances of finding ways to enhance the mental health of autistic individuals by collaborating with them and focusing on aspects that matter to them in their preferred ways.

In 2022, I co-led a team that piloted the National Autism Trainer Programme (NATP) at Anna Freud. Commissioned by NHS England, the NATP aims to support staff in enhancing the care provided to autistic individuals within mental health services. Crucially, it is designed as a model that can be implemented within your own NHS Trust to facilitate training with your colleagues, supported by our team. Currently, the training is being rolled out across five different NHS strands and one educational strand for residential special schools and colleges. The training aims to inform practice by examining perceptions of autism, offering insights and practical strategies drawn from autistic and trauma-informed experiences while acknowledging the challenges faced by autistic individuals and staff working across different settings. It is delivered in partnership with AT-Autism.

The question that has driven my work for many years and underpins the ideas of our training efforts is: "How do we transition from 'fixing' autistic individuals to fostering shared power and embracing a more democratic approach to mental health support?" It is widely acknowledged by autistic individuals, their parents, caregivers, and clinicians that children and young autistic individuals often do not receive the psychological support they deserve.

This is due to a lack of training among those delivering evidence-based therapies in adapting their approaches for individuals with autism and/or learning disabilities. Conversely, those with extensive experience working with these groups may lack training in evidence-based therapeutic methods. How can we ensure that everyone is actively engaged and learning from each other?

The training programmes I co-run at Anna Freud aim to address these challenges by helping mental health staff understand and meet the needs of autistic and other neurodivergent patients. Our approach goes beyond mere knowledge transfer; it provides opportunities for staff to share vulnerabilities and concerns and encourages them to reframe their understanding of how their behaviour impacts their interactions with autistic individuals.

Collaborative practices aiming at improving mental health for autistic children and their families are central to our training programme. A primary objective of the book is to provide readers with a framework for promoting self-agency among autistic individuals, along with a range of techniques and ideas for nurturing this agency. All co-authors emphasise the importance of creating supportive environments that foster autistic acceptance and well-being. The involvement of autistic authors and editors was crucial in ensuring that innovations in practice draw on collaborative work with autistic individuals and their families, rather than relying on assumptions about them. This approach has been a dominant theme throughout my professional and research career. This principle of collaboration signifies mutual respect and appreciation for individual skills and lived experiences – a key theme of our book. I am grateful for all the opportunities I have had so far to work with autistic people and amplify their voices. I am also very proud of working with tireless autistic advocates to co-create, at Anna Freud, a space for all to negotiate, grow, and actively listen to each other.

This book offers a humanising approach, setting it apart from many others that primarily focus on the clinical features of autism and corresponding responses. Instead, this book aims to summarise autistic perspectives and experiences on service improvement. It explores ways for professionals at all career stages to shift from a mindset of "fixing" to one of sharing power and co-designing models of support.

I am delighted to have had the opportunity to collaborate with Dr Russell Hurn, Dr Damian Milton, Professor Laura Crane, our Young Champions, and several autistic and non-autistic experts by experience and science to record some of the key ideas that shape Anna Freud Centre's best practices in autistic mental health.

A key question addressed by this book is: How can we implement collaborative approaches to support the mental health of autistic children and young people (CYP) in neuro-inclusive services? Specifically, the book aims to move beyond a deficit model when working with autistic CYP and their families within educational and healthcare systems.

The book will offer practical tips for improving mutuality in therapy and establishing support networks for autistic CYP and their families. Emphasising **partnership and involvement**, these strategies are informed by clinical, empirical, and theoretical understandings that recognise the fundamental significance of agency and selfhood in promoting recovery.

Throughout the book, contributions from autistic children and adults are interwoven, presenting ideas that challenge conventional perspectives on autism and autistic mental health. By involving autistic children and their families in the process, the book offers a transformative approach to how therapists conceptualise and engage with autism.

The importance of fostering a **neuro-inclusive service culture** based on acceptance and learning from autistic people's experiences will be discussed, particularly in the context of supervision. The book will describe a model of supervision that considers how both autistic and non-autistic individuals mentalise and predict each other, aiming to help professionals maintain their capacity for critical thinking and continuous learning in their work.

To avoid mechanistic and ableist formulations, the consideration of therapy outcomes must inherently involve reflecting on the needs, contexts, and perspectives of autistic individuals. This concept circles back to the central theme introduced at the beginning of the book – the recognition of the agency and selfhood of autistic people and their families in therapy is paramount.

Throughout this collaborative journey, I had the privilege of sharpening our book proposal by listening to the insights of young advisors who provided clear direction on our objectives for the book. Some of these young individuals also eagerly offered feedback at various stages, including the final draft of our manuscript. Their input, alongside that of Russ, Laura, and Damian, helped us define the necessary space for effective collaborative working relationships to form and develop.

Furthermore, their contributions informed approaches that delineate the underlying processes and guiding beliefs of a system designed to support autistic individuals. We were honoured to co-author the final chapter of the book with young people who expressed a keen interest in becoming co-authors. Others made comments and preferred to stay anonymous. Some of them agreed for their anonymised blurbs to be published here.

People who will read this book should try to not be too loud with us and to be nice. We have enough stress in everyday life. If you want to help us, make us feel safe and connected. We have enough worries about disappointing everyone around us and feeling disconnected, trying to fit in constantly. If we feel it's not getting well with the people who are around to help us, we will lose all hope. Then, ask people to read this book to understand a little bit more about what it is like to be autistic and interact with professionals. Many autistic people gathered to write this book. Oh, and next time they meet someone like me … or even me, please believe me. Listen to me even when I can't use my words to tell you what I am going through.

10-year-old autistic human with a diagnosis of autism and ADHD also known as Sloth

This book aims to provide insight into the experiences of neurodivergent young people facing mental health challenges and the support they receive. It challenges traditional approaches that may not fully value the individuality of the young person or positively impact their engagement with support services. There is hope that professionals can improve their practice to create a more supportive environment where young people feel empowered to take care of themselves.

In the past, therapy and mental health services have often been perceived negatively, even frightening, for many of us. However, from personal experience and the experiences of others, I know the difference it can make to feel valued and at the centre of clinical work. Simple gestures, like showing interest in our hobbies or providing the tools we need, can help us feel comfortable opening up honestly, setting goals, and working towards them. It's important for interactions to feel less clinical and more like a collaborative discussion, where we can take on a leading role.

My greatest hope is that professionals will implement the insights from this book and be inspired to make their positive changes and adaptations. While this book may not capture everything or everyone's experiences, it serves as a starting point. Often, the smallest gestures, such as genuine kindness and being well-informed, can have a significant impact on everyday life.

21-year old autistic advisor.

To further support readers' engagement with autistic narratives about autistic mental health we have co-created animation videos that cover the following topics: communication, senses, the eight dimensions of an experience-sensitive approach, double empathy problem, monotropism, the five elements of the SPELL framework, reasonable adjustments, safety in predictability, siblings, low mood and depression, victimisation, and trauma.

These were funded by an anonymous funder via the School Division at Anna Freud and are also featured in the National Autism Trainer Programme e-library.

Please visit link below to access the videos:

https://drive.google.com/drive/folders/1C3W_9nY5ftrqcuMzFU7xJ4e3hBF KsokU?usp=drive_link

Acknowledgements

I am deeply grateful to the many individuals who have contributed to the ideas expressed in this book. This includes the diverse cohorts of trainees and delegates I have had the privilege of training over the years, spanning across NHS, education, UCL programs, and autistic individuals from around the world. A special thanks goes to Chloe Campbell and my good colleague Dora Kokosi for their invaluable and unwavering support in preparing the manuscript. Their sharp insights and tireless dedication ensured that this book remains true to the preferences and needs of the neurodivergent creators who contributed to this project.

I would like to extend my gratitude to the remarkable individuals with whom I have engaged in fascinating discussions about mental health. Special thanks to Claire Evans, Irina Neldecu, Hasan Wazir, Peter Fuggle, Cos Michael, Karolina Sauciunaite, Ann Memmott, Christina Malamateniou, Richard Mills, Zachary Walker, Chris Papadopoulos, Anna Stenning, Nick Midgley, A 2nd Voice, Mask Off, Edmund Sonuga Barke, Sylvan Baker and the RE-STAR team, Myrto Kakoulidou from UCL's Group for Research in Relationships And NeuroDiversity (GRRAND), and everyone at the National Autism Trainer Programme (NATP). Your insights and discussions have been a continuous source of inspiration for many of the ideas expressed in this book. I am also indebted to the authors who contributed with love and passion, illuminating ways in which we can strive for neuro-affirming and neuro-inclusive practice.

Foteini, my sister, you are my witness and my support. We need to travel together again soon.

Mark Devonport, I love you and I could only do this (and anything else) with you by my side.

Georgia Pavlopoulou, PhD
Little Venice, London 2024

Contributors

Jon Adams is a freelance British artist, autistic advocate, trauma researcher, and expert consultant for AT-Autism. He also works as Research Associate at the Strathclyde Institute of Education. Jon's research includes work on autistic peer participation, inertia, suicidality, belonging, trauma, mental health, and creativity. He is also interested in solving barriers to inclusion for both the arts and research participants, creatives, and audiences.

Julia Avnon is a child and adolescent psychologist with 20 years of experience in working with children and young people with a variety of psychological, neurological, and neurodevelopmental differences, including autism, ADHD, complex epilepsy, and learning disability. Julia is also a clinical tutor at Anna Freud.

Vanessa Bobb is the mother of three young adults between the ages of 17 and 22 years old, and the two youngest have a diagnosis of autism and ADHD. Vanessa is the founder of A2ndvoice, an autistic speaker, a content developer at the Anna Freud, and an AT-Autism Associate.

Tiegan Boyen is an independent researcher, public speaker, content developer, and author. She advocates based on her personal experiences and reflections of being neurodivergent and an adoptee. She is co-researcher at RE-STAR, Regulating Emotions – Strengthening Adolescent Resilience (RE-STAR) project at King's College London.

Laura Crane is Professor of Autism Studies at the University of Birmingham, where she is Director of the Autism Centre for Education and Research (ACER).

Mairi Evans is Systemic Psychotherapist, Clinical Director, and Neurodiversity Lead. She has worked across several contexts including Child and Adult Mental Health, Social Care, and Neurodevelopmental Services. Mairi's doctoral research focused on autism diagnosis, mothers, and girls. She is informed by both her lived, and her professional, experience.

Nikita K. Hayden is Research Associate in iHuman and the School of Education at the University of Sheffield, England. Nikita's research includes a focus on families, including child and adult siblings of people with intellectual (learning) and developmental disabilities. Nikita is a volunteer research associate for the UK charity Sibs and is a sibling herself.

Russell Hurn is Chartered Counselling Psychologist and Programme Director for the CYP IAPT Programme at Anna Freud. Russell has spent 20 years working in child and adolescent mental health in the NHS, voluntary sector, and private practice. He specialises in trauma and is an EMDR consultant/supervisor.

Clare Kassa joined Sibs as CEO in 2018. Clare has worked in the voluntary sector supporting disabled children, siblings, and adults and their families for over 25 years. Clare is a sibling herself; she has an older brother with a learning disability.

Ellie Kollatsi has worked in inner city London, mainly in mainstream educational settings offering therapeutic and emotional support to children, young people, and families from diverse backgrounds. Her interests are in reducing the stigma and isolation of autistic and neurodivergent people in the Greek and Greek Cypriot community.

Roslyn Law is a consultant clinical psychologist, who specialises in Interpersonal Psychotherapy, which she uses as a clinician, supervisor, and trainer working internationally and across the lifespan. She leads on workforce development training for professionals working with children, adolescents and adults in health, education, and community settings.

Virginia Lumsden is a consultant clinical psychologist with a clinical leadership role in the NHS focusing on how schools can support the emotional well-being and mental health of all children and young people. She is Associate Clinical Tutor and honorary Clinical Lecturer at University College London and Research Supervisor at Salomons Centre for Applied Psychology.

Maciej Matejko is an autistic EFL (English as a Foreign Language) teacher and independent autism researcher/research advisor, who is passionate about working with autistic people and helping make the science relevant. Maciej is also a member of the Youth Researcher Panel, as part of the Regulating Emotions – Strengthening Adolescent Resilience (RE-STAR) project at King's College London.

Lucy Matthews is a late-diagnosed autistic, cis woman, and proud lesbian. She has lived experience of long-term mental health problems, including anxiety, self-harm, and suicidal ideation. She is passionate about getting involved in projects where her experience may help others.

Andy McDonnell is a consultant clinical psychologist and Director of Studio III Clinical Services, as well as Visiting Professor of Autism Studies at Birmingham City University. Andy is the originator of the Low Arousal Approach, a method for managing distressed behaviour and reducing environmental stress. Andy is passionate about not only reducing the use of restrictive practices but also eliminating them from caring environments.

Ann Memmott is an autistic Research Consultant, blogger, trainer, and adviser. With more than three decades of experience in the field of autism, Ann's skills in a wide range of healthcare, charitable, Government-level, and general organisations have been well received.

Richard Mills is an autism researcher and practitioner who holds several roles, including Associate Consultant at AT-Autism, UK; Visiting Professor at Taisho University, Japan; Honorary Research Fellow, at the University of Bath, UK; and Senior Research Fellow at Bond University, Australia. For 25 years, Richard was Director of Services, and later Director of Research at the National Autistic Society, UK.

Damian Milton works part-time for the University of Kent as Senior Lecturer in Intellectual and Developmental Disabilities.

Ruth Moyse is Director and Associate Consultant at AT-Autism and Visiting Research Fellow in the Department of Psychology at the University of Southampton. A teacher by profession, her research interests are mental health and the experiences of autistic children and young people in mainstream schools.

Georgia Pavlopoulou is Associate Professor at University College London, a psychotherapist, Director and Co-strategic Lead of the NHS-funded National Autism Trainer Programme at Anna Freud, and founder of UCL's Group for Research in Relationships And Neurodiversity-GRRAND. Georgia's focus is closing the gap in educational and health professionals' skills using creative and co-produced methodologies.

Amy Pearson is Assistant Professor at the University of Durham and Autistic Autism Researcher at the Centre for Neurodiversity and Development. She is also Associate at UCL's Group for Research in Relationships And NeuroDiversity (GRRAND). Her work focuses on understanding the impact of interpersonal victimisation among autistic people and the relationship between autistic identity, masking, and stigma.

Prithvi Perepa is Associate Professor at the University of Birmingham, based within the Autism Centre for Education and Research (ACER). His research interests include family experiences, intersectionality of autism and culture, and developing good educational provision. He has authored books and journal articles focusing on some of these themes including a book titled *Autism, Ethnicity, and Culture*.

Alexis Quinn was a schoolteacher for over ten years, is a former professional athlete, and is the author of two books: her ground-breaking memoir *Unbroken*, as well as *Autistic and Expecting*, a guide for autistic parents to be. Alexis now works as Manager of the Restraint Reduction Network, is Associate at the National Autism Trainer Programme, and is also pursuing an MSc in Psychotherapy at the University of Greenwich.

Kieran Rose is an autistic consultant and trainer to organisations worldwide. He is a published academic researcher specialising in autistic masking and content creator for the NHS-funded National Autism Trainer program (NATP). He is also the co-author of the ground-breaking book: *Autistic Masking: Understanding Identity Management and the Role of Stigma*. Kieran was diagnosed as autistic in 2003 and has three autistic children.

Suzy Rowland is a late-diagnosed ADHD, and a mother of two, one of whom is ADHD and autistic. She is a best-selling author, with her books helping thousands of families educate autistic and ADHD young people. Suzy is a qualified Cognitive Behavioural Practitioner, and she founded the #happyinschool project in 2018, delivering bespoke neurodiversity training, consultancy, and public speaking, rooted in lived experience.

Introduction

This book is structured into five interconnected sections, each of which was co-produced with a group of young people by the lead editor. Subsequently, co-authors were invited to respond to the aims and objectives of each section, sharing their own lived experiences.

Every chapter of this book is a result of co-creation with lived experience experts, many of whom also hold positions as scientific directors, researchers, and academics in autistic mental health, and have contributed to the National Autism Trainer Programme. This collaborative effort ensures that this book amplifies autistic narratives and reframes negative or limiting perceptions of the autistic community.

Section 1: Overview: integrating autistic understanding for better delivery of evidence-based mental health interventions

In this section, we introduce readers to various theoretical models that have been used to conceptualise autism. We contrast traditional medical models of autism, which view autism as a disorder requiring cure and remediation, with more contemporary social models that recognise autistic individuals as being disabled by societal barriers rather than their inherent characteristics. We provide examples illustrating how adhering to a medical model perspective and receiving interventions aligned with it could have detrimental effects on the mental health of autistic children and young people (CYP).

Central to these discussions is the focus on the dynamic between service users and therapists. Drawing upon the concept of the 'double empathy problem,' we explore how autistic CYP may encounter difficulties in understanding and empathising with non-autistic professionals, and vice versa. We advocate for an experience-sensitive approach that prioritises the lived experiences of young people, moving away from narratives centred solely on behaviour. This approach enables scientist-practitioners to better understand and address autistic individuals' perceived needs, leading to greater real-life impact in areas chosen by the individuals themselves.

DOI: 10.4324/9781003352327-1

We stress the urgent need for change and seek to demystify what change entails by highlighting examples of good practice, such as validating lived experiences and providing sensory accommodations. Readers are encouraged to ensure that the workforce is well-informed about both autism and mental health difficulties, with a deep understanding of the unique challenges faced by young autistic individuals with mental health problems, and a genuine commitment to their well-being.

To facilitate reflection, we include vignettes of autistic young people sharing their experiences of accessing mental health services through CAMHS. These vignettes shed light on issues related to accessibility, engagement, help-seeking behaviours, and relationships with professionals.

A core objective of this section is to underscore the importance of agency in facilitating psychological understanding collaboratively, democratically, and without pathologising. We reflect on the profound impact of lacking agency, not only hindering recovery but also potentially leading to new challenges and conditions. The chapter aims to empower practitioners to reflect on their capacity to enhance agency in everyday practice, employing a neurodiversity-affirmative perspective.

Section 2: Overview: understanding autistic mental health

In this section, our aim is to enhance understanding of anxiety, depression, and trauma in autistic CYP. We begin by exploring the concept of 'intolerance' and the role of both certainty and uncertainty in the lives of autistic CYP, reframing these notions to better support their needs. We delve into the school environment to identify daily uncertainties for autistic CYP and examine the impact of unpredictability on their anxiety levels, juxtaposed with the expectation for them to self-regulate their emotions. Clinicians are encouraged to adopt a curious stance toward the causes of uncertainty and to consider how viewing uncertainty through an autistic lens may alter the support provided to autistic CYP. We offer three key suggestions for professionals seeking to reframe intolerance of uncertainty into safety in predictability.

Furthermore, we emphasise the importance of understanding the physiological and neurological functioning of aι ιistic bodies, as well as the specific psycho-social factors and environments that affect autistic CYP. This understanding is crucial in discerning the underlying causes of the high prevalence of low mood, shutdowns, and burnout experienced by this group. Too often, autistic CYP are unfairly blamed for their experiences, with issues centred within them and assumptions made about their ability to exert influence over narratives beyond their control. We discuss therapeutic approaches to interpreting these experiences and explore how therapists can validate, contextualise, and navigate these ideas within the framework of their therapy modality.

Additionally, we underscore the importance of adopting a trauma-informed approach when working with autistic individuals, shifting from viewing trauma as a diagnostic label to understanding the experiences that have occurred. It is essential not only to be informed about general principles of trauma but also to understand the individual's specific experiences. Chapter 6 will delve into painful experiences (trigger warnings), sensitising readers to the significance of trauma-informed care.

Section 3: Overview: Autism, gender, and ethnicity

Gender non-conformity and diverse sexual identities are prevalent within the autistic population, with autism being common among these groups. Individuals with multiple minority identities may face significant marginalisation, potentially leading to active discrimination. Moreover, LGBTQIA+ individuals are more susceptible to mental health problems. It is imperative for therapists working with these communities to be aware of and sensitive to these diverse identities. To support readers in understanding this critical topic, we include case studies highlighting various experiences.

Autistic CYP from global majority ethnic backgrounds who experience mental health difficulties may encounter specific challenges in receiving a mental health diagnosis and accessing appropriate services. In this chapter, authors employ a blend of identity-first and person-first language to reflect the preferences of CYP with multiple identities. These individuals may prioritise other aspects of their identity, such as ethnicity, religion, or sexuality, over their autistic identity, considering them to be more prominent and significant.

Section 4: Overview: working in partnership with autistic CYP and their families

In this section, we underscore the significance of adopting a holistic and collaborative approach to mental health care. Autistic CYP, with or without learning disabilities, often exhibit behaviours of concern. Traditional support models tend to view these behaviours as deficits within the child and prioritise addressing the behaviour and its functions. We introduce readers to a low arousal approach, emphasising shared responsibility between clinicians and autistic CYP. This approach encourages reflection on our own behaviour and interactions with the child, aiming to provide the right level of environmental support to foster positive behaviours. Key aspects for practitioners to consider in home and school environments are outlined, along with practical recommendations for practice.

Furthermore, we advocate for the involvement of all family members in supporting autistic CYP, including siblings. Despite the importance of siblings' involvement, clinicians often neglect to provide guidance on meeting siblings' needs and fail to recognise the expertise and positive contributions they bring. Readers will gain insights into the experiences of siblings, enabling mental health and school professionals to offer appropriate and proactive support.

Autistic young people may face heightened levels of school exclusion and daily challenges in the school environment, potentially leading to severe behaviours of concern. However, this does not have to be the norm. We explore strategies for working with schools, focusing on a method for addressing behaviours of concern that centres on teacher character, mindset, well-being, influences, and actions. This approach supports teachers and school staff, both individually and as a group, to understand and focus on factors within their control. By fostering reflection, examining impressions and narratives, and devising realistic plans for response, teachers can shift from emotional to rational reactions and develop proactive and reactive strategies to regulate their own behaviour and model regulation to students.

Section 5: Overview: developing curiosity in service delivery and service transformation

In this section, our aim is to present ideas on how engaging with autistic individuals and narratives led by autistic voices can enhance our collective learning journey, ultimately fostering a shared understanding of the situation. We illustrate this concept through an example featuring two authors – one autistic and one not – who found common ground by embracing discomfort and recognising their mutual similarities. They describe creating a safe space where they can authentically share vulnerabilities as they navigate uncharted territory together.

Additionally, a clinician with over 20 years of experience in Child and Adolescent Mental Health Services (CAMHS), who is also a parent to two neurodivergent children, explores the evolving awareness of autism within CAMHS over time. They discuss the increasing number of autistic children accessing specialist CAMHS services and invite readers to contemplate current CAMHS commissioning structures and how they can evolve to better serve autistic children.

Throughout this book, we have integrated perspectives from academics, therapists, service users, and the neurodivergent community to examine the current landscape of mental health provision and explore innovative approaches to working with and understanding the needs of autistic CYP, and their families. Drawing from autistic-led theories like the double empathy model and the diverse experiences of all stakeholders, the final chapter synthesises key themes discussed in preceding chapters. We propose a model of neuro-affirming and neurodiversity-informed practice and service delivery, aiming to provide a framework for personal and service reflection to enhance mental health support for autistic children, young people, and their families. While this chapter may not address every reader's question or concern, we hope it serves as a catalyst for meaningful dialogue and positive change in mental health support practice.

Integrating autistic understanding for better delivery of evidence-based mental health interventions

Chapter 1

From disorder to difference

Shifting the narrative

Amy Pearson

Throughout the 20th century and for much of the 21st, the way that we thought about autism and autistic people remained fairly static. Since Kanner's use of the term 'infantile autism' to describe a group of 11 children with unusual behaviour that he encountered in his clinic in the 1940s, autism has primarily been understood as a disorder of social behaviour and communication. Kanner's interactions with these children led him to believe that they had 'Autistic disturbances of affective contact', noting that they found it difficult to relate to people in a normative way and that whilst they had an excellent memory for information of interest, they tended to take what others said literally and were more interested in objects than people. The term 'autism', derived from the Greek 'autos' or 'self' was first used by Eugene Bleuler to describe how schizophrenic patients would retreat inwards, and Kanner found it an apt description for the children he worked with, who appeared to prefer their own company to that of others.

Kanner was almost certainly not the first person to recognise characteristics of what we now call autism. In 1925, a Russian child psychiatrist named Grunya Sukhareva used the term 'schizoid psychopathy' (later changed to 'autistic psychopathy', Sher & Gibson, 2021) to describe 11 children who displayed flattened emotional affect and expressiveness, strong interests, and sensory sensitivities. The same term was used later in 1938 by Hans Asperger to describe a subset of children he encountered in his work, who displayed difficulty with social interaction and communication. He made no reference to the work of Sukhareva, despite it having been translated to German in 1926. Somewhat ironically, Kanner himself made no reference to Asperger's in his own formulations, despite working closely with an ex-colleague of Asperger's (Georg Frankl) who had recently moved to the US. Whilst there is considerable debate about Asperger's affiliation with the National Socialist Party his interactions with the children in his clinic should be contextualised within the prevailing narrative of the time. Asperger's job was primarily focused on deciding which of the children he encountered were 'treatable' and could be taught to be 'productive' members of society, and which of them were not. Children who were deemed 'feeble-minded' and ineducable would be entered

DOI: 10.4324/9781003352327-3

into the child euthanasia programme at Am Spiegelgrund, and those deemed capable of 'productive' contributions to society received intervention (Czech, 2018). Asperger noted that both children with and without intellectual disability displayed these 'autistic' characteristics, but only the latter were thought to have the potential to be educated.

In more modern times we may view the segregation and institutionalisation of disabled children as abhorrent, but in the early 20th century it was very much the norm, and this history still impacts how we think about autism today. The National Socialist Party was not the only government to legally codify disabled children as defective. Prior to the Second World War, disabled children in the United Kingdom were forcibly institutionalised under the Mental Deficiency Act of 1913, with the role of psychologists being to identify these 'defectives' (Evans, 2014). In the post-war period, a series of parliamentary acts established a new focus on child health and welfare, which included some disabled children (e.g. deaf children, or those labelled as maladjusted), but not all (i.e., those who were labelled as defective). This change in the law led to the establishment of Child Psychiatry as a legitimate practice and attempts by psychiatrists to formulate new diagnoses for children that would see them labelled as 'mentally ill' and kept within their family, rather than 'mentally defective' and institutionalised. A new diagnosis of 'childhood psychosis' was developed during this time period, characterised by a 'triad of malfunctions', including the formation of a stable and coherent sense of self, difficulty with interpersonal relationships and a preference for objects over people, and a confused distinction between self and other. This triad of malfunctions would later be refined by Lorna Wing and Judith Gould into the 'triad of impairments'. They proposed that autism (thought at the time to be a form of childhood psychosis) could be characterised by core difficulties in three distinct areas: social communication (e.g. a lack of eye contact, unusual facial expressions), social interaction (e.g. a lack of engagement in reciprocal conversation), and social imagination (e.g. difficulties with changes to routine). Thus, this body of work led to autism being added to the Diagnostic and Statistical Manual (DSM) in 1968, labelled as a psychiatric condition. The DSM is used to classify and diagnose 'mental disorders' and is used primarily in the United States, with the "International Classification of Diseases" (or ICD) used more commonly in the UK and other countries. In 1980, the classification of autism was amended, and autism was instead listed as a pervasive developmental disorder, listing the triad of impairments as core features. This classification has undergone minor changes since, with the 2013 update re-characterising autism as a 'dyad of impairments' in social features (i.e. social communication and social interaction), and non-social features (i.e., restricted, repetitive patterns of behaviour, interests, or activities).

With the introduction of autism as a distinct diagnostic category, the enshrinement of a medical approach to autistic people was reified. The medical model views autism as a series of 'deficits' or 'impairments', positioning able-bodiedness and neurotypicality as the ideal societal standard (or, what is 'normal'). Under the medical model, deviations from this standard can be identified, treated, and ameliorated. It is critical to consider how the historical context of autism has influenced our understanding and our modern-day approach, as very little has changed since the addition of autism to the DSM. Whilst autistic people display many tangible differences to non-autistic people that can be disabling in and of themselves (e.g., sensory sensitivities), early formulations of autism were based on early 20th-century standards of normality, whereby a pathological approach to difference was prevalent. This historical context, and the categorisation of autism as a disorder of childhood development, led to two distinct issues: (1) autism being relegated to niche status, primarily the concern of developmental psychologists, and (2) a focus on identifying 'core deficits' of autism in order to best identify how to intervene.

Deficit theories of autism

Several theories have been proposed since the 1980s to account for the core challenges faced by autistic people, focusing mostly on understanding the social features of autism. These theories drew upon a medical model approach, attempting to identify specific deficits (see Milton, 2019).

One of the most enduring deficit-based theories of autism is that autistic people lack a theory of mind. Theory of mind (or mentalising) is a term used to encapsulate the capacity to recognise that others have minds distinct from our own and understand the contents of those minds (Frith & Frith, 2006). Baron-Cohen et al. (1985) conducted pioneering research into autistic theory of mind in the 1980s, finding that autistic children were less accurate at estimating the mental states of others compared to their non-autistic counterparts. This research sparked a pervasive interest in whether autistic people are 'mind blind' and egocentric, incapable of understanding or distinguishing the thoughts, beliefs, and emotions of other people from their (our) own. This theory attempted to explain socio-communicative difficulties between autistic and non-autistic people through the lens of autistic deficits in mentalising. This framing led to multiple suggestions that autistic people's lack of consideration of other minds might also lead to difficulty understanding other people, and a lack of social motivation (Chevallier, 2012).

Baron-Cohen (2009) later proposed that difficulties with intuiting the thoughts and feelings of others stemmed from autistic people having an 'extreme male brain' (EMB). The EMB theory of autism posited that empathising (e.g., the ability to recognise and respond to the feelings of other people) and systemising (e.g., an interest in understanding mechanisms) existed along a continuum, with empathising more strongly associated with women, and systemising more strongly associated with men. Baron-Cohen argued that autistic people were at the 'extreme male' end of this continuum, with strengths in understanding systems, but weaknesses in understanding and responding to people. This theory was based on research showing that autistic people demonstrated strengths in tasks requiring local detail processing (e.g., identifying embedded figures, Shah & Frith, 1993) but difficulties with identifying mental states (e.g., identifying emotions from images of the eye region, Baron-Cohen et al., 2001).

These perceptual differences autistic people display (e.g. a detail-focussed attentional style) were also explained primarily through deficit theories. Weak Central Coherence (WCC) theory (Frith & Happé, 1994) explains autistic attentional focus as a result of poor integration of 'multiple parts of a whole', focusing less on the global features (like neurotypical individuals do) and more on the local aspects. This theory acknowledged that autistic people could display strengths on tasks where local detail processing was an advantage, as highlighted in several less deficit focussed explanations of the attention to detail often seen in autistic people (e.g., Enhanced Perceptual Functioning from Mottron & Burack, 2001; Monotropism from Murray et al., 2005).

The academic acceptance that autistic people's cognition and behaviour were abnormal also led to a skewed interpretation of tasks where autistic performance was the same, or better than that of their neurotypical counterparts. Where no 'impairments' were present, autistic performance was referred to as 'intact', framed as compensatory (e.g., balancing out social deficits) or considered an 'islet of ability' (Shah & Frith, 1983). Social differences that did not result in poorer performance but differed to the neurotypical group (e.g., fairer performance on a task where participants have to split a pot of money between multiple people) were framed as 'abnormal' by virtue of being different.

A focus upon the deficits associated with autism has had a negative impact on autistic people. Both within and beyond academia, there are many misconceptions grounded in academic research (i.e., that autistic people lack empathy, or do not value relationships), and these impact on how autistic people are perceived (Sasson et al., 2017) and stereotyped (Wood & Freeth, 2016). These outsider conceptualisations of autism have also led to the development of many treatments and therapies that aim to 'fix' autistic people, such as Applied Behavioural Analysis, (see, for example, debates around Applied Behavioural Analysis; Chapman & Bovell, 2020). Up until recently the development of such treatments lacked the input of autistic people themselves on the assumption that they were not capable of self-knowledge and reflection (Pellicano et al., 2019). These misconceptions are still highly prevalent across academia (Botha & Cage, 2022) and the general public (Turnock et al., 2023).

A neu(rodiversity) approach?

More recently, there have been major changes in the way we understand autistic people. We are seeing a shift away from a medicalised understanding of autism, towards an approach more consistent with the social model of disability (Oliver, 1983), with more value placed on the role of autistic expertise in the creation of knowledge about autism. The social model of disability argues that the difficulties faced by disabled people are primarily due to living in an inaccessible society (e.g., buildings become more accessible to people with mobility difficulties when ramps are available instead of stairs). A social model approach to autism has been embedded through the development of a neurodiversity approach to understanding neurological difference, and through the advocacy work associated with the neurodiversity paradigm. Reconceptualising autism and other forms of developmental difference such as attention deficit hyperactivity disorder (ADHD) and dyslexia as a form of neurodivergence emerged from discussions between neurodivergent (Asasumasu, 2016) community members (see Dekker, 2023; Singer, 1999). The neurodiversity approach draws upon theories of biodiversity that we see in nature to argue that autism is just one variation that a human brain (and a human) might exhibit.

The neurodiversity movement (Kapp et al., 2013) and neurodiversity paradigm (Glenn, 2022) took the concept of neurodiversity and politicised it. Key neurodiversity theorists and advocates argue that the natural variations we see in human cognition and behaviour associated with neurodiversity are not just natural, but value-neutral. While being neurodivergent is not inherently negative (or positive), neurodivergent people are often positioned negatively due to dehumanising or medicalised narratives of difference. The neurodiversity paradigm seeks to emancipate autistic (and other neurodivergent people) from the perspective of 'normal' and 'abnormal', creating a society where normativity is not the goal, and diversity is accepted.

A neurodiversity-aligned approach to autism was drawn upon by autistic scholars such as Milton (2017), to argue that our understanding of autism had neglected one crucial component: the input of autistic people themselves. Milton proposed that the focus on cognitive explanations for autistic differences had driven the assumption that the core indicators of autism are externally visible and could be measured (i.e., behavioural measures of cognitive abilities such as mentalising). He drew upon the work of autistic advocates such as Williams (1996), suggesting that we instead approach autism from 'the inside-out', exploring the notion that subjective differences present among autistic people may give us a more accurate understanding of what it means to be autistic, rather than relying upon second hand, outsider interpretations of behaviour. Autistic advocacy (both in and outside of academia) is leading to the gradual acceptance that autistic people might be able to contribute towards knowledge of what it is like to be autistic. The involvement of autistic people in research has led to the development of new research areas that address the genuine priorities of autistic people (Pearson et al., 2022) such as sensory processing and mental health.

Autistic-led theory

The growth in autistic-led autism research has led to major developments in the field that have helped researchers to rethink and reframe the way we approach autistic cognition. One major theoretical contribution to autism research has been the development of the Double Empathy Problem (DEP; Milton, 2012). The DEP positions the socio-communicative difficulties between autistic and non-autistic people as bi-directional, recognising that social interaction is, by its very nature, social (Gernsbacher, 2006). Within our interactions with others, we are mutually responsible for any misunderstandings or breakdowns in communication. The majority of research prior to the DEP had focussed on autistic difficulties in recognising the contents of neurotypical minds (e.g., through facial expressions), but there had been very little exploration of how accurate non-autistic people were at recognising autistic emotions, or mental states. The assumption that autistic people were deficient by virtue of their neurotype and that non-autistic people knew the best way to intervene was sharply called into question following the results of several research studies. For example, empirical evidence for the DEP has shown that neurotypical people are less accurate at recognising the emotions of autistic people (Alkhaldi et al., 2019), are less likely to want to interact with autistic people based on thin-slice judgements (Sasson et al., 2017), and that autistic and neurotypical people are as effective as transmitting information to another person of the same neurotype (e.g., autistic to autistic) but communication is less effective between neurotypes (e.g. autistic to NT, Crompton et al., 2020).

An alternative explanation for perceptual and attentional differences among autistic people has also been proposed by autistic researchers. Murray et al. (2005) developed the theory of *monotropism*, suggesting that autistic global/local processing can be understood through the allocation of attention. They argue that non-autistic people have a polytropic attentional style, meaning that they can spread their attention and cognitive resources across multiple stimuli. In contrast, autistic people may have a more monotropic attentional style, meaning that we allocate our attention in a more singular manner to a particular stimulus whilst filtering out (or attempting to filter out) others. Empirical research into monotropism is still in its infancy, however, monotropism has been linked to understanding autistic rumination (Hallet, 2021), developing engaging educational environments (Wood, 2019), and autistic flow states (Milton, 2018).

Both of these theories encourage researchers and practitioners to explore and understand autistic experience through an autistic lens, leading to a more autistic-affirming approach. These theories provide space to examine and support autistic strengths **and** challenges without reinforcing stigma towards autistic people. Instead of focusing on encouraging autistic people to think and behave in the same way as neurotypical people, we can use these theories as a starting point to explore what a good life looks like for autistic people in and of themselves.

Shifting the narrative

Researchers and practitioners have the power to affect this change and shift the narrative about autism from a deficit focussed view, and towards one that fosters compassion and empathy. However, this shift also means taking the responsibility (and the time) to develop a more up-to-date knowledge of autism and being open to a potentially unfamiliar approach. Shifting the narrative around autistic people is crucial to our well-being and our self-understanding. As a late-identified autistic adult, part of my own struggle to recognise that I was autistic (despite overwhelming similarities between my experiences, and those of other autistic people) was based on not recognising myself as 'socially impaired' or 'mind blind' (see Pearson, 2021). The way I described my own experiences (e.g., that I 'didn't like change') did not align with the terminology used to describe autistic 'behaviour' (e.g., 'an insistence on sameness'). Recognising that I was autistic had an important impact on my own flourishing; from learning how to manage the sensory environment more effectively, to being more compassionate toward myself. I would never have gotten to that point without the support of other autistic people and witnessing a shift away from conceptualising autism as a tragedy, as relying solely on academic descriptions only reinforced internalised ableism.

We still have a lot of work to do to improve autistic outcomes. Autistic young people are more likely to experience mental health difficulties than their non-autistic counterparts, as well as bullying and stigma (Crane et al., 2019). Historically, interventions for autistic young people have involved an attempt to minimise autistic characteristics and help them achieve a more 'normative' appearance (Leadbitter et al., 2021). These approaches centred on the comfort of non-autistic people (e.g., peers, teachers, parents) as opposed to seeking to develop strengths in areas that the autistic person valued. Whilst research into the 'masking' of autistic characteristics is still in its infancy (see Chapter 6), evidence is starting to show that the suppression or masking of autistic ways of being (e.g., stimming) has a negative impact on autistic people and increase stress (Bradley et al., 2021; Pearson & Rose, 2023; Ross et al., 2023).

One way to ameliorate the impact of deficit-focused narratives is to embed a double empathy-informed approach in mental health practice (Jellett & Flower, 2023). This approach emphasises the importance of recognising that autistic young people may struggle to build a bond with their practitioners (particularly those of a different neurotype), and importantly, that practitioners may struggle to understand and empathise with autistic young people.

Autistic young people have personally highlighted the importance of having a good relationship with practitioners: "What I'd like is somebody I can trust, someone to talk to and someone who understands autism; 'a professional person.'" (Crane et al., 2019, p. 476). Building a successful relationship means recognising that the way that non-autistic people conceptualise positive well-being does not necessarily align with the aims or preferences of autistic people themselves (Chapman & Carel, 2022; Lam et al., 2021).

Taking a double-empathy approach means meeting someone where they are, and not where we expect them to be, and recognising that mutual misunderstandings and misalignments of priorities and expectations may occur. As a practitioner, this might involve recognising for example that an autistic person's interests and goals may not appear to 'have function' to an outsider, but that they might bring a deep sense of joy and calm to an autistic person's life. Whereas historically autistic interests may have been framed as pathological, or through the lens of intervention (e.g., attempts to use sources of interest such as trains to train emotion recognition), the DEP provides space to reconsider outsider framings of autistic behaviour, and look for ways to build bridges (see Pavlopoulou et al., 2022).

Chapman and Botha (2022) emphasise how practitioners should take a relational approach to understanding their clients' challenges and recognise that the clients themselves are the experts of their own experience. One potential framework for reimagining the relationship with autistic clients is Pavlopoulou and Dimitriou's 'lifeworld framework' (Pavlopoulou & Dimitriou, 2019, see Table 1.1). This approach emphasises working *with* (and not on) autistic people and their family members, to explore their needs, goals, challenges, and strengths together. The lifeworld framework situates eight core values within practitioner-client relationships, aiming to shift away from outsider perceptions of external behaviour to insider understandings of motivations built upon the recognition of the young person as the expert of their own experience. The development of a genuinely mutual relationship helps both the practitioner and young person to make sense of the young person's experiences and the journey that they are on, focusing on what makes them unique. In turn, this fosters a sense of agency for the young person, and a feeling of togetherness in the practitioner-client relationship. The approach validates the young person, and instead of seeking to change who they are, looks for ways to use their unique personal insight to further develop their flourishing.

Pavlopoulou, Usher and Pearson (2022) used the Lifeworld Framework to examine autistic young people's engagement in online gaming from their own perspectives, moving past outsider perceptions of 'healthy gaming behaviour' to explore what the young people had to say about their own motivations. The young people in the study gave important insights on their own motivations, highlighting how gaming helped them to regulate their emotions, gave them a chance to display agency and make choices (which they felt did not occur often in daily life), but also could cause friction with caregivers who did not see the value of gaming as a hobby or were concerned it was detracting from self-care. By refraining from a pathologising interpretation of the young people's perspectives, the authors were able to see how insider insights could be used to better align the priorities of young people and their caregivers. By shifting the narrative and recognising Insiderness as a positive, we can begin

Table 1.1 Lifeworld framework

Insiderness	Valuing the subjective experiences of the young person
Agency	Promoting autistic decision making in collaboration with caregivers and practitioners
Uniqueness	Recognising the unique aspects that make up an autistic young person's identity (e.g. friend, male, son, pupil)
Sense making	Listening to autistic interpretations of their own experiences
Personal journey	Recognising and facilitating individual pathways and aspirations
Sense of place	Ensuring autistic young people feel included and welcome across their home, school and wider community
Embodiment	Exploring the experience of autistic ways of being without defaulting to a deficit narrative and enabling them in their personal development
Togetherness	Creating a safe place for autistic young people to share their worries and joys

to foster better outcomes for autistic young people. The lifeworld framework (also known as an experience-sensitive approach by McGreevy et al., 2024 as referenced in Chapter 15) can therefore help to create a more meaningful dialogue between autistic young people and those who support them (e.g., parents, clinicians, and teachers) across different contexts (Pavlopoulou & Dimitriou, 2019), aligning with what Beardon (2008) calls the golden equation: autism + environment = outcome.

Conclusion

This chapter highlights the importance of considering where our framing of autism comes from, and what we can do to create a more affirming approach to supporting autistic people. Historically autism has been considered as a disorder characterised by deficits, which frames the autistic person as inherently impaired. More recent neurodiversity-affirming approaches recognise that autistic strengths and challenges arise through interaction between that person and their environment. By seeking to understand autistic people through a non-pathologising lens that recognises them as a whole person, professionals can develop genuine relationships and provide support that contributes towards autistic flourishing.

References

Alkhaldi, R. S., Sheppard, E., & Mitchell, P. (2019). Is there a link between autistic people being perceived unfavorably and having a mind that is difficult to read? *Journal of Autism and Developmental Disorders, 49*(10), 3973–3982. https://doi.org/10.1007/s10803-019-04101-1

16 Amy Pearson

Asasumasu, K. (2016). *PSA from the actual coiner of "neurodivergent"*. *Shit bor-derlines do: Tumblr.* Retreived from: https://shitborderlinesdo.tumblr.com/post/121319446214/psa-from-the-actual-coiner-of-neurodivergent

Baron-Cohen, S., Leslie, A. M., & Frith, U. (1985). Does the autistic child have a "theory of mind"? *Cognition*, *21*(1), 37–46.

Baron-Cohen, S., Wheelwright, S., Hill, J., Raste, Y., & Plumb, I. (2001). The "reading the mind in the eyes" test revised version: A study with normal adults, and adults with Asperger syndrome or high-functioning autism. *The Journal of Child Psychology and Psychiatry and Allied Disciplines*, *42*(2), 241–251. https://doi.org/10.1017/S0021963001006643

Baron-Cohen, S. (2009). Autism: The empathizing–systemizing (E-S) theory. *Annals of the New York Academy of Sciences*, *1156*(1), 68–80. https://doi.org/10.1111/j.1749-6632.2009.04467.x

Beardon, L. (2019). *Autism, masking, social anxiety and the classroom.* Teacher education and autism: A research-based practical handbook.

Botha, M., & Cage, E. (2022). "Autism research is in crisis": A mixed method study of researcher's constructions of autistic people and autism research. *Frontiers in Psychology*, *13*, 7397. https://doi.org/10.3389/fpsyg.2022.1050897

Bradley, L., Shaw, R., Baron-Cohen, S., & Cassidy, S. (2021). Autistic adults' experiences of camouflaging and its perceived impact on mental health. *Autism in Adulthood*, *3*(4), 320–329. https://doi.org/10.1089/aut.2020.0071

Chapman, R., & Bovell, V. (2022). Neurodiversity, advocacy, anti-therapy. In J. L. Matson, & P. Sturmey (Eds.), *Handbook of autism and pervasive developmental disorder: Assessment, diagnosis, and treatment* (pp. 1519–1536). *Autism and Child Psychopathology Series.* Cham: Springer. https://doi.org/10.1007/978-3-030-88538-0_67

Chapman, R., & Carel, H. (2022). Neurodiversity, epistemic injustice, and the good human life. *Journal of Social Philosophy*, *53*(4), 614–631.

Chapman, R., & Botha, M. (2023). Neurodivergence-informed therapy. *Developmental Medicine & Child Neurology*, *65*(3), 310–317. https://doi.org/10.1111/dmcn.15384

Chevallier, C., Kohls, G., Troiani, V., Brodkin, E. S., & Schultz, R. T. (2012). The social motivation theory of autism. *Trends in Cognitive Sciences*, *16*(4), 231–239. https://doi.org/10.1016/j.tics.2012.02.007

Crane, L., Adams, F., Harper, G., Welch, J., & Pellicano, E. (2019). 'Something needs to change': Mental health experiences of young autistic adults in England. *Autism*, *23*(2), 477–493. https://doi.org/10.1177/1362361318757048

Crompton, C. J., Ropar, D., Evans-Williams, C. V., Flynn, E. G., & Fletcher-Watson, S. (2020). Autistic peer-to-peer information transfer is highly effective. *Autism*, *24*(7), 1704–1712. https://doi.org/10.1177/1362361320919286

Czech, H. (2018). Hans Asperger, national socialism, and "race hygiene" in Nazi-era Vienna. *Molecular Autism*, *9*(1), 1–43. https://doi.org/10.1186/s13229-018-0208-6

Dekker, M. [@autimodo]. (2023, July 13). I credited #JudySinger with coining the term 'neurodiversity' in error. I have found evidence that the #neurodiversity concept was. [Tweet]. Twitter. Retrieved from: https://twitter.com/autimodo/status/1679506905394282497?s=20

Evans, B. (2014). The foundations of autism: The law concerning psychotic, schizophrenic, and autistic children in 1950s and 1960s Britain. *Bulletin of the History of Medicine*, *88*(2), 253. https://doi.org/10.1353/bhm.2014.0033

Frith, C. D., & Frith, U. (2006). The neural basis of mentalizing. *Neuron*, *50*(4), 531–534. https://doi.org/10.1016/j.neuron.2006.05.001

Frith, U., & Happé, F. (1994). Autism: Beyond "theory of mind". *Cognition*, *50*(1–3), 115–132. https://doi.org/10.1016/0010-0277(94)90024-8

Gernsbacher, M. A. (2006). Toward a behavior of reciprocity. *The Journal of Developmental Processes*, *1*(1), 139.

Glenn, D. (2022). Neuroqueer heresies: Notes on the neurodiversity paradigm, autistic empowerment, and postnormal possibilities: Walker, N. *Neuroqueer Heresies: Notes on the neurodiversity paradigm, autistic empowerment, and postnormal possibilities*. Fort Worth, TX: Autonomous Press, 2021, https://doi.org/10.1080/02604027.2022.2094194

Hallet, S. (2021). Loops of concern. [Blog post] In *Medium.com*. Retrieved from: https://medium.com/@sonyahallett/loops-of-concern-ff792eebad03 Retrieved on 22/2/23.

Jellett, R., & Flower, R. L. (2023). How can psychologists meet the needs of autistic adults? *Autism*, *28*(2). https://doi.org/10.1177/13623613221147346

Kapp, S. K., Gillespie-Lynch, K., Sherman, L. E., & Hutman, T. (2013). Deficit, difference, or both? Autism and neurodiversity. *Developmental Psychology*, *49*(1), 59. https://doi.org/10.1037/a0028353

Lam, G. Y. H., Sabnis, S., Migueliz Valcarlos, M., & Wolgemuth, J. R. (2021). A critical review of academic literature constructing well-being in autistic adults. *Autism in Adulthood*, *3*(1), 61–71. https://doi.org/10.1089/aut.2020.0053

Leadbitter, K., Buckle, K. L., Ellis, C., & Dekker, M. (2021). Autistic self-advocacy and the neurodiversity movement: Implications for autism early intervention research and practice. *Frontiers in Psychology*, *782*. https://doi.org/10.3389/fpsyg.2021.635690

Milton, D. E. (2012). On the ontological status of autism: The 'double empathy problem'. *Disability & Society*, *27*(6), 883–887. https://doi.org/10.1080/09687599.2012.710008

Milton, D. (2017). *A mismatch of salience* (pp. 883–87). Hove: Pavilion. Pavilion Press.

Milton, D. (2018). *The double empathy problem: Salience and interpersonal flow*. In: PARC Fringe, 8–9 Nov 2018, Glasgow, UK.

Milton, D. (2019). Difference versus disability: Implications of characterisation of autism for education and support. *The Sage Handbook of Autism and Education*, 3–11.

Mottron, L., & Burack, J. A. (2001). Enhanced perceptual functioning in the development of autism. In J. A. Burack, T. Charman, N. Yirmiya, & P. R. Zelazo (Eds.), *The development of autism: Perspectives from theory and research* (pp. 131–148). New York: Lawrence Erlbaum Associates Publishers.

Murray, D., Lesser, M., & Lawson, W. (2005). Attention, monotropism and the diagnostic criteria for autism. *Autism*, *9*(2), 139–156. https://doi.org/10.1177/1362361305051398

Oliver, M. (1983). *Social work with disabled people*. Basingstoke: Macmillan.

Pavlopoulou, G., & Dimitriou, D. (2019). 'I don't live with autism; I live with my sister'. Sisters' accounts on growing up with their preverbal autistic siblings. *Research in Developmental Disabilities*, *88*, 1–15. https://doi.org/10.1016/j.ridd.2019.01.013

Pavlopoulou, G., Usher, C., & Pearson, A. (2022). 'I can actually do it without any help or someone watching over me all the time and giving me constant instruction': Autistic adolescent boys' perspectives on engagement in online video gaming. *British Journal of Developmental Psychology*, *40*, 557–571. https://doi.org/10.1111/bjdp.12424

Pearson, A. (2021). Rehumanising the study of humans. [Conference presentation]. *Interdisciplinary Festival of Autism Research*. Online. https://youtu.be/E4EPL7MvYzU

Pearson, A., Surtees, A., Crompton, C. J., Goodall, C., Pillai, D., Sedgewick, F., & Au-Yeung, S. K. (2022). Addressing community priorities in autism research. *Frontiers in Psychology*, 6189. https://doi.org/10.3389/fpsyg.2022.1040446

Pearson, A., & Rose, K. (2023). *Autistic masking: Understanding identity management and the role of stigma*. West Sussex: Pavilion.

Pellicano, E., Den Houting, J., du Plooy, L., & Lilley, R. (2019). Knowing autism: The place of experiential expertise. *Behavioral and Brain Sciences*, *42*. https://doi.org/10.1017/S0140525X18002376

Ross, A., Grove, R., & McAloon, J. (2023). The relationship between camouflaging and mental health in autistic children and adolescents. *Autism Research*, *16*(1), 190–199. https://doi.org/10.1002/aur.2859

Sasson, N. J., Faso, D. J., Nugent, J., Lovell, S., Kennedy, D. P., & Grossman, R. B. (2017). Neurotypical peers are less willing to interact with those with autism based on thin slice judgments. *Scientific Reports*, *7*(1), 1–10. https://doi.org/10.1038/srep40700

Shah, A., & Frith, U. (1983). An islet of ability in autistic children: A research note. *Journal of Child Psychology and Psychiatry*, *24*(4), 613–620. https://doi.org/10.1111/j.1469-7610.1983.tb00137.x

Shah, A., & Frith, U. (1993). Why do autistic individuals show superior performance on the block design task? *Journal of Child Psychology and Psychiatry*, *34*(8), 1351–1364. https://doi.org/10.1111/j.1469-7610.1993.tb02095.x

Sher, D. A., & Gibson, J. L. (2023). Pioneering, prodigious and perspicacious: Grunya Efimovna Sukhareva's life and contribution to conceptualising autism and schizophrenia. *European Child & Adolescent Psychiatry*, *32*(3), 475–490. https://doi.org/10.1007/s00787-021-01875-7

Singer, J. (1999). Why can't you be normal for once in your life? From a problem with no name to the emergence of a new category of difference. *Disability Discourse*, 59–70.

Turnock, A., Langley, K., & Jones, C. R. (2022). Understanding stigma in autism: A narrative review and theoretical model. *Autism in Adulthood*, *4*(1), 76–91. https://doi.org/10.1089/aut.2021.0005

Williams, D. (1996). *Autism--an inside-out approach: An innovative look at the mechanics of 'autism' and its developmental 'cousins'*. London: Jessica Kingsley Publishers.

Wood, C., & Freeth, M. (2016). Students' stereotypes of autism. *Journal of Educational Issues*, *2*(2), 131–140. https://doi.org/10.5296/jei.v2i2.9975

Wood, R. (2021). Autism, intense interests and support in school: From wasted efforts to shared understandings. *Educational Review*, *73*(1), 34–54. https://doi.org/10.1080/00131911.2019.1566213

Chapter 2

Something needs to change
Making CAMHS accessible to autistic CYP and their families

Ann Memmott

Our understanding of autism has been transformed in recent years by new research and improved engagement with autistic people (Pellicano & den Houting, 2022). What was widely believed to be a behavioural condition is now often better understood as a sensory and social processing difference (Gonçalves & Monteiro, 2023), with autism situated amongst the wider picture of neurodiversities such as dyslexia, dyspraxia, and ADHD (see Chapter 1). As reviewed in Chapter 1, this positioning of autism as a neurodiversity challenges existing medical-model approaches viewing autism in terms of disorder and deficit (Shaw et al., 2021). Significant changes in ethos are emerging, in part through the insights from networks of autistic clinicians such as those within Autistic Doctors International (Shaw et al., 2022). There is a clear ethical and scientific obligation to consider the new evidence around autistic sensory processing and autistic communication differences, the ethical debates around Human Rights to an autistic identity, and the vital research into the extent and impact of trauma on autistic lives.

Child and Adolescent Mental Health Services (CAMHS) teams are increasingly ensuring that a modern approach to autism is embedded within training and that their therapeutic environments match autistic access needs wherever possible. This chapter describes how CAMHS might be best adapted to meet the needs of autistic CYP. If left in repeated situations of sensory or social overwhelm, autistic CYPs may experience anxiety and develop related distress behaviours. The need to avoid sensory and social overwhelm often drives the quest for certainty and routine that autistic people need (Powell et al., 2022). Autistic CYP tend to function well when enabled to anticipate, avoid, or regulate sensory and social input. In addition, autistic CYPs tend to thrive when in good contact with autistic peers, communicating in authentically autistic ways (Huang et al., 2022).

DOI: 10.4324/9781003352327-4

Setting the scene, example scenario 1: Carly, age 17 and recently diagnosed as autistic after being on a two-year waiting list

Carly has been having increasing difficulties with extreme anxiety, preventing her from accessing school and many other aspects of daily life. She has been harming herself, leading to admission to a unit three months ago. Carly edged into the care review meeting, hesitating at the doorway. A sea of mostly unfamiliar faces peered at her from various chairs around the long conference table. Overhead, a fluorescent light bulb flickered, casting a strobe-light effect across the room. In the corner, an air conditioning unit hissed, deafeningly. Laptop keyboards clacked as individuals typed their notes. Chairs scraped on the hard flooring as people pulled them into position. The stench of some 70 different perfumes, aftershaves, shampoo fragrances, tubes of toothpaste, and other products filled the air. The Clinician gestured to her to sit in a particularly hard, uncomfortable, unsupportive plastic chair. A few conversations were still taking place, the voices forming a cacophony of competing and indecipherable noise. If only she knew why she was there, or who people were, but no one had said. The explanatory leaflet she held, now crumpled in her hand, made no sense. Anxious and overwhelmed, Carly had no idea if she was to speak, or when. The overhead lighting was making her feel sick and dizzy and she really wanted to run out of the meeting, back to the safety of her bedroom. The team members were asked about how Carly was doing, and ended each statement with, "...isn't that right, Carly?" Carly couldn't respond, even if they'd left her enough time to do so. Carly was in an autistic shutdown, unable to speak. A key team member explained that in their view, Carly was 'making a mountain out of a molehill' with some of her sensory requests, and surely, she needed to be more resilient. After all, they continued, the outside world wasn't always going to be able to offer sensory accommodations. Carly returned to another day of sensory and social hell, waiting to be released one day. She needed to remember not to 'misbehave', become 'controlling' during distress, or appear to be autistic in any way; she knew there would be painful restraint, removal of even more of her needed and loved items, fewer chances to see family, and even fewer chances to regulate and recover.

Something needs to change

Many autistic young people are either undiagnosed, misdiagnosed, or unsupported after diagnosis. Commonly, adolescent girls are misdiagnosed with personality disorders or other psychiatric conditions (e.g., Iversen & Kildahl, 2022). Setlhare and Rafi (2022) set out the range of presentations of undiagnosed autistic CYPs receiving mental health services. These presentations included two-thirds having a significant sensory difference, and autistic girls having a greater incidence of self-harm. Misunderstandings around the variation in autism presentations may be a factor in underdiagnosis and misdiagnosis, and the authors recommend that clinicians should be seeking autism assessment where anxiety, sensory differences, and/or self-harm are present. Further difficulties in therapeutic settings can ensue if teams are unaware that a significant number of autistic individuals have prosopagnosia (face blindness) and may not immediately recognise team members from their faces, relying instead on other clues from hair, height, build, voice, or similar personal features (Minio-Paluello et al., 2020). If any of those identifiers change, mistaken identity becomes much more likely. It can be very helpful for staff to identify themselves each time they meet an autistic person.

Mental health teams need to be aware of the dangers of assuming that an optimal outcome looks like an autistic CYP resembling and mimicking a non-autistic individual. Hanlon et al. (2022) note that autistic CYP experience higher rates of mental health problems than non-autistic peers, but mental health assessment tools and evidence-based interventions have typically been developed to address non-autistic needs. They also observed the common mislabelling of autistic CYP experiences as a result of a lack of training and understanding of autism. The sometimes catastrophic impact of having to perform 'neurotypicality' ('masking' or 'camouflaging') in order to avoid significant negative outcomes is also discussed. Bernardin et al. (2021) also explore the factors around mental health for autistic CYP, observing that masking often predicted depression, anxiety, stress, and suicidality.

On account of Carly, we might consider the obstacles that she may have encountered in her journey towards appropriate mental health support till date, such as a late diagnosis of autism, a long wait for community services, and increasing levels of anxiety. Having received little support, Carly's increased distress led to the admission within a unit. Once there, it appears that the staff was unaware of Carly's sensory and communication needs, her autistic distress behaviours such as shutdown, and her human rights, including good family contact and dignified care and support that respected her autistic identity (UN Convention on the Rights of Persons with Disabilities, 2007).

There are considerable misunderstandings relating to training around resilience and exposure, including assumptions that autistic individuals lack the determination or skills to work through difficulties that others cope with. 'Making a mountain out of a molehill' is a common expression relating to this kind of misunderstanding. In reality, autistic individuals are rarely overreacting. Their life experiences are often repeatedly traumatic. Their sensory experiences, cultural and communication needs, and ways of socialising are different for their entire life. Indeed, research shows that autistic individuals generally experience repeated traumatic incidents in life, and from a wider range of incident-categories (Rumball et al., 2020).

An August 2022 report by a UK charity highlighted how over 1,200 autistic people were in inpatient mental health hospitals in England, and around 180 of these were under the age of 18. This report by the National Autistic Society (2022) notes that

... care in an inpatient unit is rarely helpful – in fact, it can be deeply damaging. Wards can be noisy, bright, and unpredictable. Without reasonable adjustments to the environment, and support from a professional who understands autism and how to adapt care, it can be completely overwhelming...we continue to hear alarming cases of overmedication, seclusion, and unnecessary restraint.

The report gives a clear indication of why it is so important for community services to provide the right support at the right points for autistic CYP.

The National Development Team for Inclusion is a not-for-profit organisation in the UK whose work on autism and learning disability has been commissioned by many NHS bodies. Its report, 'It's not Rocket Science' details supporting statistics, personal accounts from young autistic people who have been treated by Mental Health teams, the challenges of obtaining an autism diagnosis, and key information on necessary change (Memmott et al., 2021). The changes recommended apply to all CAMHS settings and have informed the recommendation at the end of this chapter. Of particular note is the checklist for sensory/self-regulation accommodations, which may be helpful to individuals in CAMHS settings, including:

- use of noise-cancelling headphones/earbuds, sunglasses, hats, or caps,
- ability to make contact with walls or other objects around them for better proprioception,
- use of blankets to help with self-regulation, choice of location where possible,
- taking time out to access to personal items and hobbies where safe,
- acceptance and encouragement of safe stimming (repeated movement or sound to aid self-regulation), and
- access to family, friends, and pets.

A good and adaptable sensory room or quiet space is also often much appreciated.

Acting in ways that best support autistic CYP is essential if we are to promote good outcomes. First, however, one needs to identify that they are autistic. A large number of autistic CYP in CAMHS settings are either undiagnosed or unsupported after diagnosis. There are multiple reasons for such situations, including underlying narratives that prevent useful identification and diagnosis of individuals who do not fit into problematic stereotypes of, for example, a young white male with challenging behaviour, who collects toy trains or solves equations. Many will be only diagnosed after encountering mental health services at a point of crisis. For some, this crisis involves a traumatic experience where their level of distress from sensory/social overload becomes such that they are brought to the attention of the police, who may misidentify signs of escalating distress as anger. With no opportunity to self-regulate with soothing stimming, sensory accommodations or hobbies, the painful and terrifying experiences of the day may lead to entry to mental health settings, or indeed to arrest.

Current approaches in some talking therapies and other interventions are often not highly rated by many autistic participants (Wang et al., 2021), and may, for example, focus on the normalisation of autistic CYP, rather than outcomes meaningful for them (Nicholls, 2018; Shum et al., 2019). Such attempts at normalisation may be a breach of Human Rights, for example, within the United Nations Convention on the Rights of Children with Disabilities (Article 3h, 2006).

What has enabled this problematic approach to autistic CYP to develop and continue? One must consider the underlying narratives around autism (as detailed in Chapter 1). For example, in some philosophies of behaviour from the 1940s to 1980s, autistic individuals, and indeed some other groups such as individuals with learning disabilities, were regarded as sub-human, for example, as outlined by Ivar Lovaas (Chance, 1974). Autistic focus and stimming were often seen as meaningless and to be prevented, a belief that continues in some behaviourist settings (Verriden & Roscoe, 2019). Autistic distress, causing shutdowns, flight responses, or meltdowns, was understood as anger, defiance, insanity, or an inability to understand how to behave 'correctly'.

Within some institutions, there are also issues around power and control, combined with the notion of autistic CYP as complex and in need of extreme measures (Joint Committee on Human Rights, 2019). Staff are sometimes chosen for their physical strength and speed, and not for their empathy, compassion, modern autism training, or willingness to communicate well from an autistic perspective. Meaningful goals are often framed in ways suited to non-autistic individuals, and quality of life measures may assume incorrectly that autistic individuals will achieve happiness from the same things as the average non-autistic person (Kim, 2019).

Getting it right from the start

Amidst all this backdrop, there are several important questions clinicians must reflect on.

- How do CYP mental health teams hear autistic CYP?
- How do they engage with them as therapeutic partners?
- How do they win their trust, establishing safe relationships with staff who are genuinely curious about that young person's lived experiences, and are genuinely caring?

- How do we ensure quality teams who are sensitive to the presence and expertise of excellent autistic colleagues at their side?
- How do we use words and descriptions that enable trust, relationship, confidence, collaboration, and excellence in outcomes?

Hanlon et al. (2022) recommend several changes to improve service design and delivery. These changes include rapid access to mental health diagnosis and early support, and improved understanding of the range of communication needs that autistic CYP may need to achieve good outcomes. Other recommendations are approaches that centre the individual needs of autistic CYP rather than formulaic methods designed for non-autistic individuals, which would include improved knowledge and accommodation of sensory processing needs. Also in the recommendations, co-production with autistic CYP was emphasised, so that services can adapt in ways that match autistic end goals rather than non-autistic assumptions of what a 'good life' might look like. There is also careful thought around whether parents may also be neurodivergent, and how teams in the community and within mental health units need to reflect on differences in autistic cultures and communications before ascribing blame or judgement of parenting styles.

Bernardin et al. (2021) recommend that treatment focuses on improving self-acceptance and self-esteem. More broadly, they recommend interventions targeting increased autism acceptance in those around the autistic CYP. Of note also, is the work of Monk et al. (2022) who give clear guidance on the use of language that aids minimisation of stigma, marginalisation, and exclusion of autistic people. Indeed, individuals continually referred to as disordered and in terms of a list of deficits rarely have positive self-esteem and good mental health outcomes. Factors contributing to a Neuro Affirming and Informed Service are considered in the last chapter of this book.

Given research showing high levels of bullying, exclusion, trauma, and other negative outcomes for autistic individuals, distress in autistic individuals is to be expected. Rather than framing the situation as a lack of resilience within the autistic individual, one may commission therapeutic approaches that better match the needs of the autistic CYP seeking mental health support. Therapeutic teams need excellent modern training on autism, using training programmes co-produced with autistic specialists and based around a neurodiversity-affirming, autistic-led approach, which can lead to a very real change of perspectives and approaches. Recently, NHS England funded the National Autism Trainer Programme via the Anna Freud Centre in collaboration with AT-AUTISM to ensure that teams are accessing up-to-date, person-centred, and trauma-informed/relationally framed training to support them in improving outcomes when working with autistic people. Notable, this is authentically produced by and co-delivered with autistic people of all ages.

Significantly improved outcomes tend to occur when those supporting autistic individuals reflect on their own behaviour and approaches, using low-arousal methods (McDonnell et al., 2018; see also Chapter 10 in this book) and showing a willingness to build empathetic relationships (Milton, 2012). Of vital importance is the co-creation of understanding around key areas of well-being, including agency and sense of belonging (Pavlopoulou, 2021). Whilst good practice is increasing, some teams may be unaware of their environment's sensory impact, and unaware of the impact of their own ways of communication.

Talking therapies may have value for some and should be appropriately adapted, although data as yet is limited and rarely includes a large CYP patient group. Adapted Cognitive Behavioural Therapy has shown some usefulness for some adult autistic individuals (Russell et al., 2019) as has adapted Dialectical Behaviour Therapy (Cornwall et al., 2021). However, some autistic individuals have raised concerns about such approaches (Hallett & Kerr, 2020). It is vital to acknowledge the autistic CYP's expertise in their own lives and adopt a flexible cognitive approach when working with manualised approaches. For instance, framing responses as unhelpful thinking and/or catastrophising thoughts may need to be used carefully or dropped completely if these prove to invalidate the autistic experience of navigating a non-autistic world.

It is also important to reflect deeply on the need for 'double empathy' (Milton, 2012), in other words, the acknowledgement that both the therapist and the patient will need to understand each other's communication and empathy styles. Therapies such as Eye Movement Desensitisation and Reprocessing (EMDR) are gaining traction and are sometimes particularly suited to autistic individuals who have experienced high levels of traumatic incidents (Lobregt-van Buuren et al., 2019).

The need for trauma-informed approach

The trauma that many autistic people face is discussed extensively in Chapter 7. While many services claim 'trauma-informed' status, it is often not clear what is meant by this. For instance, are they fully trained in the range, depth, and variety of autistic experiences of trauma, and how those may be exhibited? Are staff reflective around traumas from repeated exposure to painful environmental factors such as blinding lighting and deafening noise? Are teams considering communication traumas from repeat exposure to negative, stigmatising language around autism, and repeated insistence on normalisation of verbal and non-verbal communication? Are staff familiar with the need for trust-building, warm relationships, and a low-arousal approach to environment and interaction? Are staff aware of masking and how that may disguise depths of distress? Much more research is needed in this field, but the work of Benevides et al. (2020), gives good starting points on trauma and wider mental health priorities, for reflection within teams. Recommendations included research informing trauma-informed care, greater focus on inclusion and acceptance of autistic individuals; improved community approaches enabling self-management of mental health; better evaluation of adverse effects from current mental health interventions, and better measures of outcomes meaningful to autistic lives.

The importance of involving family members

When meeting families of autistic CYP, it is wise to assume that they may also be autistic or otherwise neurodivergent (Rylaarsdam & Guemez-Gamboa, 2019). Establishing good levels of trust between parties will often happen when the same steps are taken for family members as we take for the young person, namely compassion, empathy, clear and timely communication, and an environment that is low-sensory, for example. Assuming a degree of face blindness, as discussed earlier, may also be of use, with clarity as to who the family is meeting. In many meetings, autistic parents who are applying excellent autistic-informed practice to the care of their autistic CYP may be assumed to be incompetent, due to misunderstandings about how one achieves good outcomes for autistic CYP. There is a clear need for reflective discussion and compassion in such conversations. In some circumstances, parents and carers are assumed to be the consenting party, with the autistic individual assumed to be unable to assent or consent in any meaningful way and are therefore not offered the proper opportunity to understand and collaborate. There is much to do to improve in this regard so that autistic CYP are *truly* placed at the centre of their own care.

Finally, siblings often want to be valued and informed when their families work with professionals but report feeling invisible/not included in family meetings. They may have information, possible solutions, and worries for themselves to share. Often, they will not share their worries in front of their parents and may find it difficult to express their needs in order not to 'burden' others. Some siblings may be night and day carers of their brothers and sisters, but they will rarely identify as such at a young age. Some siblings may also have undiagnosed neurodivergencies which may not be noticed by the parents.

What enables a good outcome?

Example scenario 2:

Hemal, a 14-year-old autistic boy, was referred to CAMHS after experiencing severe depression for more than a year. The therapist working with Hemal and his family had good modern autistic-led training on autism, understanding autism as neurodiversity with different communication and cultural protocols. The centre's team ensured that the website for the service had clear, easily accessible information on it, using positive language around autism. It showed photographs of the centre and its main therapy rooms, and photographs of the staff, with a description of their roles and the therapies they offered. Hemal was asked which appointment time might suit him best, and where possible the team ensured this was respected. If there was a delay, Hemal could wait in a quiet, low-arousal area where he could use for example noise cancelling headphones or sunglasses to cut down sensory overload further. Hemal was given advance information on the sort of questions that would be asked, which were phrased in clear ways. He had the opportunity to position himself in the most comfortable space in the room, and time to think about each question he was asked. He could answer either verbally, in writing, or in drawn responses. The centre could accept email responses if Hemal would prefer to answer the next day, and Hemal and their family were given careful instructions about boundaries for this. The therapist was skilled in using affirming language, and in understanding the need for a calm, kind, attitude, full of curiosity and positive regard for Hemal's experiences. This approach enabled a relationship of trust and respect to build, and a good outcome for Hemal. The transition to other services was well planned, with Hemal and the family as active and valued partners in all parts of the process, where possible.

Checklists for mental health teams working with autistic CYP

1 Advance information is vital, where possible. A sensory report on the building should be available so that CYP and their families can predict the sensory load ahead of them. This information should include maps of car parking areas, bus stops nearby, and similar navigation tips. What is going to happen when they arrive? What options might they have, for example, delaying an initial medical evaluation for a few hours until they feel settled? [See further examples in Memmott et al. (2021)].

2 Ensure all staff, including cleaning and kitchen teams, have modern training from autistic experts, giving vital experience in working respectfully and collaboratively with autistic individuals, and giving a deeper understanding of autistic communication and sensory needs. Approaches need to be holistic.

3 Assess each autistic individual's sensory needs on admission and prepare a sensory plan with the individual. Assume that they may be autistic and screen accordingly. This information should include what they need to encourage self-regulation, such as stimming, hobbies, possessions, quiet spaces, good quality noise-cancelling headphones, or other accommodations. This is a common expression, but what benefits autistic people often benefits all anyway. It's not just that this benefits autistic people, but it's about making the service better generally too.

4   Consider communication and social needs. Be aware that autistic individuals communicate differently and are not usually seeking to be rude. Working with Speech and Language Therapists and Occupational Therapy enables good communication, including the use of devices or picture boards where the person finds those helpful. 'Blanket bans' on the use of technology for communication may be unlawful, and with many autistic people sometimes or usually unable to use spoken language, may prevent effective care.

5   Consider your own impact on the young person's sensory and social experiences. Reduce the use of highly fragranced products, e.g., perfumes. Use a low-arousal, friendly, calm approach with minimal eye contact and a gentle, slower voice tone. The one thing we know we can change is our own approach, so this is key to success (see Synergy in Chapter 11).

6   Where are you meeting the young person? Can lighting be switched off? Is the room likely to have a lot of echo or background noise? Autistic hearing can be exceptional, and seemingly quiet spaces may be filled with distracting noise. Ask, and be prepared to adapt where possible, or allow the use of noise-reducing equipment. Do alarms in the centre have to be alarming? If budgets permit, there are alert systems that replace alarm systems.

7   Consider the impact of touch and texture. This may relate to allowed clothing and shoes, towels, and bedding, and to the safe use of cutlery, stair handrails, taps, door handles, and toilet flush mechanisms.

8   Consider sleep. Most autistic individuals are exhausted from a lack of quality sleep and may need their room adapted to enable better sleep to occur. In particular, many units have curtains or blinds that block little or no light, flickering fluorescent lighting over the young person's bed, noisy air conditioning, noise from adjoining rooms and shower units, and noise from laundry facilities in the vicinity.

9   Consider goals. Make these truly person-centred, fully engaging with what will be a meaningful quality of life for that person, rather than an assumed set of goals suited to non-autistic lives. It is not realistic to expect the best outcomes from group work, or from standardised approaches such as CBT. Think laterally and be prepared to 'meet them where they are'.

10 From the outset, consider the right pathway to discharge, working collaboratively with family and with community services. A safe and caring community setting is the right place for most autistic individuals, supported by a team they know and trust.

Whilst good practice is increasing, some teams may be unaware of their environment's sensory impact, and unaware of the impact of their own ways of communication. Recently, NHS England funded the National Autism Trainer Programme to ensure that teams are accessing up-to-date, person-centred, and trauma-informed/relational approaches in working with autistic people.

Notable, this is authentically produced by and co-delivered with, autistic people of all ages. Significantly improved outcomes tend to occur when those supporting autistic individuals reflect on their own behaviour and approaches, using low-arousal methods (McDonnell et al., 2018; see also Chapter 10 in this book) and showing a willingness to build empathetic relationships (Milton, 2012). Of vital importance is the co-creation of understanding around key areas of well-being, including agency and sense of belonging (Pavlopoulou, 2021).

Example scenario 3:

Sam was given advance information on what the professional team meeting was about, and who would be there. Photos of people were given, where possible, along with photos of the room. The team asked Sam what accommodations would support her, and which member of staff she would like to be there. Sam was allowed into the room first, to choose her own best place to sit. Each person who came in engaged in a friendly wave or a few words of encouragement to Sam, respecting her own choices about such matters. The tone of the meeting was set by the friendly, well-informed, kind calm Responsible Clinician. Sam's parents were allowed in, and the professionals were warm and friendly towards them. Throughout the meeting, Sam was put at the centre of the meeting's pace and content, enabled to chair or co-chair it if they wanted to. Sam was in charge of when breaks happened, though supported to take some regularly if they forgot. Sam and the parents were given refreshments, and there was good communication throughout, to check that each person was comfortable and coping well. Sam's own goals were centred in the clear, well-summarised paperwork. Everyone in the room knew what hobbies, interests and people were important to Sam, and what Sam needed support with on a difficult day. Everyone was focused on providing the right care and a timely discharge when safe and appropriate to do so. Community services were present, well-informed, and planning well. Everyone could relax and engage.

Scenarios such as Sam's happen, and the difference in autistic young people's lives can be extraordinary. By considering autistic CYP as partners in their own care and treatment, as individuals with valid but sometimes different ways of moving, thinking, encountering the world, and thriving, we can enable meaningful therapeutic outcomes and excellent relationships.

Conclusion

There is no doubt that something needs to change, to ensure good outcomes for more autistic CYP accessing mental health services. By collaborating with autistic individuals, their families, and teams embedding autistic specialists, services can bring about significant improvements and excellent outcomes. Access to early diagnosis and appropriate support is a vital step, as is a thorough assessment of sensory and communication needs for the individual. Co-production of solutions means better outcomes, and this includes valuing and supporting not only the individual and their own way of interpreting the world but also valuing family insights. Listening with genuine interest, and framing ways of coping in positive ways, are also important steps towards a therapeutic recovery. Of prime importance are the training, attitudes, and actions of the team around the autistic individual, and excellent early results are being achieved from the new programmes which focus more on this aspect. A holistic approach encompassing well-being, agency, and excellent relationships with trusted team members yields success in so many cases and a genuine improvement in quality of life.

References

Benevides, T. W., Shore, S. M., Palmer, K., Duncan, P., Plank, A., Andresen, M. L., ... Coughlin, S. S. (2020). Listening to the autistic voice: Mental health priorities to guide research and practice in autism from a stakeholder-driven project. *Autism*, *24*(4), 822–833. https://doi.org/10.1177/1362361320908410

Bernardin, C. J., Lewis, T., Bell, D., & Kanne, S. (2021). Associations between social camouflaging and internalizing symptoms in autistic and non-autistic adolescents. *Autism*, *25*(6), 1580–1591. https://doi.org/10.1177/1362361321997284

Chance, P. (1974). A conversation with Ivar Lovaas. *Psychology Today*, *7*(8), 76–80, 82–84.

Cornwall, P. L., Simpson, S., Gibbs, C., & Morfee, V. (2021). Evaluation of radically open dialectical behaviour therapy in an adult community mental health team: Effectiveness in people with autism spectrum disorders. *BJPsych Bulletin*, *45*(3), 146–153. https://doi.org/10.1192/bjb.2020.113

Gonçalves, A. M., & Monteiro, P. (2023). Autism Spectrum Disorder and auditory sensory alterations: A systematic review on the integrity of cognitive and neuronal functions related to auditory processing. *Journal of Neural Transmission*, *130*(3), 325–408. https://doi.org/10.1007/s00702-023-02595-9

Hallett, S., & Kerr, C. (2020). *Autistic adults' experiences of counselling – full report*. Retrieved from https://autisticmentalhealth.uk/creportfull/

Hanlon, C., Ashworth, E., Moore, D., Donaghy, B., & Saini, P. (2022). Autism should be considered in the assessment and delivery of mental health services for children and young people. *Disability & Society*, *37*(10), 1752–1757. https://doi.org/10.1080/09687599.2022.2099252

Huang, Y., Arnold, S. R., Foley, K. R., & Trollor, J. N. (2022). Experiences of support following autism diagnosis in adulthood. *Journal of Autism and Developmental Disorders*, *54*(2), 518–531.. https://doi.org/10.1007/s10803-022-05811-9

Iversen, S., & Kildahl, A. N. (2022). Case report: mechanisms in misdiagnosis of autism as borderline personality disorder. *Frontiers in Psychology*, *13*. https://doi.org/10.3389/fpsyg.2022.735205

Joint Committee on Human Rights. (2019). *The detention of young people with learning disabilities and/or autism*. Retrieved from https://publications.parliament.uk/pa/jt201919/jtselect/jtrights/121/121.pdf

Kim, S. Y. (2019). The experiences of adults with autism spectrum disorder: Self-determination and quality of life. *Research in Autism Spectrum Disorders, 60*, 1–15. https://doi.org/10.1016/j.rasd.2018.12.002

Lobregt-van Buuren, E., Sizoo, B., Mevissen, L., & de Jongh, A. (2019). Eye Movement Desensitization and Reprocessing (EMDR) therapy as a feasible and potential effective treatment for adults with Autism Spectrum Disorder (ASD) and a history of adverse events. *Journal of Autism and Developmental Disorders, 49*(1), 151–164. https://doi.org/10.1007/s10803-018-3687-6

McDonnell, A., Milton, D., Page, A., Kendall, S., Kaur Johal, T., & O'Connell, A. (2018). The low arousal approach: A practitioner's guide.

Memmott, A., Corbyn, J., Williams, G., & Newton, K. (2021). *"It's Not Rocket Science": Considering and meeting the sensory needs of autistic children and young people in CAMHS inpatient services.* Retrieved from https://research.brighton.ac.uk/en/publications/its-not-rocket-science-considering-and-meeting-the-sensory-needs-

Milton, D. E. (2012). On the ontological status of autism: The 'double empathy problem'. *Disability & Society, 27*(6), 883–887. https://doi.org/10.1080/09687599.2012.710008

Minio-Paluello, I., Porciello, G., Pascual-Leone, A., & Baron-Cohen, S. (2020). Face individual identity recognition: a potential endophenotype in autism. *Molecular Autism, 11*(1), 1–16. https://doi.org/10.1186/s13229-020-00371-0

Monk, R., Whitehouse, A. J., & Waddington, H. (2022). The use of language in autism research. *Trends in Neurosciences, 45*(11), 791–793. https://doi.org/10.1016/j.tins.2022.08.009

National Autistic Society. (2022). *Number of autistic people in mental health hospitals: Latest data.* Retrieved from https://www.autism.org.uk/what-we-do/news/number-of-autistic-people-in-mental-health-hos-aug

Nicholls, A. (2018). *Why doesn't standard talking therapy work for autistic people?* Retrieved from: https://www.dralicenicholls.com/why-doesnt-standard-talking-therapy-work-for-autistic-people/

Pavlopoulou, G. (2021). "A good night's sleep: Learning about sleep from autistic adolescents' personal accounts": Corrigendum. *Frontiers in Psychology, 12*, Article 657385. https://doi.org/10.3389/fpsyg.2021.657385

Pellicano, E., & den Houting, J. (2022). Annual research review: Shifting from 'normal science'to neurodiversity in autism science. *Journal of Child Psychology and Psychiatry, 63*(4), 381–396. https://doi.org/10.1111/jcpp.13534

Powell, H., He, J., Wodka, E., DeRonda, A., Edden, R. A., Vasa, R. A., Motofsky, S. H. & Puts, N. (2022). Investigating the associations between perceptual alterations, sensory reactivity, intolerance of uncertainty and anxiety in autistic children.

Hill, R. M., & Katusic, M. (2020). Examining suicide risk in individuals with autism spectrum disorder via the interpersonal theory of suicide: Clinical insights and recommendations. *Children's Health Care, 49*(4), 472–492.

Rumball, F., Happé, F., & Grey, N. (2020). Experience of trauma and PTSD symptoms in autistic adults: Risk of PTSD development following DSM-5 and non-DSM-5 traumatic life events. *Autism Research, 13*(12), 2122–2132. https://doi.org/10.1002/aur.2306

Russell, A., Gaunt, D., Cooper, K., Horwood, J., Barton, S., Ensum, I.,... & Wiles, N. (2019). Guided self-help for depression in autistic adults: The ADEPT feasibility RCT. *Health Technology Assessment (Winchester, England), 23*(68), 1. https://doi.org/10.3310%2Fhta23680

Rylaarsdam, L., & Guemez-Gamboa, A. (2019). Genetic causes and modifiers of autism spectrum disorder. *Frontiers in Cellular Neuroscience*, *13*, 385. https://doi.org/10.3389/fncel.2019.00385

Setlhare, K., & Rafi, S. (2022). Presenting symptoms of undiagnosed autism spectrum disorder among young boys and girls in community CAMHS between 2018–2019. *BJPsych Open*, *8*(S1), S172–S173. https://doi.org/10.1192/bjo.2022.482

Shaw, S. C., Doherty, M., McCowan, S., & Eccles, J. A. (2022). Towards a neurodiversity-affirmative approach for an over-represented and under-recognised population: Autistic adults in outpatient psychiatry. *Journal of Autism and Developmental Disorders*, *52*(9), 4200–4201. https://doi.org/10.1007/s10803-022-05670-4

Shaw, S. C., McCowan, S., Doherty, M., Grosjean, B., & Kinnear, M. (2021). The neurodiversity concept viewed through an autistic lens. *The Lancet Psychiatry*, *8*(8), 654–655. https://doi.org/10.1016/S2215-0366(21)00247-9

Shum, K. K. M., Cho, W. K., Lam, L. M. O., Laugeson, E. A., Wong, W. S., & Law, L. S. (2019). Learning how to make friends for Chinese adolescents with autism spectrum disorder: A randomized controlled trial of the Hong Kong Chinese version of the PEERS® intervention. *Journal of Autism and Developmental Disorders*, *49*(2), 527–541. https://doi.org/10.1007/s10803-018-3728-1

UN General Assembly, Convention on the Rights of Persons with Disabilities: resolution / adopted by the General Assembly, 24 January 2007, A/RES/61/106. Retrieved from: https://www.refworld.org/docid/45f973632.html [accessed 1 October 2023]. https://www.ohchr.org/en/hrbodies/crpd/pages/conventionrightspersonswithdisabilities.aspx

Verriden, A. L., & Roscoe, E. M. (2019). An evaluation of a punisher assessment for decreasing automatically reinforced problem behavior. *Journal of Applied Behavior Analysis*, *52*(1), 205–226. https://doi.org/10.1002/jaba.509

Wang, X., Zhao, J., Huang, S., Chen, S., Zhou, T., Li, Q., ... Hao, Y. (2021). Cognitive behavioral therapy for autism spectrum disorders: A systematic review. *Pediatrics*, *147*(5). https://doi.org/10.1542/peds.2020-049880

Chapter 3

The role of autistic agency in recovery from mental health illness

Alexis Quinn and Suzy Rowland

The role of autistic agency in recovery from mental distress

This chapter, written by two neurodivergent women and parents of neuro-divergent children, illuminates the difference that being in the driver's seat makes when it comes to recovery from mental distress. The first half of this chapter considers the need for personal agency, how it might be constricted and the impact this can have on autistic lives. The second half of this chapter explores how we might promote the agency to aid recovery – establishing the right setting, which is adequately resourced, with an internal sense of hope and external personal support enabling autistic people to thrive, despite the misfortunes or distress interpersonal misalignment and societal expectation may invite.

Agency

A sense of personal agency might be defined as perceiving ourselves as able to influence our own actions and life circumstances. Having a sense of personal agency can help people feel psychologically stable and flexible in the face of conflict or change (Gallagher, 2000). Creating opportunities to experience feelings of agency must take into consideration the beliefs, perceptions, feelings, and choices of the young person. Yet this opportunity may not be apparent for autistic youth when well-meaning supporters such as teachers, support staff, parents, and mental health professionals believe the principal aim of helping is to encourage conformity to neurotypical norms.

Growing up as a neurodivergent child and adolescent, Alexis Quinn, co-author of this chapter, often experienced the comments, 'why are you doing that?', 'what's wrong with you?', and 'why are you so weird?' In school, teachers would berate her for being disorganised, losing equipment, forgetting what she was supposed to be doing and taking too long to process and act on instructions. People found little favour or merit in her autistic disposition and Alexis soon came to realise that warmth, respect, and acceptance

DOI: 10.4324/9781003352327-5

would only be extended when she fulfilled some particular (usually neurotypical) expectation.

Struggling to manage the sensory-charged environment of classrooms, Alexis would often cover her ears and engage in self-stimulatory behaviour such as bouncing her foot/leg. Her teachers responded by rewarding *appropriate* behaviour (e.g., giving a point/merit for being still) and berating her neurodivergent coping strategies (e.g., by sending her outside, putting her in isolation, or making her face the wall). Such experiences led to overload and meltdown where Alexis would flee the classroom and run around the school field until calm. Her parents were called in to address her 'truancy'. Predictably, Alexis began to mask her neurodivergence resulting in anxiety, depression, loneliness, and isolation, coming to fear interaction and her own autistic nature.

Constricting agency, fracturing identity

What was once considered true and irrefutable around autism 'disorder' and within the person deficit must be rigorously challenged and re-defined as explained in Chapter 1 of this book. Oftentimes, mental distress is thought to occur in autistic people, precisely because they are autistic. However, experiences of powerlessness where one is not free to act in the ways they find most comfortable, are strongly associated with psychological distress (Proctor, 2018), far outweighing biological or genetic causes (e.g., Bentall, 2003). This explanation is significant as almost from the moment autistic people are born, our environments can be experienced as *too much* – too noisy, too chaotic, too confusing, too spoken communication based, too bright! Given we express our discomfort of living in a world not sensitive to our needs, we are unforgivingly compared to "culturally preferred ways of being" (White, 1995, p. 16) and exposed to messaging that suggests autistic preferences are abnormal and/or impaired (Botha & Frost, 2020; Milton, 2017; Rose & Vivian, 2020).

Much of our autistic stereotypy is rated negatively by non-autistic people (Botha & Frost, 2020; Evans, 2013; Wood & Freeth, 2016), and rather than being supported, we are stigmatised and considered on the fringe of human normality (Botha & Frost, 2020; Cage et al., 2019; Gernsbacher, 2007; Pearson & Rose, 2021; Rose & Vivian, 2020). On TV, at school and in public, we have incurred slights, insults, or unfavourable comparisons e.g., "have you tried a gluten-free diet?", "perhaps she needs some discipline", and "why doesn't she speak?" These microtraumas, however well-intentioned, inflict damage over time (Crastnopol, 2015), and are hidden in the neuronormative that infuses interpersonal relating. Thus, it becomes impossible for autistic people to express their frustration because to do so would be to rock the relational boat after all, we are the weird ones, and 'so-and-so was only trying to help!' The environment around us then creates a pattern of distorting influences that suppress our ability to be in our own driver's seat and exercise agency over our lives.

As injurious moments accumulate, our identities become fractured, and our sense of self is undermined. Many of us will have internalised a negative self-concept – a 'bad me' (Sullivan, 1953). This 'bad me' comprises our worst, most undesirable qualities, which garner the most disapproval. We do fewer and fewer things that are part and parcel of autistic culture to avoid harmful messaging and 'bad me' experiences.

Many of us 'mask' in the hope that we might avert disapproval (see also Chapters 5 and 12). These acts of pseudo-agency have the immediate advantage of relieving external consequences (e.g., bullying/microtrauma), yet come at a cost. (Un)consciously we realise that our autistic selves are the 'bad me', and we, therefore, cannot ward off 'bad me' experiences – we get caught in a double bind in which we cannot do the right thing. This gross constriction of agency caused by an inability to accept neurodivergent ways of being thwarts our efforts to manage and cope with the anxieties of our unpredictable relationships.

As we realise the extent to which we are not welcome, we get anxious, depressed, and eventually burnout. These are all common reactions among masking autistics (Botha et al., 2022; Cage & Troxell-Whitman, 2019; Cassidy et al., 2023; Pearson & Rose, 2021). The authors of this chapter and their children have at best been burdened, experienced an eroded sense of worth, and at times suffered from significant mental ill-health (see Quinn, 2021). A childhood of presenting as a problem to be solved by others does not and cannot be nurturing nor enable us to realise our best selves. Surely, the way to effect positive change and diminish the difficulties that have arisen from the powerlessness created by a lack of agency to be we is not to impose further power and control, but rather create environments where the entirety of the self is accepted!

Conceptualising autism and working together as a means to increase agency and aid recovery

Contrary to some prominent theories of autism (Chevallier et al., 2012), autistic people are social beings, with prosocial tendencies. We are all wired to connect and require those supporting us to demonstrate a consistent attitude that deeply values the totality of our humanity, showing no preference for a particular behaviour or way of being (Mearns & Cooper, 2018). Because we construct our understanding of the world through language, narrative approaches such as those of White and Epston (2004) can be helpful. Where staff focus on supporting autistic people, neurodivergent-friendly narratives are foregrounded that might reduce 'bad me' experiences and self-blame, maximising agency, and freedom. Such deconstructive approaches have the potential to loosen "the grip of the most prestigious and powerful elements or tradition....freeing up the repressed senses, the silenced voices, the excluded and marginalised elements" (Caputo, 1998, p. 231).

If autistic people are exposed to greater neuro-affirming narratives, they might be able to reverse the binds of judgement and agency constriction, learning that the aspects of themselves that they have hated or feared have instead been trying to help and protect them. For instance, Alexis came to realise that she had not become isolated from peers because she was unable to connect, having been labelled anti-social and a loner. Rather Alexis had learnt, it was safer to isolate herself to avoid bullying. This realisation helped her accept and have compassion for her self-preservation strategies.

Practitioners can support neuro-affirming approaches that have the capacity to increase agency using the following tips:

1   Help young people find value in their uniqueness. How do they feel about their areas of strength and where they struggle? In what ways can you celebrate the young person's chosen accomplishments?
2   Support areas that are experienced as difficult by the person or others in a non-judgemental, loving, and accepting way. For example, what is the child's preferred method of communication? How can I communicate in a way they find comfortable?
3   Identify strengths and involve children in activities that highlight these so that they might gain mastery and build their innate worth and value. What does the child like? Can you set achievable, empowering goals that are meaningful to the child?
4   Reauthor medical model narratives/experiences from a neuro-affirming perspective. Do you have the knowledge, vocabulary, and understanding to reframe?
5   Build systems around the child that are capable of supporting the realisation of chosen goals.
6   Build circles of friendship and support. Who are the young person's cheerleaders? How can you support the person to find friends who are neuro-affirming/neurodivergent?

In all the above, it is important that those supporting the young person come from a place of unknowing where they do not presume anything or fall prey to cultural stereotypes. This support might first involve approaching the young person and their family as experts in their uniqueness. Here the supporter has no expectations of similarity to other autistic people and they do not try to fit them into behavioural models or agendas. For Alexis, this was freeing as she no longer needed to convince others of her perspective or to defend against their ideas. When her supporters were non-directive and demonstrated an abundance of curiosity, new narratives emerged that promoted agency and freedom.

Promoting agency via collaborative family iterations across school

One way to increase acceptance and promote agency is the meaningful involvement of parents of autistic children in the school environment. Data highlights the positive impact of parental engagement on the general school population (Hattie et al., 2008). From personal experience and many anecdotes, we hear, that many parents of autistic children find it difficult to partner with schools and teachers due to stigma, and a sense of feeling ostracised and blamed. Yet, if we align with the idea that genuine child and parental involvement builds self-esteem, it follows that when a child requires additional educational support due to a specific learning difficulty, parental and child involvement will likely become a valuable component of developing the child's eventual sense of agency and well-being.

The requirement for parental contributions in Education Health and Care plans is a good example of the value of parent voice and input in the child's eventual educational and emotional well-being and the resulting feelings if their voices are not fully heard or represented (Palikara et al., 2018). Engaging parent and child voices in key decisions that impact parent and child (and usually wider family) can support agency, quieting the 'bad me' inner narrative. If this is done, however, in an environment *without* genuine mutuality and co-production, it can create an adversarial atmosphere that further shuts down any real agency for the young person.

Suzy, co-author of this chapter, worked with a family for several months supporting 'Hattie', an autistic young person with co-occurring ADHD. She presented with sensory sensitivity, high self-awareness, and difficulty in managing big emotions provoked in the school setting by daily incidents of feeling misunderstood or overstimulated. A meeting took place at Hattie's school to discuss whether she would be able to remain in that school, and what further support the school could offer to alleviate her distressed state. Suzy was surprised that Hattie was not invited to the meeting. It became clear that the school felt that the decision about her further education could be conducted without input from the principal player.

Agency is critical and excluding a young person from key decisions that affect their own lives can adversely damage self-esteem and potentially impact future decision-making skills. In Hattie's case, it meant that staff also lost a chance to hear from the young person directly about what would help them to prevent or recuperate from triggering school situations. Additionally, being able to represent yourself and be heard, it is a key part of healing some of the pain and damage that occurs to autistic people when they are either unconsciously gaslighted or bullied, often by people they look up to and respect. Providing opportunities and encouraging agency can build the self-esteem necessary for a child to raise their hand to ask a question, say 'no' to something that constricts their right to legitimate, autistic self-expression, and advocate for themselves or others. Professionals need to support this crucial work, provide small, incremental opportunities to challenge the status quo, and extend young people's ability to self-assert and express themselves in ways they find most comfortable. It is unmasking that the autistic person might find out who they are and what their wants and needs are. They must be permitted access to their truths to speak to them and feel validated.

We can improve agency by not only ensuring there is a space at the table for the young person and their family but also by making meetings accessible and enquiring how a specific activity or intervention has made the child feel. Suzy attended school meetings where her son's opinions and understanding about his learning needs and in-school support were consistently and actively sought through direct conversations, 1–2-1s with her son, and opinions and reports from individuals and social groups who knew her son outside of the educational setting. To facilitate communication visuals, rating scales and additional processing time were offered. Documents written in lay language and agendas were shared in advance. These examples represent the sort of good practice that can build confidence in young people, permitting self-exploration and self-advocacy whilst also enabling supporters to develop a deeper understanding of the individual's needs.

In genuine collaboration, it is important to hear when those seeking to help the young person or the family have gone down the wrong track. Acknowledging that we can share expertise as expert by science and expert by experience during consultations with school and mental health professionals and co-produce ideas about what helps/what does not help is a win–win. Trust and agency grow when we listen to each other carefully and respond holistically.

Relational spaces that allow for acceptance and the development of agency

Mandy, now aged 19, experienced considerable constriction of agency in her later years of primary education at a residential school. Vulnerable to sensory overwhelm, Mandy would exhibit distressed behaviour in learning settings and at break times. Staff working with Mandy misread her communication as challenging behaviour and they responded with restrictive practices, including restraint and solitary confinement.

Mandy was admitted to a CAMHS unit where greater restrictions on her agency (such as an inability to engage in her passions and interests) led to more extreme distress including self-harm and suicide attempts. Her parents have long attributed Mandy's difficulties to a lack of autism understanding in her support workers and a lack of appropriate environments. After successfully campaigning for her release, Mandy is now living happily in a bespoke home environment with an educational package that meets her needs. It does not have to be rocket science to bring positive change – starting from simple accommodations that increase agency and model empathy can bring vital improvements for all. These efforts take time as there are no quick fixes, and the profiles of the young people may often change or look spikey. Also sometimes, their requests may ask professionals to think differently about things they have learnt in their original training and academic study.

Mandy's story demonstrates the effectiveness of what we might call *relational spaces* in extending agency. The physical space was low demand, low arousal, and provided time to settle Mandy's sensitive cognitive, emotional, and sensory systems. Supportive people were recruited by Mandy and were invited to get to know her. Each member of the support team respected Mandy's ways of being as valid and meaningful. They did not always understand, but they did not dismiss aspects of her either. Instead, they entered her world rather than forcing her to enter theirs. This approach offered Mandy a different relational experience, letting her know that it was safe to embrace her uniqueness. Supporters, therefore, had to be open to their own transformation to participate 'in' the relationship rather than standing 'outside' judging it.

Relational spaces can be set up anywhere – they are interactive and function as a safe laboratory full of possibility and critique. Some supporters might feel worried about the status of their work without a theoretical, scientific-based structure. It can be scary to adopt a not-knowing, young-person-led approach. An important point to consider here is whether an autism theory or approach opens the agency of the young person or constricts their agency and/or understanding. If supporters become trapped within the confines of scientific, medical models or other such autism theories, they will continue to find in the young person what that theory leads them to expect – usually deficit and disorder. Being youth-led in a relational space aims to help supporters see what that young person's uniqueness brings. The space therefore attempts to express uncertain knowing rather than claiming to erase knowing; it emphasises the importance of holding any autism-related theories or approach with uncertainty.

Anyone can create a relational space. They can be in family homes, classrooms, or clubs; anywhere that there is no normal, and no specific way any person must be. An ideal relational space is characterised by unconditional positive regard, interdependence, connectedness, and openness. Helpers might:

- understand that autistic people are pro-social and want to form trusting relationships.
- welcome autistic culture and be curious about ways to engage from an autistic perspective.
- level up power imbalances.
- get rid of standardised ways of working and coproduce solutions.
- be encouraging and willing to take *risks*.
- always be agile, flexible, dynamic, and evolving, understanding that a person's agency is theirs. It should not be task specific or dependent on helpers *allowing* it.

Mandy's relational spaces meant she no longer felt alone, isolated, and weird. Her confidence to express her concerns increased resulting in an ability to communicate her needs more readily knowing they will be acted upon. She has recently won an award for her studies in health and social care in a mainstream college.

Agency, ethnicity, and neurodivergencies

Where there is an intersection of a racialised young person who is also neurodivergent, their neurodivergence may remain unseen behind the more obvious signifier of their 'race.' The bias sometimes directed towards black and other minoritised groups, can result in a severe lack of agency, compromising their right to have a say in decisions about their life, including in education, employment, and relationships (see also Chapter 7).

Anecdotally, numerous non-white families observe that their undiagnosed or diagnosed autistic children in school settings are perceived solely through the prism of dysregulated or 'challenging' behaviours, and social emotional or mental health difficulties, before a possible neurodivergent presentation. This was Suzy's experience and correlates with that of many parents of a neurodivergent child racialised as black. As a result of these misperceptions, these autistic children are treated punitively, in ways that can further traumatise them and delay their ability to build the self-esteem required to self-advocate (Rowland, 2020). Similarly, Vincent et al. (2023) described black students' struggles to claim a positive learner identity in the face of some teachers' negative attitudes, assumptions, and misunderstandings of autism. This was reported to also have an impact on mothers to maintain their credentials as 'good' mothers.

Suzy once attended a 'return to school' meeting with her autistic son, after a one-week exclusionary period. The SENCO, parents, and deputy head of the school sat around the table discussing how seriously the school took her son's behaviour outbursts, with the veiled threat of permanent exclusion. While struggling to keep her composure, the meeting was interrupted by a soft knock at the door as Suzy's five-and-a-half-year-old yet undiagnosed autistic son came into the room, ostensibly to atone for his 'transgressions.' Suzy and her son had not previously been informed that her son would be invited into this highly charged adult space. The whole experience felt diminishing and shameful for both, effectively leaving them powerless and voiceless.

Conclusion

It is only by encouraging acceptance and promoting unconditional positive regard that we will make a positive contribution to autistic people's mental health. The reality is that irreparable, interpersonal damage can be caused directly by well-meaning but ultimately damaging interactions and interventions that insist on people fitting in at all costs (Crastnopol, 2015; Rogers, 1959; Stern, 2003). Autistic people need and deserve to have their views heard, choosing, or refusing to engage in interventions that target their development. Without this sense of personal agency coping strategies cannot be personalised and are unlikely to be of benefit (Quinn, 2021). We suggest that relational spaces should be adopted in settings that care for and educate autistic people. These provide opportunities for connection with peers and supportive helpers that enable people to heal in the safe company of others.

References

Bentall, R. P. (2003). *Madness explained: Psychosis and human nature*. Allen Lane.

Botha, M., & Frost, D. M. (2020). Extending the minority stress model to understand mental health problems experienced by the autistic population. *Society and Mental Health*, *10*(1), 20–34. https://doi.org/10.1177/2156869318804297

Botha, M., Dibb, B., & Frost, D. M. (2022). "Autism is me": An investigation of how autistic individuals make sense of autism and stigma. *Disability & Society*, *37*(3), 427–453. https://doi.org/10.1080/09687599.2020.1822782

Cage, E., & Troxell-Whitman, Z. (2019). Understanding the reasons, contexts and costs of camouflaging for autistic adults. *Journal of Autism and Developmental Disorders*, *49*(5), 1899–1911. https://doi.org/10.1007/s10803-018-03878-x

Cage, E., Di Monaco, J., & Newell, V. (2019). Understanding, attitudes and dehumanisation towards autistic people. *Autism*, *23*(6), 1373–1383. https://doi.org/10.1177/1362361318811290

Caputo, J. D. (1998). Heidegger. In S. Critchley & W. Schroeder (Eds.), *A companion to continental philosophy* (pp. 223–236). Oxford: Blackwell.

Cassidy, S., McLaughlin, E., McGranaghan, R., Pelton, M., O'Connor, R., & Rodgers, J. (2023). Is camouflaging autistic traits associated with defeat, entrapment, and lifetime suicidal thoughts? Expanding the integrated motivational volitional model of suicide. *Suicide & Life-Threatening Behavior*, *53*(4), 572–585. https://doi.org/10.1111/sltb.12965

Chevallier, C., Kohls, G., Troiani, V., Brodkin, E. S., & Schultz, R. T. (2012). The social motivation theory of autism. *Trends in Cognitive Sciences*, *16*(4), 231–239. https://doi.org/10.1016/j.tics.2012.02.007

Crastnopol, M. (2015). *Micro-trauma: A psychoanalytic understanding of cumulative psychic injury*. London: Routledge.

Evans, B. (2013). How autism became autism: The radical transformation of a central concept of child development in Britain. *History of the Human Sciences*, *26*(3), 3–31. https://doi.org/10.1177/0952695113484320

Concept of Child Development in Britain. *History of the Human Sciences*, *26*(3), 3–31. https://doi.org/10.1177/0952695113484320.

Gallagher, S. (2000). Philosophical conceptions of the self: Implications for cognitive science. *Trends in Cognitive Sciences*, *4*(1), 14–21.

Gernsbacher, M. A. (2007). On not being human. *APS Observer*, *20*(2), 5.

Hattie, J. (2008). Visible learning: A synthesis of over 800 meta-analyses relating to achievement. Routledge.

Mearns, D., & Cooper, M. (2018). *Working at relational depth in counselling and psychotherapy* (2nd ed.). London: Sage.

Milton, D. (2017). *A mismatch of salience: Explorations of the nature of autism from theory to practice*. Hove: Pavilion Press.

Palikara, O., Castro, S., Gaona, C., & Eirinaki, V. (2018, April). Capturing the voices of children in the education health and care plans: are we there yet?. In *Frontiers in education* (Vol. 3, p. 24). Frontiers Media SA.

Pearson, A., & Rose, K. (2021). A conceptual analysis of autistic masking: Understanding the narrative of stigma and the illusion of choice. *Autism in Adulthood*, *3*(1), 52–60. https://doi.org/10.1089/aut.2020.0043

Proctor, G. (2018). *The dynamics of power in psychotherapy and counselling: Ethics, politics and practice*. Monmouth: PCCS Books.

Quinn, A. (2021). *Unbroken: Learning to live beyond diagnosis*. Welbeck Publishing.

Rogers, C. R. (1959). Therapy, personality and interpersonal relationships. In S. Koch (Ed.), *Psychology: A study of a science*, Vol. 3: Formulations of the Person and the Social Context. New York: McGraw-Hill.

Rose, K., & Vivian, S. (2020). *Regarding the use of dehumanising rhetoric*. Retrieved from: https://theautisticadvocate.com/2020/02/regarding-the-use-of-dehumanising-rhetoric/

Rowland, D. (2020). Trauma induced autism—an update. *Journal of Neurology, Psychiatry and Brain Research*, 3.

Stern, D. N. (2003). *The interpersonal world of the human infant: A view from psychoanalysis and developmental psychology* (2nd Ed.). London: Karnac.

Sullivan, H. S. (1953). *The interpersonal theory of psychiatry*. New York: Norton.

Vincent, C., Oliver, C., & Pavlopoulou, G. (2023). Lessons from lockdown: Autistic students, parents and mainstream schools. *British Educational Research Journal*, *49*(3), 522–537.

White, M. K. (1995). *Re-authoring lives: Interviews & essays*. Dulwich Centre Publications.

White, M. & Epston, D. (2004). Externalizing the problem. In C. Malone, L. Forbat, M. Robb, & J. Seden (Eds.), *Relating experience: Stories from health and social care* (pp. 88–94). London: Routledge.

Wood, C., & Freeth. (2016). Students' stereotypes of autism. *Journal of Educational Issues*, *2*(2), 131–140. http://doi.org/10.5296/jei.v2i2.9975

Understanding autistic mental health

Chapter 4

Uncertainty and stress in autistic CYP

Ruth Moyse and Ellie Kollatsi

Reframing 'intolerance' of uncertainty

There is considerable evidence that many autistic CYP experience higher levels of anxiety (Simonoff et al., 2008; van Steensel & Heeman, 2017), and to a much greater degree, than CYP in the community (Kuusikko et al., 2008). Is it true, then, that autistic people are inherently more anxious, or do their experiences make them so? And how does our understanding of anxiety in autistic CYP influence the support with which they are provided?

Autistic CYP are often described as not liking change and as finding change stressful, and this is not without reason. Research has demonstrated a significant relationship between anxiety and what is described as an 'intolerance of uncertainty' in autistic CYP (Boulter et al., 2014; Cai et al., 2018; Rodgers et al., 2017). Furthermore, studies have shown that autistic participants with the greatest 'intolerance of uncertainty' were also the most highly anxious (Buhr & Dugas, 2009). Understanding the link between these two concepts is thought to be an important step towards developing 'better treatments' for autistic and non-autistic populations (Jenkinson et al., 2020, p. 1933). How we frame anxiety and intolerance of uncertainty in autistic CYP also determines whether we see 'intolerance' as a problem that requires a 'fix', or as a naturally occurring difference that requires a different approach.

Intolerance of uncertainty is typically defined as the 'overvaluation of predictability and the tendency to become overwhelmed by the unexpected or unknown' (Jenkinson et al., 2020, p. 1934). A model by South and Rogers (2017) proposes that uncertainty in autistic people is created by sensory processing differences and alexithymia (the term for difficulties in understanding and describing your own emotions, which many autistic people experience). This uncertainty leads to high levels of anxiety which, it is argued, leads autistic people to seek to make the world a more predictable place (e.g., through repetitive behaviours). However, these attempts can be thwarted by alexithymia, which is challenges in recognising, expressing, sourcing, and describing one's own emotions and which can make emotional regulation difficult (Gaigg et al., 2018).

DOI: 10.4324/9781003352327-7

Differences in sensory processing can impact how well someone is able to use predictive processing to manage incoming sensory information. Typically, the brain uses prior experiences to make predictions about incoming sensory information and compares it with the actual input, instead of processing all sensory input. The brain then makes perception changes based on the discrepancy between the two. This experience is argued to be less active or reduced in autistic people, as compared to non-autistic people (Stark et al., 2021). It is suggested that this experience may account for an autistic desire for 'sameness' to achieve maximum predictability in a changing world (Stark et al., 2021). When these autistic-led efforts to achieve sameness are dismissed or interrupted, distress behaviours or shutdowns are possible. Following these lines of thought, intolerance of uncertainty could be perceived as a peculiarly autistic problem. Being critical of an autistic person's emotional *response* to uncertainty also frames that *response* as unacceptable, as 'inappropriate emotionality' (Bervoets et al., 2021, p. 3). Both the 'intolerance' *and* the reaction are seen as problems located within the individual. The solution, according to this approach, is to somehow teach the autistic person to tolerate uncertainty – or at least to better self-regulate. Yet this approach raises several questions:

- Do practitioners sometimes prioritise shutting down the response over understanding and resolving or preventing the uncertainty? And what does this say about *our level* of tolerance to autistic CYP experiencing overwhelm or distress?
- What message does it send to our autistic CYP when we tell them to simply be more resilient, to make less of a fuss? Could it be that we create *more* uncertainty for them when we tell them their 'intolerance' of uncertainty is irrational, or when we tell them they must think differently? Is the result more fear, not less? Less hope, not more?
- Do we stifle or remove their coping mechanisms, instead of adding to them, when we tell them to be more tolerant of uncertainty? What is the impact of telling them to suppress their emotions? Should we be trying to change the child, or should we instead be examining the environment, and the role we play in it?

If we regard a response to uncertainty as rational, rather than unreasonable, our attitude and our approach to support may both change. Reframing 'intolerance' of uncertainty as a *rational* response shifts our focus to the nature of the uncertainty, and our interventions to removing or reducing the cause. This reframing moves us to consider and accept the importance of predictability in the lives of autistic people, in making them feel safe and grounded. Instead of being intolerant of the autistic child's response to uncertainty, we can identify and help address uncertainty in their lives.

Identifying uncertainty in the environment and social factors

There is evidence that 'uncertainties are not objective (and equal)', but instead subjective and contextual (Bervoets et al., 2021, p. 2). As such, the location of uncertainty that creates anxiety is likely to be different for autistic people compared to non-autistic people (Bervoets et al., 2021). Therefore, practitioners should seek to understand autistic experiences of the world as the key to reducing their anxiety.

As the same experience or event may be felt qualitatively differently, non-autistic clinicians and practitioners may struggle to notice instances and situations that create uncertainty for autistic CYP. In addition, they may not appreciate the significance of uncertainty for autistic CYP and can perhaps unwittingly underestimate or brush aside the impact on them. This next section identifies some examples of uncertainty in the school environment, on the basis that this is where autistic CYP spend most of their time, and where great demands are made on their sensory processing and emotional regulation abilities. It usefully highlights issues that – unaddressed – may ultimately result in admission to specialist CAMHS or crisis care.

If we think of uncertainty as a firework – unexpected, overwhelming, unpredictable, sometimes frightening – it is easier to see that schools are full of 'fireworks'. From a sensory perspective, just being in a school environment – with vast amounts of competing information produced in the classrooms, the hallways, the canteen, and the playground – can be problematic. Autistic CYP may be unable to filter out excess or unnecessary information, leading to overwhelm (Donaldson's Trust, 2020; Rose, 2018). They may be hyper- or hypo-sensitive to sensory information, or both. This unpredictability can lead autistic CYP to feel unsafe. In research by Moyse (2020), an interviewee named Alex[1] said 'At any point someone, someone could just shout...so I constantly have to be on guard for someone going to make a noise'. Rosie, meanwhile, described school corridors and playgrounds as places that are 'out of control'. Being bombarded with sensory input, particularly that which is unpredictable in terms of occurrence but certain in terms of likelihood, is therefore very challenging to manage; more so when you are given no support or know what you need but lack the agency to affect change.

Multiple other aspects of the school day can also create uncertainty (see Table 4.1 for some examples). Whilst autistic CYP may depend on things being as they are told they are, or will be, confusion and uncertainty can be created *by others*. In many cases, this results in the autistic person questioning whether they feel safe, something which may not be noticed or understood by others. For example, the significance of a class seating plan seems particularly great for autistic CYP, who report wanting to sit by the door, with their back to a wall, or next to a trusted friend. All relevant for a child who perhaps feels

Table 4.1 Examples of aspects of the school day that can create uncertainty

Example	Some reasons for uncertainty	Thoughts autistic YP may have
School rules	Some rules are enforced by some staff but not others. Some rules are not enforced. Some rules are enforced some of the time. Rules are not enforced when peers break them.	When will rules be enforced? How will peers behave? Why is it a rule if it is not enforced? Why am I criticised or punished if I tell a staff member that someone has broken a rule? *Do I feel safe?*
Seating plans	Seating plans change without warning. New table layout without warning. Quiet pupils sat between disruptive pupils.	Why has the plan changed? How will I know if the seating plans will be the same tomorrow? Why am I sat between people who don't follow the rules? How can I work? *Do I feel safe?*
Peer relationships	Peers are inconsistent in their behaviour. Group dynamics are confusing. Expectations of friendships differ.	Will my friend be my friend tomorrow? How will I know if I can trust them? I don't want to be bullied again. *Do I feel safe?*
Timetable	Fancy dress days Sports days Surprise assembly	What will I have to wear? How will it feel? Will I wear the right thing? How will I manage the extra sensory input from assembly? *Do I feel safe?*
Dining hall	Changes to the published menu. Some items on the menu run out. Multiple sources of sensory input. Groups of peers who are in the dining hall at the same time. Staff on duty.	Will there be something I can eat? Will I find somewhere to sit? Will the smells overwhelm me? Who will be in the queue? *Do I feel safe?*

unsafe in school, who may be bullied by peers, and who is always checking if they can escape.

Of course, these sensory processing differences and changing, unpredictable days are not limited to the school environment. As practitioners, have you considered the impact of the environment in which you work and in which you meet autistic young people? As described more fully in Chapter 2, examples of the impact of unmet sensory needs of autistic CYP in CAMHS inpatient services can be found in the NDTi report, 'It's not rocket science' (2020). This report outlines some different sensory challenges caused by physical environments. One of the top ten recommendations of this report is for services to assess everyone's sensory needs and to consider how these can be accommodated. There is also an emphasis on enabling autistic young people to self-regulate through engagement in favoured interests, stimming (repeated movements) and wearing noise-cancelling headphones and caps to cut out light (NDTi, 2020).

The environment can also be said to include the practitioner, who has some agency over whether their actions increase predictability or create uncertainty, and thus greater anxiety. In a mental health hospital setting, planning for the former is important as this is a space where levels of anxiety are likely to be higher for all people. Being seen by multiple people means having to interpret and adjust for multiple unknown attitudes and beliefs, whilst not knowing who you will be seen by or when. Time can stretch and stand still. Waiting can seem endless. Autistic young people visiting a crisis community support service may have a rational and increasing need for certainty. The crisis team are more likely to minimise distress if they view the young person's need to ask for information on what will happen and when as a normal response to the uncertainty they experience.

Impact of uncertainty on autistic people

Society is full of messages pushing the benefits of uncertainty for opportunities and creativity. Uncertainty is portrayed as bringing risk and reward. For many autistic people, however, uncertainty makes everyday tasks impossible. It is impossible to focus, to settle, to think. Accumulating uncertainty may lead to mental health difficulties, such as stress, anxiety (Ong et al., 2023), or low mood (Cai et al., 2018). An excess of uncertainty can lead to complete shutdown and loss of functionality (Goodwin et al., 2022) and to physical illness (Larkin et al., 2023) and fatigue. It is exhausting. There is nothing secure to hold on to; uncertainty is uncontained and unending.

Some autistic people find uncertainty so stressful and upsetting – at the time, and afterwards – that they do everything to avoid it (e.g., by not attending school). But is this purely the effect of uncertainty, or the cumulative result of unmet needs and a lack of understanding from others (Milton's double empathy problem)? Some research has found that 'social anxiety' increases in autistic CYP as they age, whilst it decreases in other CYP in the community (Kuusikko et al., 2008). This is attributed to deficits in autistic CYP who, it is argued, 'begin to recognize their own impaired social skills' in adolescence, becoming 'self-conscious, apprehensive, or worried about their competency in social situations' (Kuusikko et al., 2008, p. 1707).

Such an explanation fails to consider the impact of potentially multiple instances of trauma caused by previous interactions with peers, which may lead to masking. These traumas mean it is the actions *of others* that contribute to withdrawal, and a strong disinclination for autistic CYP to engage, even though the events may not be assessed or experienced as trauma by others. However, it is often the social skills of autistic YPs that are criticised, rather than the bullying of their peers.

A consequence of not having support needs met can result in trust degrading in an autistic young person. They may feel they are not believed, or their needs taken seriously. They may feel they are not sufficiently cared about, or undeserving of support. Not addressing uncertainty results in confusion and can add to self-doubt and self-blame. All lead to increased levels of anxiety and a state of continuous, exhausting high vigilance, of feeling permanently unsafe. Such feelings impact other areas of their life, such as reduced quantity and quality of sleep. It is a vicious circle. But do autistic CYP have the agency to remove uncertainty? Rarely.

What professionals can do to help

'An overly anxious state is a potential but not essential outcome for autistic people' (Bervoets et al., 2021). So, what can professionals do to help?

Move from 'fixing' to validating and supporting

It is important to recognise that anxiety arising from uncertainty is often a perfectly rational response for autistic CYP. Reducing that anxiety, therefore, must start with identifying and addressing the causes of uncertainty. Starting at this point demonstrates to the YP that you are interested in solutions, not sticking plasters. By contrast, starting with teaching emotional regulation strategies conveys to the YP that it is more important to not show how they feel than it is to do anything about the thing that made them feel that way. This may add to their trauma.

Consider how you can give the autistic young person control of their own narrative around the importance of certainty and predictability for their wellbeing. This is vital to avoid assumptions on the part of the practitioner, and of the young person responding in a way they feel they should. Finding creative ways to engage collaboratively with the YP is helpful, so they can share their thoughts in a way that is meaningful to them. Arts-based research tools can be particularly helpful because they are designed to elicit unpredictable responses without a dependency on the autistic young person using the spoken word (see Table 4.2 for examples). Reflect on what they tell you when you listen to understand when you are more curious.

Table 4.2 Examples of creative engagement tools

Creative tool	Description
Photo voice	The young person is given a camera and asked to take photos of, for example, things that make them feel safe.
Digital storytelling	This is a method of creating and sharing stories using digital media. For example, a 2-minute film about the young person's interests.
Drawing	The young person is asked to draw their response to a question, or series of questions. For example, the elements of their ideal school.
Body mapping	A method that combines drawing and narrative to explore embodied experience, for example to explore emotional and physical feelings.
Topical life charts	This method starts with a simple T template, and the young person is asked to mark on it events of significance to them. For example, positive and negative memories of home life.
Cartoon strips	The young person is asked to draw a series of cartoon-style drawings, for example to explain a sequence of events and what they were thinking.

Make sense of the void

'For many autistic people the world can be a very scary place. It's our job to make it less so' (Wing, 2008). SPELL (Beadle-Brown & Mills, 2018) is an evidence-based framework that provides practitioners with five key elements to do just that, to understand and support good practice with autistic people. These elements are:

- Structure
- Positive attitudes and approaches
- Empathy
- Low arousal
- Links

Always work with the autistic young person to provide structure and increase predictability in the different areas of their life, which will help reduce anxiety.

Structure should be meaningful to the individual, using tools that they value, and not imposed. Age-appropriate visual schedules are useful for many – but not all – autistic people in helping them plan. Positive attitudes and approaches reflect the need to move away from unhelpful deficit-based narratives of autism. Empathy reminds us to see the world from the perspective of others. We need to provide clear explanations; to make time to answer the 'why'. This approach is important in terms of processing information, forming an understanding, reassuring, and enabling action. Provide context, too – the details of a situation aid processing and comprehension, whereas generalisations can increase anxiety. Don't give vague advice; be specific. Low arousal approaches help to reduce stress by reducing sensory input. Finally, links are about having a consistent approach to the individual, and creating connections.

Co-create a plan

Proactively providing strategies to make an appointment more predictable and support for sensory processing differences can reduce anxiety generated by uncertainty.

So, make a plan. Make a back-up plan. These plans should be co-created with autistic CYP and their families. Looking through the lens of the child facilitates understanding and compassion. Build on the young person's strengths and insights. Ask for and incorporate parental knowledge. The simple act of being listened to, as a child or a parent, can be transformational. Empower parents to support their children at home and to advocate for them at school and in healthcare settings. Make sure the focus is on reducing uncertainty instead of increasing tolerance. Then, make a plan for how this co-designed plan will be implemented. Agree with the CYP when the plan will be reviewed, and how a review is triggered. Ensure the CYP is a partner in this process. Give warnings of changes that are going to happen. Plan to give time to process unexpected change. If something isn't working, revisit and adjust. Always be curious as to why and what is happening.

Advocate a Low Arousal approach. Conduct a sensory audit of the spaces used by the CYP (e.g., home and school) and reduce anxiety 'by making learning environments calmer and more predictable' (Leek, 2022). Recognise, too, that 'whilst we want to proactively & longitudinally teach [YP] self-regulation and awareness skills...most adults co-regulate with others throughout life' (Boot, 2022). Autistic YP should not be expected to regulate alone. Reduce input, reduce demands. Hold the space. Hold the words. Stop. Wait.

Solutions can be simple sometimes – if we take the time to listen to the young person and reframe what seems to be the issue and co-design models of support with them. Recognise that predictability helps to create certainty, and that certainty is needed to feel safe.

Key practice/reflection points and case scenario

We finish with an activity to help you reflect on the key learning from this chapter. The case below is based on a real person, though their name has been changed. As you read the scenario, note down your thoughts about each of the three elements. Can you identify:

a   Elements of uncertainty;
b   The possible impact of uncertainty on Jessica's daily life, including on her eating and sleeping;
c   Ideas or protocols to reduce uncertainty.

Jessica

Jessica attends a nurturing and inclusive school. She likes her teachers, and she likes learning. Unfortunately, her class teacher had a bad accident before the end of the first term in Y2. The teacher's accident means Jessica's class must be taught by a 'supply' (temporary) teacher until their return. Jessica does not know when her class teacher will return. The class is frequently taught by a different supply teacher each day. Some of the supply teachers return and teach the class on several occasions; some don't. Jessica's class teacher does not return for the rest of the academic year. During this period, Jessica develops physical symptoms of stress and starts resisting going to school.

Jessica

a   Some of her thoughts on uncertainty and supply teachers:

- Who will it be? Will I have met them before?
- What will they be like? Will they be kind? Strict? Will they be impatient? Or understanding? How do I find out? How long will it take me to find out?
- What mood will they be in when they arrive? Will they stay in that mood or change all the time?
- If they've taught me before, will they remember me? Do they like me?
- Will they know I'm autistic? Will they know what I need? Will they know how to help? Will they want to help me? What will I do if I don't understand?
- Will they move my seat? Will they expect me to sit in my seat a certain way?
- Will they have the lights on? Will they leave the door open?
- Will they have different rules? Will they shout? For what will they shout at people? Will they shout if I twiddle my pencil or rock on my chair? Will they make me look them in the eye?

- Will they punish people? For what? What punishments will they give?
- When is my own class teacher coming back?

b Impact on other areas of her life:

- Less sleep, poorer quality of sleep, constantly tired
- Reduced variety of food eaten
- Felt ill much of the time (physical symptoms of anxiety), which she didn't understand wasn't sickness
- Reluctance to go to school
- Less interactions with peers
- Stigma from other parents, who were less likely to invite her to play with their children

c Strategy used by the school in collaboration with the parents

- Head and parents met to discuss the possible causes of Jessica's reluctance to attend school. It was a positive, collaborative relationship, putting Jessica and an understanding of her needs at the centre. All felt her anxiety was arising from the increased uncertainty of each day.
- A plan was made *with Jessica* to provide a known structure and transitional path into school each morning, which was based on removing stress and increasing consistency and care. The plan was:

  - The parent phoned the school office before the start of the school day if Jessica was reluctant to attend
  - The Head phoned the parent back to provide reassurance and to confirm the plan. It was important that the plan was led by authority, in this case, the Head. Any changes to the plan, for example, if the Head was not going to be available later, he could be stated and re-planned.
  - The pressure of time was removed: the agreement was to assume Jessica would get to school, but at her own pace; she led. This removed stress from the parent and supported her in maintaining a state of low arousal as she supported her daughter.
  - Jessica was taught about physical symptoms of anxiety, compared with symptoms of illness.
  - When Jessica and her parent got to school, the Head met her at the gate and walked with her to her office area, where she spent time reading (her passion) in a low-arousal environment until she was reading to transition to the class. The Head was calm and understanding. Jessica had familiar surroundings each morning, and the reassurance of being met by the Head or another member of staff she trusted.
  - The school worked to reduce the number of different supply teachers, which benefited all the children in the class.

- The school worked with a smaller number of supply teachers to provide a more consistent approach. They were made aware of Jessica's requirements (e.g.: knowing what was going to happen; having the teacher check her understanding, as she didn't like to put her hand up to ask for help), and those of the other children in the class.
- The parents worked with Jessica to remove uncertainty at home by co-developing a structure for their time after school. This reduced her energy expenditure, leaving her with more capacity to manage the uncertainties of school.

- **Outcome of the plan**: Jessica continued attending school on this basis for the rest of the year, with these 'minor' adjustments, with increasing confidence. She re-engaged fully with school at the start of the next academic year and had no subsequent difficulties with attendance or well-being at her primary school.

Conclusion

It is thought that differences in sensory processing and emotional regulation contribute to high levels of anxiety in autistic CYP, as they perceive the world to be an unpredictable and consequently unsafe place. Rather than taking a deficit-based understanding that views autistic CYP as irrationally intolerant of uncertainty, this chapter argues that a better approach is to create safety where possible and understand their perspective. Rather than encouraging autistic CYP to mask their distress – to pretend to tolerate that which they find intolerable – make the world safer and more predictable for them, in collaboration with them. This will reduce their anxiety – and show you care.

Note

1   Names are pseudonyms.

References

Beadle-Brown, J., & Mills, R. (2018). *Understanding and responding to autism: The SPELL framework self-study guide* (2nd edition). West Sussex: Pavilion Publishing. https://www.pavpub.com/learning-disability/autism/understanding-and-responding-autism-spell-framework-self-study-guide-2nd-edition

Bervoets, J., Milton, D., & Cruys, S. V. de. (2021). Autism and intolerance of uncertainty: An ill-fitting pair. *Trends in Cognitive Sciences*, 25(12), 1009–1010. https://doi.org/10.1016/j.tics.2021.08.006

Boot, K. (2022, November 13). *I think whilst we want to proactively & longitudinally teach self-regulation & awareness skills. My lived experience shows me that I also still need the co-regulation time & safe spaces to reflect after an event. I don't think this should ever be withheld from a child.* [Twitter]. https://twitter.com/AuDHD_SLT/status/1591904976355442688

Boulter, C., Freeston, M., South, M., & Rodgers, J. (2014). Intolerance of uncertainty as a framework for understanding anxiety in children and adolescents with autism spectrum disorders. *Journal of Autism and Developmental Disorders*, *44*(6), 1391–1402. https://doi.org/10.1007/s10803-013-2001-x

Buhr, K., & Dugas, M. J. (2009). The role of fear of anxiety and intolerance of uncertainty in worry: An experimental manipulation. *Behaviour Research and Therapy*, *47*(3), 215–223. https://doi.org/10.1016/j.brat.2008.12.004

Cai, R. Y., Richdale, A. L., Dissanayake, C., & Uljarević, M. (2018). Brief report: Inter-relationship between emotion regulation, intolerance of uncertainty, anxiety, and depression in youth with autism spectrum disorder. *Journal of Autism and Developmental Disorders*, *48*(1), 316–325. https://doi.org/10.1007/s10803-017-3318-7

Clark, A. (2015). *Surfing uncertainty: Prediction, action, and the embodied mind.* Oxford: Oxford University Press.

Donaldson's Trust (Director). (2020, May 12). *Walk in my shoes.* https://www.youtube.com/watch?v=KSKvazfTLv8.

Gaigg, S., Crawford, J., & Cottell, H. (2018). *An evidence based guide to anxiety and autism.* London: City University.

Goodwin, J., Rob, P., Freeston, M., Garland, D., Grahame, V., Kernohan, A., Labus, M., Osborne, M., Parr, J. R., Wright, C., & Rodgers, J. (2022). Caregiver perspectives on the impact of uncertainty on the everyday lives of autistic children and their families. *Autism*, *26*(4), 827–838. https://doi.org/10.1177/13623613211033757

Jenkinson, R., Milne, E., & Thompson, A. (2020). The relationship between intolerance of uncertainty and anxiety in autism: A systematic literature review and meta-analysis. *Autism*, *24*(8), 1933–1944. https://doi.org/10.1177/1362361320932437

Kuusikko, S., Pollock-Wurman, R., Jussila, K., Carter, A. S., Mattila, M. L., Ebeling, H.,… Moilanen, I. (2008). Social anxiety in high-functioning children and adolescents with autism and Asperger syndrome. *Journal of Autism and Developmental Disorders*, *38*, 1697–1709. https://doi.org/10.1007/s10803-008-0555-9

Larkin, F., Ralston, B., Dinsdale, S. J., Kimura, S., & Hayiou-Thomas, M. E. (2023). Alexithymia and intolerance of uncertainty predict somatic symptoms in autistic and non-autitic adults. *Autism*, *27*(3), 602–615. https://doi.org/10.1177/13623613221109717

Leek, R. (2022, October 31). *Behaviour management—Try tinkering around the edges.* The Headteacher. Retrieved from: https://www.theheadteacher.com/attainment-and-assessment/teaching-practice/behaviour-management-try-tinkering-around-the-edges

MacLennan, K., Rossow, T., & Tavassoli, T. (2021). The relationship between sensory reactivity, intolerance of uncertainty and anxiety subtypes in preschool-age autistic children. *Autism*, *25*(8), 2305–2316. https://doi.org/10.1177/13623613211016110

Milton, D. E. M. (2012). On the ontological status of autism: The 'double empathy problem'. *Disability & Society*, *27*(6), 883–887. https://doi.org/10.1080/09687599.2012.710008

Moyse, R. (2020). *Missing: The autistic girls absent from mainstream secondary schools* [PhD, University of Reading]. https://centaur.reading.ac.uk/97405/

National Autism Trainer Programme. (Director). (2023, September 1). *CAMHS crisis care.*

NDTi. (2020). *It's not rocket science.* NDTi. Retrieved from: https://www.ndti.org.uk/assets/files/Its-not-rocket-science-V6.pdf

Ong, C. S., Magiati, I., Maybery, M. T., Rodgers, J., Uljarevic, M., & Alvares, G. A. (2023). Parental perspectives of the everyday experiences of uncertainty among young children on the autism spectrum. *Research in Autism Spectrum Disorders, 101*, 102087. https://doi.org/10.1016/j.rasd.2022.102087

Rodgers, J., Herrema, R., Honey, E., & Freeston, M. (2018). Towards a treatment for intolerance of uncertainty for autistic adults: A single case experimental design study. *Journal of Autism and Developmental Disorders, 48*, 2832–2845.

Rodgers, J., Hodgson, A., Shields, K., Wright, C., Honey, E., & Freeston, M. (2017). Towards a treatment for intolerance of uncertainty in young people with autism spectrum disorder: Development of the coping with uncertainty in everyday situations (CUES©) Programme. *Journal of Autism and Developmental Disorders, 47*(12), 3959–3966. https://doi.org/10.1007/s10803-016-2924-0

Rose, K. (2018, January 7). An Autistic Education. *The Autistic Advocate*. Retrieved from: https://theautisticadvocate.com/2018/01/an-autistic-education/

Rose, K. (2023). *Safety in predictability*. [Animation]. National Autism Trainer Programme.

Simonoff, E., Pickles, A., Charman, T., Chandler, S., Loucas, T., & Baird, G. (2008). Psychiatric disorders in children with autism spectrum disorders: Prevalence, comorbidity, and associated factors in a population-derived sample. *Journal of the American Academy of Child & Adolescent Psychiatry, 47*(8), 921–929. https://doi.org/10.1097/CHI.0b013e318179964f

Stark, E., Stacey, J., Mandy, W., Kringelbach, M. L., & Happé, F. (2021). Autistic cognition: Charting routes to anxiety. *Trends in Cognitive Sciences, 25*(7), 571–581. https://doi.org/10.1016/j.tics.2021.03.014

Van de Cruys, S., Evers, K., Van der Hallen, R., Van Eylen, L., Boets, B., de-Wit, L., & Wagemans, J. (2014). Precise minds in uncertain worlds: Predictive coding in autism. *Psychological Review, 121*, 649–675. https://doi.org/10.1037/a0037665

van Steensel, F. J. A., & Heeman, E. J. (2017). Anxiety levels in children with autism spectrum disorder: A meta-analysis. *Journal of Child and Family Studies, 26*(7), 1753–1767. https://doi.org/10.1007/s10826-017-0687-7

Wing, L. (2008). *For many autistic people the world can be a very scary place. It's our job to make it less so*. Research Autism conference on Challenging Behaviour, London.

Chapter 5

Understanding low mood, shutdown, and burnout in autistic CYP

Kieran Rose and Julia Avnon

Understanding context is key to addressing low mood, shutdown, and burnout in autistic CYP

There is so much misinformation and misperception regarding autistic people that impacts negatively on the way that autistic people are perceived, treated, and supported that it is of little surprise that both mental health and life outcomes for autistic CYP are so dire.

Earlier chapters in this book explore the context of how autism has been conceptualised historically and the misconceptions that have arisen because of this. On a superficial level, the concept that autistic people are 'different' exists, but when it comes to many non-autistic professionals what that understanding of difference actually is, is up for debate. Generally, autistic people are seen as neurotypical people with 'bits that don't work well enough', rather than the 'radical' conception that autistic people are fundamentally different *types* of human beings, experiencing and responding to the world very differently, on multiple intersectional levels (Walker, 2021). In this chapter, Kieran, an autistic autism trainer, and Julia, a psychologist, worked together to discuss key considerations around the emotional burdens that pose autistic people at higher risk of burnout and/or depression.

Burnout, shutdown, and low mood in autistic people all tend to be a cumulative response to the same psycho-social barriers such as ongoing invalidation, sensory and emotional overwhelm, stigma, and the extra effort it takes to exist as an autistic person in a world that is centred on normative behaviours, communication, and sensory experiences.

For example, an autistic child within mainstream education may, daily, be experiencing overwhelming sensory input which can cause them to be emotionally dysregulated and require a need to shut down or meltdown. They may be struggling to communicate normatively and/or interpret normative communication. Their attention and interest needs may not be met, despite these being fundamental aspects of how they need to engage with their environment and their ability to learn (Wood, 2021). Their way of playing and behaving

DOI: 10.4324/9781003352327-8

may not conform to normative expectations around play and behaviour and they may be criticised or corrected because of this. They may be experiencing interpersonal victimisation or bullying as a result of these experiences and their vulnerabilities. They also may be engaging in high levels of self-monitoring and autistic Masking, a developmental and unconscious attempt to suppress responses to all these things, change behaviours and project a version of themselves to others that others expect and find acceptable, driven by stigma and trauma in order to find a level of acceptance and safety, but which comes with a deep psychological, physical and emotional toll (Chapman et al., 2022; Pearson et al., 2023).

Normative society tends to assume that the reason for all this happening is centred with the autistic person because autism is seen as a series of deficits, rather than how they are being treated because they are autistic; and this centring of normative, non-autistic perspectives also extends then to how autistic people's experiences of low mood, shutdown, and burnout are both perceived and treated. There is often a failure to understand that low mood, burnout, and shutdowns within autistic people are a response to poor environments, rather than issues centred within autistic people that need to be treated in normative ways.

When addressing burnout, shutdown, and low mood experienced by autistic CYP, we have to consider the contexts within which autistic experience exists and what poor mental health is a response to. While it's imperative to address poor mental health in populations of autistic CYP as a direct response to something centred within them, it's equally imperative to address the environments autistic CYP are in and validate how much autonomy they have over those environments. In the spirit of understanding differences and meeting need in an informed way, we also *have* to understand *how* trauma is experienced by autistic CYP, understand *why* trauma is experienced by autistic CYP, and understand *what* the responses to that trauma, things like autistic burnout, shutdowns, and low mood, look like for autistic CYP; *before* we consider directly addressing it (see Chapter 6 for further discussion of trauma in autistic people).

An ecology of stigma feeding poor mental health outcomes

For autistic CYP, developing an authentic sense of identity in environments where we are stigmatised daily, is difficult (Botha & Frost, 2020). Persistently, our sensory experiences, attention, movement, eating habits, play, communication, thinking, interactions, and emotional responses, can be invalidated in some way, coupled with constant ignorance of the fact that our social motivations, instead of being absent as has been historically reported, are very different to neurotypical people's social motivations.

Autistic CYP are often poorly informed and rarely constructively validated as to why we feel discombobulated socially, why we feel disconnected from others and detached from ourselves, and why we struggle with normative ways of playing, communicating, and forming and maintaining relationships. Sometimes we aren't even told that we are autistic, but that does not mean we aren't experiencing *being* autistic; our differences are obvious to us. We still experience the overwhelm from all of this singly and collectively, which causes us to sometimes melt, down or oppositely internalise our overwhelm, causing us to shut down.

When we are told, it's often unfortunately inadequately explained by parents who are not adequately supported to understand, their information retrieved from professionals steeped in a stigmatising, medicalised narrative. Due to this, for those of us who know we are autistic, often our personal understanding of autism is stigmatised, so we commonly distance ourselves from the notion of being autistic. And none of this accounts for the many who go missed completely.

Diagnosed and undiagnosed, autistic CYP are more likely to experience bullying (Hebron & Humphrey, 2014) and interpersonal victimisation across the lifespan (Pearson et al., 2023). For many autistic CYP, it is often safer to conform to particular social groupings, fit particular social roles, or even withdraw altogether. At this time, being 'different' or 'standing out' is often an invitation to be targeted, rather than something to celebrate. This highlights the importance of community amongst autistic people.

Community connectedness has been identified as a crucial missing factor in identity development and mental well-being for autistic people (Cage et al., 2022). To reinforce this, the bi-directional gap between non-autistic and autistic social communication is starting to be defined as one of a difference in cultures and communities, rather than autistics having 'deficits in Neurotypicality' (Qualls, 2022; Rose, 2021). Research is also now validating that autistics have our own innate forms of social skills and social communication (Crompton et al., 2020), which in turn can be evidenced by the significant differences in autistic cognitive styles in comparison to non-autistic cognitive styles.

The theory of monotropism, for example, describes how autistic people focus attention differently, requiring intrinsic motivation to be able to engage and give things our full attention. This can be followed by the building of a state of flow where all our attention becomes focused on that thing (Murray et al., 2005). To give an example, when an autistic young person is in a position where they are in poor environments, feeling excluded and forced to mask; and alongside this are experiencing constant interruptions to their need to be monotropic, because of the normative demands and pressures of the education systems they find themselves within, the physical and emotional toll taken on them is significant, often leading to extreme the physical, cognitive and emotional exhaustion now being identified as autistic burnout (Raymaker et al., 2020; Rose, 2018). In turn, due to normative interpretations of non-normative behaviours, this experience is often misperceived and medically identified as depression. It is undeniable that low mood has contributed to reaching this point, but the distinction between burnout and depression is vital, as the outcome of a depression diagnosis usually results in medication and therapy, which in turn risks (again) centring these issues as innate problems in a person with deficits, rather than acknowledging the external factors and the level of invalidation the person has experienced.

It is not unusual for autistic monotropic brains to focus on extrapolating as many of the potential outcomes for differing social scenarios as possible before we enter them, based on the information we have. When humans are experiencing low mood, or feel particularly anxious or unsafe, it is natural for our thoughts to become negative. It explains why, when the autistic brain is extrapolating while experiencing low mood, scenarios framed around death and suicide are increasingly common. Equally, when our autonomy is at a minimum it is not unusual to grasp for or seek agency in any way possible.

This hypothesis also goes towards explaining rumination experienced by autistic people. Rumination describes the action of hyperfixating on the persistent deconstruction of experiences. This post-event deconstruction is common for autistic people but can be monotropically exacerbated significantly by dysregulation, anxiety, and trauma. These and other intrusive thoughts are often 'treated' or intervened with, without considering either the underlying neurology or the environment in which that person exists which has brought them to that point, compounding a narrative that these are 'irrational' and unreasonable responses. When factually, with context accounted for, they are actually rational and reasonable responses. This is not a disordered brain, but a response to a disordered experience in a stigmatised life.

Our experience of this external blame from both therapies and society at large, forces an internalised, ableist, narrative onto autistic CYP that we carry into later life. One which tells us the multitude of ways in which we are wrong and that we need to change, improve, get better, stop melting down, pay more attention, be more present, stop making mistakes, sit still, listen, work harder at being like everyone else, understand better, be more like everyone else. A narrative that states clearly to us that we are not good enough.

A response to stigma that further fuels autistic burnout, shutdown, and low mood

Masking (Pearson & Rose, 2023) is a developmental response to this internal narrative and the stigmatising world around us (Rose & Vivian, 2020). It is something experienced and described by multiple marginalised groups. These narratives, outside of autism, have long been identified in both psychological *and* social theory around the impact of stigma. A good example is 'Double Consciousness' referring to the experiences of marginalised black people (Du Bois, 1897).

Understanding autistic-specific masking as a trauma response to stigma (Rose, 2023) helps us recognise the fallacies of previous understandings of autism, within which autistic people were seen as poor communicators with no social skills or social motivation, who developed within a 'social vacuum' and aren't connected to or affected by the environments around them. In much current literature, Masking is traditionally described as a form of 'choice' to 'fit in' and 'appear more neurotypical'; a contested superficial framing (Pearson & Rose, 2023).

A deeper, more insightful understanding of masking helps us recognise the differences in how it might project in alternative ways to traditional concepts about it, newly incorporating people who might be described as the 'class clown', the one who shows 'challenging behaviour', the 'average' child, the 'people pleaser' and on; an endless number of potential presentations of self that aren't based on authenticity.

Autistic masking is a complex developmental trauma response to stigma specific to autistic people, whereby one learns unconsciously to project a version of oneself to others that others deem acceptable (Pearson & Rose, 2023). While it might be considered a tool to keep the 'Masker' safe from the trauma of negative experiences, when those experiences are happening on a near-constant basis it switches from being a tool, to detrimentally life-impacting.

For autistic CYP, there may be an aspect of superficial decision-making that shapes masking contextually, but much of what happens in relation to masking involves unconscious processes that have developed over time and are grounded in previous negative experiences, and which are apparent in a number of ways.

The presence of masking is an indicator of an autistic person feeling unsafe. Unfortunately, due to normative ideologies, the stigmatising views towards autism that perceive it as a 'bad thing', and the tendency of non-autistic professionals to look only through a neurotypical lens and assume hubristically that neurotypical is the desirable way or 'right' way to be: masking is often encouraged and seen as a way of appearing 'less autistic'. There is comfort and safety in the familiar, and autistic people acting autistically are not familiar, comforting, or safe to non-autistic people (Sasson et al., 2017). Prejudice, marginalisation, and stigma are grounded in a fear of difference.

Masking takes an enormous physical and mental toll. Autistic Burnout has been openly discussed by the autistic community for about the past 30–40 years. Its recognition within academia has come very recently and, as such, only has a small but incredibly robust and growing evidence base (Rose, 2018).

Exploring, understanding, and differentiating between burnout, shutdown, and low mood

As a concept, burnout could be described as a bridge between an autistic person who may be struggling in some way, and an autistic person experiencing a serious depressive state. Burnout has been defined academically as:
"A long-lasting pervasive state of exhaustion, loss of function, and reduced tolerance to a stimulus that is conceptualised as resulting from chronic life stress and a mismatch of expectations and abilities without adequate support" (Raymaker et al., 2020) and "a condition involving exhaustion, withdrawal, problems with thinking, reduced daily living skills and increases in the manifestation of autistic traits" (Arnold et al., 2023).

Some autistic people experience severe burnout for a few weeks or months, and others have experienced Burnout over a number of years. Burnout often coincides with states of depression but is usually differentiated by recognising frustration over despondency and the continuing wish to do things and for the state to pass, rather than a want to withdraw from doing things and leaning into the state.

Burnout is a distinct state of being which is often confused with low mood. A recent study has identified that autistic people with burnout received diagnoses of depression, anxiety, or bipolar disorder, with clinicians failing to recognise it (Arnold et al., 2023). Autistic burnout in adults has only recently been recognised by the Royal College of Psychiatrists (RCPSYCH, 2020). Why this thinking has not yet been extended to autistic CYP going through the same experiences is unclear.

Burnout for autistic people can be partly defined as a lack of internal resources leading to a loss of skills. What that loss of skills may look like differs from person to person. A critical point to focus on is that autistic Burnout means a lessened ability to engage in autistic Masking, leaving that person vulnerable and unprotected in a number of ways, exposing them to further unsafety from external influences. For autistic young people, for example, this may present as an inability to access school environments any longer. This is termed 'school refusal' (which carries its own stigmatising and victim-blaming narrative).

Burnout highlights an autistic person who is deeply struggling and overwhelmed in numerous ways, and who needs an intensive reduction in demands. It is an indicator that how life was being lived previously was unsuitable and detrimental.

In order to have a paradigm shift, one must first conceive that there are possibilities outside of the mindset one has trapped oneself within the autism narrative as a whole needs reframing, but reframing the autistic Mental Health narrative needs specific attention.

What concerns me most about current practice is the interpretation of genuine autistic behaviours as pathologised behaviours because they are seen through a neurotypical gaze, again centring a notion that neurotypical is the 'right way' to be. An example of that is how a consistently dysregulated autistic person, who repeatedly experiences low mood, shutdowns, meltdowns, burnout, and emotional dysregulation, may have that behaviour interpreted as Bipolar, or as evidence of a personality disorder, or depression. In reality, it is an autistic person rationally expressing distress to sensory and emotional dysregulation, because they are consistently placed in unsuitable environments, and/or experiencing negative treatment; all of which goes unconsidered and unreflected on practitioners who cannot conceptualise this.

Another factor in this is Alexithymia, a common co-occurring condition for autistic people whereby there is a disconnect and delay in the processing of one's emotional state (Cuve et al., 2022). It is common for autistic young people to struggle to be able to identify with our emotional states because emotional and sensory dysregulation is a common factor for us. We're also on a different developmental pathway, something often stated and even more often completely ignored; so they are consistently experiencing invalidation over our emotional and sensory responses, from an early age. That invalidation leads to the self-doubting of what one's brain and body are telling oneself.

So, in order to understand low mood, shutdown, and burnout in autistic CYP we need to understand those experiences from a point of empathy. What underlines the too-common failure of therapeutic practice for me is the fundamental lack of recognition of, understanding of, and validation of autistic experience and the context within which it resides, and that is something that critically needs to change. It denotes a fundamental lack of empathy towards autistic experiences and highlights an enormous and hypocritical power imbalance whereby autistic people are both made victims *and* blamed for being victims by those with power around us.

Sharpening our tools

Supporting autistic CYP with burnout, intervention tends to require the inverse of strategies around activation used in depression instead of focusing on:

- Reducing demands as much as possible; these include social and interpersonal demands.
- Encouraging engaging with personal interests on their own terms.
- Remove children or young people from the situations that cause or maintain burnout as appropriate.
- Increasing sensory support.
- Ensuring that you allow for much time to do things that come naturally for them, so they do not engage in masking.
- Listening to them and validating their experience.
- Identifying what helps them to distress and inducing a sense of calm.
- Encouraging self-regulation e.g. stimming, spending time in nature.

- Re-introduction to daily functioning should be gradual and individually determined; a system of monitoring fatigue levels such as simple diaries can be helpful in monitoring progress.

In the long term, to prevent burnout, clinicians need to focus on a journey that includes all of the above but will also help the young person work through their experiences of trauma, embrace their autistic self, cultivate agency and authenticity, and encourage self-advocacy.

CYP have limited autonomy in determining the daily life demands placed on them, it is crucial to help parents, carers, and educators to understand what autistic burnout is, so that they can collaboratively devise a recovery and care.

Cognitive Behavioural Therapy (CBT) and interpersonal therapy are the current interventions for addressing low mood and depression in autistic CYP. There are studies, such as the recent Delphi study, where researchers interviewed expert clinicians and clinical researchers: adaptations to the structure and process of therapy were consistently endorsed, and an individualised formulation-derived approach was favoured (Spain et al., 2023). These involved adapting the process methods, e.g., enhanced use of visuals, adapting worksheets; modifying techniques to reflect a formulation-based as opposed to protocol-based approach; capacity to work with the broader system of family and school; addressing service issues such as facilitating access to assessment and therapy and practitioner's knowledge and skills in working with autistic people.

CBT aims to help the clients identify, evaluate, and modify distorted cognitions and produce more adaptive ones. However, it is essential to acknowledge that focusing on modifying the cognitions of autistic CYP to 'more neurotypical' ones, learning neurotypical social skills and ways of being, and camouflaging autistic traits inevitably foster a sense of self-deficiency. It also leads to distress and helplessness, as autistic CYP are encouraged to push themselves to do the things that make them ill. It is essential for therapists working with autistic CYP to understand, respect, and follow a client's frame of reference and their individual experience of being autistic. Acceptance of the client's unique experience, an emphasis on strengths, and validation of the client's experiences of rejection and marginalisation, alongside consideration of the need for environmental and relational change, should constitute the base of the therapeutic relationship.

If CBT is your modality of choice, it is essential to consider that for many autistic CYP, an intervention requiring them to change their cognitive style, without adaptations, can be harmful (Riches et al., 2023; Spain et al., 2023). A focus on the behavioural aspect of therapy can be beneficial and effective, however, the therapist needs to understand the nature of behaviours that autistic CYP use adaptively. For example, avoiding sensory-rich environments such as crowds can be viewed as avoidance behaviour due to low mood. Encouraging autistic CYP to change these behaviours without understanding their function can be highly detrimental.

The focus on the behavioural aspect of CBT does not mean exploring cognitions cannot be helpful. As mentioned before, low self-esteem and a sense of confusion about one's identity play an important role in the development of low mood for many autistic CYP. Exploring associated cognitions and the more realistic and balanced alternatives can be very helpful. However, clinicians need to understand that the social experiences that led to the development of distorted cognitions associated with self-esteem are often traumatic. In a study by Golan and colleagues, the authors found that among autistic young people, social incidents of rejection and exclusion predict post-traumatic stress disorder more strongly than ones of great magnitude, such as war, terror, or abuse, which are highly prevalent in Israeli society. This was the opposite for neurotypical peers (Golan et al., 2022). This means that simply challenging cognitions is not helpful. Exploring trauma and the nature of associated symptoms, identifying the contributing factors, and advocating for putting in place adequate support are essential drivers of therapy.

Whose agenda are we serving?

CBT relies on the ability of the clients to verbalise their emotions, which can be incredibly complex for autistic CYP. One should be careful not to apply neurotypical standards to reading or assessing autistic emotions. As mentioned earlier, a large proportion of autistic people experience alexithymia (Kinnaird et al., 2019). This calls for therapists to do 'grounding work' before embarking on traditional CBT strategies, such as helping their clients to recognise sensations as they arise (interoception strategies) and linking these to emotions, using visuals such as art activities, movies, or video clips; music; body mapping aimed at fostering awareness of the physiological and cognitive aspects of emotions or identifying the best way for the individual client to communicate emotions.

CBT is a goal-directed intervention, and often therapists will attempt to foster social involvement to foster behavioural activation. Many autistic CYP feel socially isolated and struggle to make and maintain friends, so while social involvement can be a valuable goal, it needs careful consideration. A therapist might unwittingly encourage autistic CYP to participate in detrimental activities that might lead to sensory and mental overwhelm. Many autistic children dread going to crowded and noisy places, such as parties and clubs; how they dread being asked to stay long hours for family gatherings with numerous people; how they are told they are 'difficult', 'stubborn', 'inconsiderate', 'boring', and let people down. An essential aspect of behavioural activation intervention is an understanding of the nature of social activities and interactions that are beneficial for one's client.

Behavioural activation must foster purpose and meaning in people's lives and be consistent with the person's goals and values. It is a self-determination intervention using a person-centred approach, making it an attractive option for supporting autistic CYP with low mood. However, like with all interventions, it needs to be collaboratively agreed, planned, and implemented with autistic young people.

There is no 'one fits all' protocol, but several considerations might be helpful for clinicians to ponder when agreeing with their client to engage in behavioural activation:

1 Most importantly, discerning whether the young person is experiencing low mood, autistic burnout, or an overlap of the two, as approaches to each can be polar opposites, and will need to be varied and well-informed.
2 Fostering agency. Clients should be helped to identify what activities are intrinsically motivating, whether personal interests or serving a bigger purpose.
3 Executive functioning differences may mean that autistic CYP benefit from structure and careful pacing and having agency over those things.
4 Enhanced engagement of the broader system: family, friends, teachers, and other allies.
5 Celebrating small successes and addressing barriers with careful consideration.

Conclusion

The high prevalence of low mood, shutdown, and burnout in autistic CYP has been identified as having roots in the life experiences of autistic people. In order to address this issue, we *must* better understand, empathise, and cater to autistic people's needs, rather than perpetuating and continuing the current ideology, which centres all the 'problems', mental health or otherwise faced by an autistic child and young person within a disordered narrative, which dictates that every issue whether real or perceived occurs because the person is autistic, a narrative which perpetuates an ever-present sense of shame and self-blame.

There has been a shameful neglect of focus on the environments that autistic people are expected to exist within; and a shameful lack of responsibility from those who hold privilege, power, and authority over autistic people in recognising the impact of their practice on autistic people. Contrary to historical belief, autistic CYP do not evolve within a social vacuum, just one in which it is assumed that their social motivations are non-existent and their attempts to socialise inept; and, unrecognised until recently, that autistic people are subjected to extreme levels of victimisation, abuse, and normative practice.

The historical practice of identifying autistic responses to normative and stigmatising environments and situations as irrational and disordered, and then putting autistic people through normalising frameworks (Gore et al.,

2022) (33) and therapeutic interventions (Linden et al., 2023) that encourage masking is indicative of a failure of empathy, and the failure to do anything other than look at autistic people through a neurotypical gaze.

All this highlights the importance of professionals receiving training and understanding from autistic people along with the application of co-produced strategies and therapeutic interventions. Meticulously researched and professionally delivered Independent autistic led-and-delivered internationally accessible training such as the Autistic Advocate training and national (England) NHS-specific training like *www.annafreud.org/training/health-and-social-care/national-autism-trainer-programme/* co-produced and co-delivered with autistic people, both utilising autistic voice, experience and cutting-edge research are examples of the difference that can be made on the professional understanding that does not perpetuate stigma and misconception, but instead can be a catalyst for real change in a professional landscape which is woefully uninformed (Camm-Crosbie et al., 2019), where therapeutic interventions and modalities such as CBT, when used with autistic CYP and well informed enough, can truly be meaningful. Along with that, mental health professionals using a neurodiversity-affirming approach and looking through a lens of the Double Empathy problem can also utilise autistic-derived support and change frameworks such as the Advoc8 Framework (Pearson & Rose, 2023) which uses deep knowledge and reflective practice to promote objectives focused on agency and authenticity. When used in conjunction with an interpersonal and experience-sensitive approach using relational processes such as Pavolopoulou's lifeworld domains (Pearson & Rose, 2023); therapeutic relationships can invoke validation, connection, and empowerment.

The impact of the disorder narrative also highlights a need for the priorities of autism research to shift significantly (Pellicano et al., 2014). Rather than investing in what could be defined as 'cause and cure' research, a more impactful and meaningful justice model focus could explore the experiences of all sorts of autistic people, with a particular nod to intersectionality across the lines of age, ethnicity and race, gender, sexual orientation and disability; interventions on professionals to support them to remove and avoid normative practice; Looking into social and health supports to mitigate isolation and poor health; Creating new mental health frameworks that coming from a place of knowing and empathy; And the exploration of systemic and societal barriers and the changes needed to remove them.

All so that autistic CYP do not have to have the experiences that lead them to have such significant levels of low mood, shutdown, and burnout; and access vastly improved life outcomes to the ones autistic people currently experience.

To stop marginalised people from being framed as the problem and expecting them to come up with solutions.

Autistic CYP deserve better. They deserve us, as professionals, to do and *be* better.

References

Arnold, S. R., Higgins, J. M., Weise, J., Desai, A., Pellicano, E., & Trollor, J. N. (2023). Confirming the nature of autistic burnout. *Autism*, *27*(7), 1906–1918. https://doi. org/10.1177/13623613221147410

Botha, M., & Frost, D. M. (2020). Extending the minority stress model to understand mental health problems experienced by the autistic population. *Society and Mental Health*, *10*(1), 20–34. https://doi.org/10.1177/2156869318804297

Cage, E., Cranney, R., & Botha, M. (2022). Brief report: Does autistic community connectedness moderate the relationship between masking and wellbeing? *Autism in Adulthood*, *4*(3), 247–253. https://doi.org/10.1089/aut.2021.0096

Camm-Crosbie, L., Bradley, L., Shaw, R., Baron-Cohen, S., & Cassidy, S. (2019). 'People like me don't get support': Autistic adults' experiences of support and treatment for mental health difficulties, self-injury and suicidality. *Autism: The International Journal of Research and Practice*, *23*(6), 1431–1441. https://doi.org/10.1177/ 1362361318816053

Chapman, L., Rose, K., Hull, L., & Mandy, W. (2022). "I want to fit in … but I don't want to change myself fundamentally": A qualitative exploration of the relationship between masking and mental health for autistic teenagers. *Research in Autism Spectrum Disorders*, *99*, 102069. https://doi.org/10.1016/j.rasd.2022.102069

Crompton, C. J., Ropar, D., Evans-Williams, C. V., Flynn, E. G., & Fletcher-Watson, S. (2020). Autistic peer-to-peer information transfer is highly effective. *Autism*, *24*(7), 1704–1712. https://doi.org/10.1177/1362361320919286

Cuve, H. C., Murphy, J., Hobson, H., Ichijo, E., Catmur, C., & Bird, G. (2022). Are autistic and alexithymic traits distinct? A factor-analytic and network approach. *Journal of Autism and Developmental Disorders*, *52*(5), 2019–2034. https://doi.org/10.1007/ s10803-021-05094-6

Du Bois, W. E. B. (1897). *Strivings of the Negro people.* https://www.theatlantic.com/ magazine/archive/1897/08/strivings-of-the-negro-people/305446/

Golan, O., Haruvi-Lamdan, N., Laor, N., & Horesh, D. (2022). The comorbidity between autism spectrum disorder and post-traumatic stress disorder is mediated by brooding rumination. *Autism*, *26*(2), 538–544. https://doi.org/10.1177/13623613211035240

Gore, N. J., Sapiets, S. J., Denne, L. D., Hastings, R. P., Toogood, S., MacDonald, A.,… Williams, D. (2022). Positive behavioural support in the UK: A state of the nation report. *International Journal of Positive Behavioural Support*, *12*(1), i–46.

Hebron, J., & Humphrey, N. (2014). Exposure to bullying among students with autism spectrum conditions: A multi-informant analysis of risk and protective factors. *Autism: The International Journal of Research and Practice*, *18*(6), 618–630. https:// doi.org/10.1177/1362361313495965

Kinnaird, E., Stewart, C., & Tchanturia, K. (2019). Investigating alexithymia in autism: A systematic review and meta-analysis. *European Psychiatry: The Journal of the Association of European Psychiatrists*, *55*, 80–89. https://doi.org/10.1016/j. eurpsy.2018.09.004

Linden, A., Best, L., Elise, F., Roberts, D., Branagan, A., Tay, Y. B. E., Crane, L., Cusack, J., Davidson, B., Davidson, I., Hearst, C., Mandy, W., Rai, D., Smith, E., & Gurusamy, K. (2023). Benefits and harms of interventions to improve anxiety, depression, and other mental health outcomes for autistic people: A systematic review and network meta-analysis of randomised controlled trials. *Autism*, *27*(1), 7–30. https://doi.org/10.1177/ 13623613221117931

Murray, D., Lesser, M., & Lawson, W. (2005). Attention, monotropism and the diagnostic criteria for autism. *Autism*, *9*(2), 139–156. https://doi.org/10.1177/136236130 5051398

Pearson, A., & Rose, K. (2023). *Autistic masking: Understanding identity management and the role of stigma*. West Sussex: Pavilion Publishing.

Pearson, A., Rose, K., & Rees, J. (2023). 'I felt like I deserved it because I was autistic': Understanding the impact of interpersonal victimisation in the lives of autistic people. *Autism*, *27*(2), 500–511. https://doi.org/10.1177/13623613221104546

Pellicano, E., Dinsmore, A., & Charman, T. (2014). What should autism research focus upon? Community views and priorities from the United Kingdom. *Autism*, *18*(7), 756–770. https://doi.org/10.1177/1362361314529627

Qualls, L. (2022). *What if we view autism as a culture?* Retrieved from: https://www.youtube.com/watch?v=S4UOFiNWYWo

Raymaker, D. M., Teo, A. R., Steckler, N. A., Lentz, B., Scharer, M., Delos Santos, A., Kapp, S. K., Hunter, M., Joyce, A., & Nicolaidis, C. (2020). 'Having all of your internal resources exhausted beyond measure and being left with no clean-up crew': Defining autistic burnout. *Autism in Adulthood: Challenges and Management*, *2*(2), 132–143. https://doi.org/10.1089/aut.2019.0079

RCPSYCH. (2020). *The psychiatric management of autism in adults*. Retrieved from: https://www.rcpsych.ac.uk/improving-care/campaigning-for-better-mental-health-policy/college-reports/2020-college-reports/cr228

Riches, S., Hammond, N., Bianco, M., Fialho, C., & Acland, J. (2023). Adapting cognitive behaviour therapy for adults with autism: A lived experience-led consultation with specialist psychological therapists. *The Cognitive Behaviour Therapist*, *16*, e13. https://doi.org/10.1017/S1754470X23000053

Rose, K. (2018, May 21). *An autistic burnout*. Retrieved from: https://theautistic advocate.com/2018/05/an-autistic-burnout/

Rose, K. (Director). (2021). *An autistic identity within autistic culture*. Retrieved from: https://www.youtube.com/watch?v=WXHuUjSfNgA

Rose, K. (2023). *Autistic masking and burnout*. Retrieved from: www.theautistic advocate.com/autistic-masking/

Rose, K., & Vivian, S. (2020, February 29). *Regarding the use of dehumanising rhetoric*. Retrieved from: https://theautisticadvocate.com/2020/02/regarding-the-use-of-dehumanising-rhetoric/

Sasson, N. J., Faso, D. J., Nugent, J., Lovell, S., Kennedy, D. P., & Grossman, R. B. (2017). Neurotypical peers are less willing to interact with those with autism based on thin slice judgments. *Scientific Reports*, *7*(1), 40700. https://doi.org/10.1038/srep40700

Spain, D., Milner, V., Mason, D., Iannelli, H., Attoe, C., Ampegama, R., Kenny, L., Saunders, A., Happé, F., & Marshall-Tate, K. (2023). Improving cognitive behaviour therapy for autistic individuals: A Delphi survey with practitioners. *Journal of Rational-Emotive & Cognitive-Behavior Therapy*, *41*(1), 45–63. https://doi.org/10.1007/s10942-022-00452-4

Walker, N. (2021). Neuroqueer Heresies. *Neuroqueer*. Retrieved from: https://neuroqueer.com/neuroqueer-heresies/

Wood, R. (2021). Autism, intense interests and support in school: From wasted efforts to shared understandings. *Educational Review*, *73*(1), 34–54. https://doi.org/10.1080/00131911.2019.1566213

Chapter 6

Autistic informed trauma practice

Moving away from trauma as a diagnostic label to understanding what has happened to a person

Jon Adams

A lifetime of being the other

I've always known I was different right from an early age but believe my trauma didn't stem just from my difference if at all but rather from the way people treated and saw that difference. It seems trauma in one form, or another has been a constant companion most of my life but remained unnamed or unrecognised for many years. I started to notice, I believe aged 6, that others did not see the world about us in the same way as I did. My interests were always intense and deep, in fact, I was terminally curious, captivated by the physical world about me and our place in space. I needed to know details: what lay beneath my feet, who the Romans were, and where to find fossils. My father tacitly encouraged me, I believe sharing much of the autistic inheritance I have but was busy providing for his family. I did mix with people as my parents were gregarious and their friends had children my age. This and then school, where I met a wider range of peers, confirmed my differences. I did occasionally find one person who shared an alternative sensory view of the world but that didn't stop the repetitive reminders of difference like when my collection of curiosities was thrown out by a visiting friend: I was devastated and rescued them from the dustbin.

I'm not only autistic but share in other neurodivergent conditions including confirmed dyslexia, **synaesthesia**,[1] and suspected attention deficit hyperactivity disorder. These conditions also influence my translation of the world about me, and I feel it's really important to be informed and understand each condition, and to take these into consideration holistically. During a later trauma care session with a mental health professional, I'd not met before (there seemed no consistency of care), I mentioned to her I had synaesthesia and after I'd explained, as they'd never heard of it, they asked if I 'Heard voices'. At that moment I knew I could not trust them and felt trapped, I was not at

DOI: 10.4324/9781003352327-9

all safe. Just another let down it seemed, as usual, by those I was supposed to place my trust in for care. In fact, earlier in that session they announced they had not read my notes and asked why I was there. I explained I had PTSD and after no acknowledgement, I also added I was autistic to which they immediately replied they were sorry to hear that. I then surmised that they considered autism worse than PTSD and feared for my safety. Consistency of care is really important because all you want to do is describe your trauma once, not have to repeat it in every session which I feel just re-traumatises you. Each encounter seemingly added another stone to place in a winter coat's pocket before you were forced to go for a swim wearing it.

I found school increasingly difficult as my compensation strategies and masking ability waned. I was becoming too mentally expensive with each new year until an event that defined my life path took place in my final year of primary school, aged 10. I learnt from pictures, radio, and television as my reading was poor and I could respond to questions with accomplished verbal answers. I could also draw pictures that my peers admired, seemingly saving me, often distracting from my lack of written ability. That morning the head teacher visited our class and chose the picture I was drawing to go up on the entrance foyer wall. It was exciting as everyone on the way to assembly or visiting would pass and see it. All I had to do was to add a subject title and my name. Unfortunately, I couldn't spell Tudor House or my name. I had a choice, ask for help or try the best I could. I chose to try, as I knew if I asked for help, I would be abused verbally by my teacher who was I feel a bully, exploiting any child's weakness it seems. Once submitted, the teacher held aloft the picture to show the class and tore it into pieces. It was binned. I was shocked (traumatised, I realise now), time slowed, and I barely heard the teacher blaming me, saying I'd let myself and the class down and I would never be anything as I couldn't even spell my own name. I wasn't recognised as dyslexic at school: my dyslexia was only identified when my son, who incidentally went to the same school, was diagnosed when I was nearly 40. Ironically, I re-visited the school many times and some of the books I drew illustrations for were on the shelves in that same classroom. Looking back, my intensely low confidence and rejection sensitive dysphoria were seeded at that moment. I was so traumatised I decided my goal of art college was now out of the question even though I'd said I needed to be an artist aged six. This toxic moment changed my life but has since been dealt with by eye movement desensitisation and reprocessing (EMDR). It now holds no fear for me even though I can remember the moment and still touch and see that picture as clear as day.

That comment 'you will never achieve anything' instigated a lifelong inner monologue. I exhausted myself, challenging myself to constantly try to do better, boost skills, and be more perfect but I had failed. It seems that comment is set so deep it feels like an irretrievably part of my DNA. 'Words will never hurt you' they say but they leave wounds, scratched into your very being you read every day behind closed eyes. Remember to be considerate and thoughtful in your interactions with an autistic person. It's important to avoid making promises you might not be able to keep. Trying to cope with unresolved trauma feels as if you are constantly drowning, sinking into deep and dark places, an abyss of both physical and mental exhaustion. Flashbacks, hyper-vigilance, avoidance, fear, dysfunction, isolation, disassociation and exhausting nightmares, reliving the same emotions and fears again and again and again but with different people and surroundings. So, with all this going on, how are we supposed to maintain a relationship, fulfil work obligations, look after ourselves, challenge or even contemplate a future beyond the pain and attempt at autistic joy? The realisation of this position and the distress caused just adds to the weight of what we're going through as it steadily corrodes our personhood and even our self-will to stay in this world.

Listen. Believe

Why am I telling you these stories, a liturgy of intense fragments and moments of meaning in my life? It's because to understand trauma in autistic people you need to listen, believe, and learn from them. I've experienced and lived with traditional post-traumatic stress disorder (PTSD) caused by a single moment, a near-death experience that nearly took me. However, for most autistic people trauma is more complex than this. Each event erodes our concepts of safety and trust leaving us more exposed the next time, but more importantly, it dissolves our self-confidence and sense of belonging. If we lose belonging, what is there to stay around for? No wonder so many autistic people have already 'left', a needless tragedy for family and friends, seemingly having been failed by society and most likely mental health services. In my opinion, neurodiversity loss will be as serious as biodiversity loss and trauma is a step on that path.

I believe there have been very few times in my life where I felt truly safe. The last time was reflected in my exhibition 'In the arms of my loving father'. I was probably about four at the time. Ironically, clearing out Dad's house I found photographic evidence of the exact moment when I was gazing at the camera hugged by both my parents. Creating 'spaces of safety' is vital and basic for any trauma informed practice (TIP). Without feeling safe, why would I open up and tell my story?

For most of my encounters with Mental Health Services, I only felt safe a couple of times. I don't believe you get enough continuity or contact with 'one named person' to feel or build trust. Your treatment is either spread between agencies and multiple people, or there were not enough number of sessions/ other reasonable adjustments to engender that trust. Both are, I feel, fundamental problems with our current mental health services. Trust also is vital to trauma-informed practice, and it doesn't take much to lose an autistic person's trust. We often need more time than is available to trust someone or we rush into it and regret it later. Often, we'll sit there conditioned by previous experience, looking for signs and indicators that this person will let us down. It's an indictment of the way we've been treated by society that the first thing we do when we enter a room is look for people who may hurt us and avoid them. Betraying the trust of an autistic person is very serious. In fact, it needs to be included in any new 'autistic model of trauma' or 'autistic TIP'.

So, what does trauma informed practice entail?

The simple tenet is to be humane, to be humble, and to add in some vital autistic peer support. It is so important to do no more harm so as to avoid re-traumatisation. Instead, protect them, engage with their skills, agency, and choices, and recognise that their current behaviour and their cognitive and emotional functioning may be down to their efforts to cope with the memory of trauma. I found that not being able to ask for help was a trauma response and I exhibited a mental form of 'terminal burrowing' often found in late-stage hypothermia cases. Is this reaction an evolutionary hangover from when mammals hibernated, causing people to automatically crawl into a small space to die? I am not sure we have enough research evidence on this aspect of epigenetic trauma but it is an interesting area to explore. All I wanted to do was hide somewhere in my head and physically crawl into a small space to make the noise and pain go away.

An understanding of autistic people is even more important with autistic trauma-informed practice. You must learn to recognise what trauma does to us that is different from a non-autistic person and, importantly, not to blame autism. Refrain from thinking or mentioning 'that wouldn't have harmed me' or commonly used phrases like 'it will seem different in the morning'. Comments like those don't engender trustworthiness because we know it really can't work like that. Very often we are blamed for being in the situation that causes our trauma or told we should have stopped it from happening. An autistic person is not weak, just different. If we experience the world in an alternative fashion, then we will experience trauma in an alternative fashion. More importantly, we may need to treat it in an alternative fashion.

In my experience there seems to be a hierarchy of trauma: if you're not in the military, for example, it doesn't count or 'that wasn't that bad'. I've had both said to my face by people who should've known better. More threads to weave into the trauma tapestry. So, what would an autistic model of trauma look like? I remember sitting as a child with my grandad and watching him as he seemed to be 'elsewhere' staring into the far distance. He fought in a particularly tough nine-day battle in 1918, on his 19th birthday, as a Lewis gunner in the thick of it. Even though my Gran told my mum he was shelled, gassed, and badly affected by this incident, he never spoke about it. Recognising that look as I sat disassociated years later engendered a deeper connection, an understanding of the pain that was never communicated. Now I just want to hug him. I believe my trauma is a mix of betrayal trauma (personal, institutional, and societal), traditional PTSD and what's known as Complex Post Traumatic Stress Disorder. Betrayal trauma, I feel, seems to fit the model of why most autistic people suffer. Further, collective, or historical trauma seems likely due to the way that over many years, society and research have always seen us as something in need of 'fixing', curing or 'being rid of'. Prevention is better than a cure if at all possible because when we come through PTSD, we are changed both mentally and physically. Even preventing a few autistic people from acquiring trauma would take root and branch change the way society understands the experience of trauma for the neurodivergent population. I believe autistic trauma relates not only to our identity as autistic people but also to a wider range of intersectionalities and experiences, which may add to our susceptibility to trauma. Basically, if we were understood and treated better by society many more autistic people would be able to live fulfilled lives to thrive, not just to survive. A huge gulf of misunderstanding is apparent when autistic people are told that because they're autistic they can't have PTSD, they are too complex to treat, or autism is simply trauma. Personally, I do not believe any of these things; trauma is trauma, and autism is autism. Withholding much-needed affirmation, support, and treatment because we don't fit the official and traditional definitions of PTSD is both rigid and a disturbingly common occurrence. In fact, I feel the very act of not confirming our trauma is an act of betrayal, deepening the despair and pushing us further towards feeling worthless. People still wonder why we get into a suicidal crisis when we are simply left to face trauma on our own, compounded by a sense we are not believed. Instead, mental health care professionals need to find a way to define trauma in autistic terms, which would be a much better and more humane path rather than a blanket refusal. We now need to add unnecessary iatrogenic harm into the mix, and yet some still wonder why autistic people avoid or are fearful about mental health services.

My episode of PTSD caused by a near-death experience is much easier for me to define than autistic trauma, which I feel is a mix of what's called complex PTSD, historical and betrayal trauma. It seems a very clear thread, one step or frame after the other, a single strip of film left on the cutting room floor that's easy to see and needs filing away. I have a food allergy and I try to be vigilant where that's concerned but one day, I missed something and within a few minutes I knew I was going into anaphylactic shock. Ironically, I was actually on the way to the hospital by train to visit my mother who was very unwell. Arriving at the station I had a choice: I collapse on the platform and an ambulance is called or I run to the hospital that's three-quarters of a mile away. I chose to run, which inadvertently I believe saved my life as the running released adrenaline. At the hospital I was assessed, given drugs, and placed on a trolley in a queue in the hallway. I was very unwell but recovered in about six hours. It didn't really scare me in the traditional sense since I've been in other situations where I felt more at risk. The symptoms didn't really start to show for about another six weeks but inevitably the textbook difficulties appeared, and I was diagnosed, after five months, with PTSD. Although I had to wait to be seen by mental health services, I was immediately assigned EMDR and within eight sessions it was sorted. At this time there was no mention that I was autistic as I had not been diagnosed. The EMDR focused on a couple of events: eating, the train station, running to the hospital and being in A&E. Looking back now, it was distressing and tough, but it was relatively simple compared to what I was to go through later. Pre-autism diagnosis, there was no argument from mental health services, no excuses. I had PTSD, I needed treatment, and they got it done.

This experience contrasts greatly with a bout of complex PTSD I believe sprang from abuse and betrayal, not only by people and organisations but by mental health services as well. This was no simple strip of film to deal with, there were multiple fragments, interwoven, which needed picking apart. Yet every time I went to mental health services, they were scattered which added to the mess. I knew I had trauma, and when I was assessed, they said I had PTSD, but by then I also had an autism diagnosis. As such, when I went in for my first session, they retracted and seemingly belittled the trauma. I felt betrayed and terrified that I wasn't going to get the support I needed. Feeling misunderstood and disbelieved, plus the feeling that I was unworthy of being helped, was traumatic and added to the problems I was facing. I chose to fight but it's taken seven years, I got deeply hopeless at times but with private support, EMDR and breakthrough moments with internal family systems therapy, I managed to break free.

One of the images in my head after the causal event was of an immovable bright burning sun, right in the middle of my head. It wasn't until I had EMDR that I realised it was just a frozen film frame, the analogy being the fireball of an atomic bomb, so there had to be an actual beginning and a finality. Through the EMDR we managed to play the whole film through and silence it. Personally, I feel EMDR works very well for autistic people, especially those with synaesthesia and the ability to think in pictures, yes it was a drawback when I was experiencing flashbacks in Ultra high definition, but it was also a salvation. As well as the EMDR working, the breakthrough came with internal family systems therapy that proposes our self is not a single entity but composed of different 'parts'. Being introduced to my 'parts' and having them show me the situations and meanings of the trauma imagery I was experiencing during EMDR was a revelation and internal family systems therapy for neurodivergent people I feel needs researching further.

During those seven years, mental health services gave me all sorts of treatments that I felt were inappropriate. This process started with mindfulness and knowing your emotions. I feel some mental health care professionals often didn't tell me the truth, which made it worse. After one said to me 'Jon because you can so eloquently describe what's wrong and the support you need, you obviously don't need it'. I left. I managed to get some funding through the local clinical commissioning group, finding a private therapist who understood autistic trauma, and this made a world of difference. Even after the trauma is gone, you still need support. I sank into a massive depression when I realised all the things, I'd not been able to do over the previous seven years. I even felt guilty that I had not been strong enough to resist what had happened and I felt that I had been conditioned over many years to accept trauma's presence within me and when it was gone, mourned its absence. But the biggest lie that people tell you is that trauma builds your character, trauma makes you stronger when in reality all trauma does harm you and life becomes a seemingly 'impossible' narrative.

But what about those autistic people still trapped within mental health services? I was supported and enabled, but what about the people who aren't? We have to make a change and I feel it's the responsibility of professionals working in mental health reading this to be a catalyst for change. We need services to walk away from the 'tyranny of the functioning label', and embrace intersectionality, double empathy and monotropism. Yes, there are good people within mental health services, but I feel that 'the MHS system' actively harms autistic people and that it should be held accountable. We're not innately broken people, we're broken by other people. Remember: it's not wholly about being trauma-informed, more importantly, it's being informed about a person's experiences of trauma. Learn from that person, listening and acting on what they say, as opposed to just relying on clinical indications. Trauma isn't transitory, it won't go by itself. Flashbacks may be especially realistic due to a person's synaesthesia. Also, autistic people have had to fight through layers of marginalisation and non-autistic privilege just to get to that point of sitting in front of you. Research the narratives, experiences, and thoughts of actual autistic people. We need validation and affirmation of our experience. We need you to gain our trust, give us treatment choice and agency, and work with us to co-produce our healing. All this is now in your hands.

Top takeaways

1 Listen to the person sitting in front of you:
   This seems simplistic to state as it is a core principle of therapeutic training but often factors can remove the therapist mentally from the room through bias, the service culture or their own work and family pressures. Recognise the individuality of the client in front of you.
2 Their narrative, experiences, and feelings should be more informative and valuable than anything you have read or been taught about autism and an autistic person in distress. With children in particular listening may come following your connection, 'tuning in' to your client through their interests and creating a place of trust and safety.
3 If they say they are in distress or feel traumatised, make it your first instinct to believe them not 'It can't have harmed you as it wouldn't have

traumatized me' (remember double empathy). What traumatises autistic people may be different to what would traumatise a non-autistic person.

4 The words you say and actions you take have consequences:

If the treatment for the traumatised autistic person isn't working, consider changing that treatment to another therapy. Please do not, as was done to me say 'If it's not working you are not trying hard enough'. This is I feel potentially harmful gaslighting and places the current failure and responsibility for their healing back on the distressed person at a time they don't need it. Our approach needs to be one that identifies the contours of the client's needs and wraps a cloak of therapy around them.

5 Take a Holistic view of trauma:

If an autistic person is caught up in an ongoing traumatic situation, then that situation will need addressing before intensive treatment starts to achieve the best outcome. Autistic people are often very reluctant to ask for help as they may have had their fingers burnt in previous situations. Supporting an autistic person to face practical issues will free up space in their minds. For children, we have to consider their safety and the support system that is contained in them. Establishing safety, routine, the presence of accessible attachment figures, and a desire to connect with these attachment figures are the primary focus of any intervention. Within this context, the story is more likely to unfold. Collaboratively the therapist and autistic child/young person can work on what is still needed to facilitate working with trauma. Trauma processing may be the goal, but the success of the therapy is in the way we treat the clients and the way they are made to feel first.

6 Requiring an autistic person to trust you in an ongoing trauma situation may be impossible if they are in 'survival mode' and protecting themselves. It's right when they say trust is grown not given; don't break it by promising more than you can give. We don't react well to suggestions like: 'it will seem different after a good night's sleep when you wake in the morning', nor 'it's not as bad as it seems'.

7 Autistic people are simply people:

Autistic people are no greater or lesser than any other person. We are often broken by a society that seems to deny us belonging. When we sit down beside someone to hear their trauma story, we are humbled. If they are telling you, it is because they trust you and feel safe enough to do so. This in my book is an honour bestowed upon us and we have a duty as therapists to treasure these stories and treat each one with respect.

Note

1   A condition in which someone experiences things through their senses in an unusual way, for example by experiencing a colour as a sound, or a number as a position in space.

Autism and intersectionality

Chapter 7

Improving access to mental health services for CYP from minority ethnic communities

Prithvi Perepa and Venessa Bobb-Swaby

When people see behaviour and the colour of your skin – a personal perspective by Venessa

I have been a single mother until recently and my household consists of my three children aged 17, 20, and 22, as well as a 5-year-old grandchild. The oldest and youngest are girls and the middle is a boy. Life has been a roller-coaster, trying to keep all my children safe. The two younger children have a diagnosis of autism and ADHD, whilst the oldest has moderate language difficulties. Before they were diagnosed, I had no clue about hidden disabilities. The lack of advice, support, and trained staff recognising that all three of my children have neurological differences grieves me even today. There were missed opportunities to provide suitable and appropriate advice and support. Instead, I experienced micro-aggressions, assumptions, and cultural incompetence.

There were so many difficulties with my second daughter when it came to school, when out in the community, and when being at home. She was a happy-go-lucky child, full of energy and very confident. Once she moved into secondary school, she changed drastically. She was described as being difficult, argumentative, defiant, and controlling. She doesn't like being in crowds, she doesn't like being told what to do, she is a picky eater, she has low self-esteem, and she finds it hard to trust people. But all this detail got lost in wasted years of being told she was 'normal', that she was aware of what she was doing, and that she was choosing to be 'difficult'. It was suggested that she was a very articulate and intelligent child and that it was my parenting skills that were the cause of her behaviour. The problem was with me in the eyes of non-trained professionals, who were not neuro-informed enough to be able to identify and support her struggles.

Reports of both my daughters' behaviours were flagged, but at no time were they viewed as being neurodivergent. Both struggled academically; they thrived if they had 1:1 support but then regressed when left to do work alone or with others who did not understand their needs and strengths. The school and social services seemed to focus on my parenting skills but did not

DOI: 10.4324/9781003352327-11

recognise my children's vulnerability, or their neurodivergencies. I thought that something was amiss with my younger daughter when she started to share how her school friends would say horrible things about her. She used to tell me that her friends said she was mentally ill and needed help. Also, other parents stopped talking to me due to the way she behaved, describing her as being verbally abusive. I found her school years very challenging. Even when asking if she could get assessed for autism, I was told she did not need a diagnosis as she clearly knew what she was doing and was fooling me. I had similar experiences with my oldest too. In their eyes I was a failure, my kids were just naughty, and we were bombarded with social services, but zero referral to neurodevelopmental pathways.

The only person who I felt really made a difference and believed in helping me was a special educational needs coordinator (SENCo) at one of my daughter's schools, who unfortunately did not stay for long. She called me in and was shocked that my daughter did not have a diagnosis, given the struggles we could all identify, how much I was trying to get diagnostic support, and the fact that her brother was already diagnosed as autistic. The SENCo tried to help as much as she could, but she could clearly see that all the other professionals did not think my daughter was autistic. I believe the SENCo tried to support my daughter and assist in getting support, but the professionals did not seem to listen. The only outcome was that my daughter was put into a part-time pupil referral unit; an alternative educational provision for children who cannot be taught in mainstream school. The setting was wrong for her, but at least some of the staff were willing to listen to me. It was at this moment that I was able to take control of the situation and find out what things were going wrong. If school data is missing vital information, this can have a negative impact on how professionals and those making decisions view my child and view me as the parent.

The lack of understanding and support for my daughter's mental health issues was extremely frustrating. For years, I raised concerns about her health and well-being. However, her behaviour was blamed on me neglecting her, me not spending enough time with her, and her missing her dad. She attended school counselling, but the school felt she needed drama therapy as the previous counsellors found it difficult to support her and felt she used the counselling sessions to get out of lessons. When seeking a diagnosis of autism, I was told she had attachment disorder and social, emotional, and mental health issues, and that she was copying her brother. My daughter suffered for years. She did not sleep, and both Child and Adolescent Mental Health Services (CAMHS) and a GP were of little help. A GP told her to count sheep and have hot chocolate before bed. She felt that no one believed her. She continues to have poor sleep patterns. It was an autistic consultant who assisted in supporting my youngest daughter with her mental state. She stepped in when I found it difficult to support her. The autistic consultant helped with the processes of getting a diagnosis and support at school. She understood my family dynamics and I am grateful for this. It was another professional who had an autistic adult son who supported my entire family. This person was able to believe me when I said my child's brain is wired differently. This person understood the double discrimination I was experiencing due to disability and ethnicity; people would see the behaviour (a meltdown in public) and then the colour of my child's skin.

Over the years I have seen a great deal of improvement when it comes to sourcing information, and resources and connecting with other families. The only challenge I continue to experience is the lack of provision and understanding from professionals when it comes to working with Black and brown autistic children and their families. This is mainly because the professionals fail to understand the intersection between autism and ethnicity/culture. The lack of support and not being understood were things I found stressful as professionals felt I was using autism as an excuse for my children's behaviour, when in fact I was having issues stemming from bad reports that followed me throughout my children's years in education.

What would have helped would have been culturally appropriate materials, resources, and networks with other Black families and professionals. What would have been beneficial for my household to manage all our health and mental well-being is life skills, advice on sleep hygiene, sexual health, money management, and many other things. What I would have preferred is family and individual counselling facilitated by autistic and ADHD specialists. I wanted all sectors to be aware that I am still my young people's voice. I feel that I have to keep repeating myself about what my trio needs.

Unfortunately, these experiences are not unique to my family. For example, there is increasing awareness in the field of autism that girls are less likely to get a diagnosis of autism. Research evidence also highlights that there could be issues in how children from minority ethnic/global majority[1] communities are diagnosed, with reports of under-diagnosis in some communities (such as Gypsy Roma and Pakistani) and over-diagnosis in others (such as Black African) (Perepa et al., 2023; Roman-Urrestarazu et al., 2021). Therefore, it is possible that girls from minority ethnic communities could have further challenges compared to girls from White majority backgrounds.

Acculturalisation and self-identity

In the field of psychology, there is an emphasis on the concept of self and self-identity. Some suggest that a well-developed identity comprises an understanding of one's strengths, weaknesses, and individual uniqueness (Marcia, 1980). This rounded view of our own self can safeguard us from mental health difficulties (Erikson, 1959). As the other chapters in this book have explored, there is a high prevalence of mental health issues in CYP on the autism spectrum. This could be a result of these CYP sharing the negative representations that others associate with their 'differentness' (Corrigan et al., 2005; Link et al., 2014). For CYP from minority ethnic communities, in addition to their autism, what makes them different will include their language, customs, how they look, and perhaps the religion they follow. It is common for individuals who perceive themselves to be different to try and integrate into the norms of the majority group. When referring to such behaviour in individuals belonging to minority ethnic groups, the term acculturation is used.

Berry (2005) describes four acculturation types in his intercultural psychology work:

Marginalised – where an individual does not align with either of the cultural groups and feels they do not belong to them,

Bi-cultural – here the individual tries to align with both cultural groups and manages to maintain their dual identity,

Assimilation – this happens when an individual rejects their own minority group and aligns with the majority group,

And finally **Separated** – here the individual disengages with the majority community and associates solely with those from their own minority group.

Whichever position an individual from a minority ethnic community takes, it is acknowledged that this process can cause stress, often referred to as acculturation stress or minority stress. Some studies with CYPs from minority ethnic communities have found that there is an association between this stress and young people's mental well-being (Duarte et al., 2008). Since CYP from minority ethnic groups who have a diagnosis of autism are not only trying to navigate the majority ethnic group but also a largely neurotypical society, it is possible that these CYP will have more mental health issues compared to autistic CYP from the majority community or compared to neurotypical CYP from minority ethnic communities.

Prevalence of mental health issues

It is noteworthy that research is almost non-existent when it comes to mental health in CYP from minority ethnic communities who are on the autism spectrum. This is perhaps an indication of the systemic racism that is prevalent in the field of autism and related services (health, education, and social care) where until recently culture and ethnicity have been ignored as irrelevant factors in understanding an individual's autism.

In a study conducted by Mandell et al. (2007), the diagnostic labels that African American children were given prior to receiving an autism diagnosis were explored. They found that compared to White American children, African American children were less likely to receive an autism diagnosis on their first visit to a clinician, instead they were often diagnosed with Attention Deficit Hyperactive Disorder (ADHD). They further found that African American children were more likely to receive a diagnosis of conduct disorder than ADHD when compared to White American children. Mandell et al. (2007) hypothesise that this could be a result of how parents describe their child's characteristics, how the characteristics are presented in children from different ethnic backgrounds or a result of clinicians' interpretations of what is being reported or being observed. Whatever the cause, this study indicates that it is possible that CYPs from minority ethnic groups are likely to be misdiagnosed – as in the case of Venessa's family.

Looking more broadly at mental health prevalence in CYP from minority ethnic groups, National Health Service (NHS) data in the UK (NHS Digital, 2020) shows a low prevalence of mental health difficulties in CYP from ethnic minorities compared to White British CYP. A similar disparity has been reported in the USA by Liang et al. (2016) who argue that non-White American children often do not receive a diagnosis of mental health difficulties or are misdiagnosed. They state that compared to White American CYP, those from Hispanic communities are more likely to be diagnosed with substance abuse or disruptive behaviour than ADHD. African American youth on the other hand are less likely to be diagnosed with substance abuse or mood disorders but are more often diagnosed with disruptive behaviour or psychotic disorders. The picture of Asian Americans or Pacific Islanders is more mixed. These prevalence rates indicate that a similar combination of factors, as suggested by Mandell et al. (2007) in relation to autism, could be influencing the diagnosis of mental health difficulties when it comes to CYP from global majority communities. Alternatively, this is a result of racial stereotypes that are held about certain ethnic groups in the UK and USA, combined with a lack of cultural competence amongst professionals when diagnosing CYP from global majority communities.

Differences have also been reported in terms of access to support or care. For example, Cummings and Druss (2011) found in their comparative study of access to services for young people who had depression from different ethnic groups in the USA, that White American youth were more likely to receive treatment than African American, Asian American, or Hispanic CYP. Young people from these communities are less likely to be seen by a clinician and receive medication or any other medical treatment. It is possible that this difference is partly attributed to the way that the health system is organised within the USA, which is dependent on access to appropriate medical insurance. In the UK, where similar economic factors do not impact access to medical care, NHS data (NHS CAMHS Benchmarking, 2019) shows that although there is less prevalence of mental health difficulties in individuals from minority ethnic communities, there is an over-representation of these communities within in-patient services. The prevalence rates are based on who gets referred to CAMHS for an assessment. In a study by Edbrooke-Childs and Patalay (2019) it was found that compared to White British young people, those from minority ethnic communities are more likely to be referred via compulsory routes (such as education, social care, or the justice system) than self-referral by the individual or their family member. This would suggest that how professionals define or understand a CYP's behaviour will influence whether they receive any support. Therefore, it is important to consider structural barriers as well as socio-economic factors to fully understand the disparity experienced by CYP from global majority communities.

Different explanatory models

To a certain extent, how we understand or explain any kind of difference is socially constructed. This can be especially true for mental health or autism diagnosis where there are no concrete biomarkers. Liang et al. (2016) use the broad categorisation of individualistic and collectivist societies as a possible explanation for differences in the prevalence rates of mental health difficulties in various ethnic groups in the Western world. The term 'individualistic societies' is used to describe those in which there is a focus on personal identity and independence and where individual contributions often shape self-worth. Collectivist communities on the other hand focus more on group affinity and there is a stronger emphasis on the role of families and the importance of putting others ahead of individual needs or desires. It is often considered that Western societies tend to be more individualistic compared to communities from other parts of the world. Liang et al. (2016) suggest that it is therefore likely that psychopathology is defined, experienced, and expressed at an individual level in individualistic communities; whereas in a collectivist society, there is more interaction between how others perceive and evaluate the individual's experience within a social and cultural context. This could mean that how we describe, interpret, or label a mental health difference could vary across different societies. It can be concluded that since most of the standardised definitions for mental health difficulties are developed within Western, individualistic societies, these may not have the same meaning for families from minority ethnic communities who often come from collectivist communities.

If family plays a central role in the experiences of CYP from minority ethnic communities, then involving and understanding parental and other family members' experiences is an important element of developing appropriate services. This is especially true as parents' mental health could impact the mental health of the child. Research in the field of autism often focuses on parental stress. However, some of the emerging research suggests that this could be experienced differently in various ethnic groups. For example, a recent Australian study by Smith et al. (2021) found that Southeast Asian parents reported better well-being and higher quality of life compared to White Australian parents. Therefore, it should not be assumed that families from all ethnic communities experience the same levels of stress or anxiety.

At the same time, other research indicates that families in some minority communities may feel ostracised in their communities as a result of their child's autism diagnosis (Hussein et al., 2019) and because of the stigma within their communities (Obeid et al., 2015). Autism or mental health-associated stigma is, to a certain extent, prevalent in all communities across the world. However, levels of stigma could vary across communities. Stigma could impact whether an individual or their family members will seek a diagnosis for mental health difficulties or indeed are willing to receive any support. For example, in a study conducted by Ruphrect-Smith et al. (2023), it was found that compared to their White British peers, young people from minority ethnic communities mentioned stigma in accessing mental health services as a reason for treatment termination or not accessing support. In addition to the stigma associated with autism and mental health, CYP from minority ethnic communities and their family members may also experience discrimination due to their ethnicity. Hardy (2013) states that racial trauma can lead to internal devaluation and to a state of 'voicelessness' where individuals from minority ethnic community do not challenge the discrimination they experience. Such experiences will then lead to an increased incidence of depression in individuals from minority ethnic communities, as Bernard et al. (2021) argue.

Professional perceptions

As stated above, the conceptualisation of mental health difficulties is culturally bound. Therefore, professionals working in the field also have specific explanatory models based on their cultural background and training. A study conducted by Pottick et al. (2007) provided vignettes that met the criteria for conduct disorder along with some contextual information to experienced psychologists, psychiatrists, and social workers. They found that professionals concluded that White youth had mental health difficulties more frequently compared to Black or Hispanic youth. Further, a study conducted by Mackin et al. (2006) found that even when clinicians from different backgrounds used the same assessment tool, the interpretations varied based on professionals' backgrounds. In this study, Indian clinicians considered the patients' conditions to be more severe than American clinicians did. Meanwhile, UK clinicians considered the symptoms to be less severe compared to American clinicians. These studies highlight how contextual factors could impact the way that professionals interpret a set of behaviours and how their training and theoretical concepts could influence these judgements. This is perhaps another reason why there is a delay in accessing appropriate diagnosis or support for CYP from minority ethnic communities.

When parents and professionals have different explanatory models, this could cause conflict or lack of trust between them. For example, a study conducted by Minsky et al. (2006) found that teachers rated African American children to have more problem behaviours than their parents believed them to have. There could be many reasons for this, such as parental expectations of behaviour or different interpretations of what constitutes 'difficult behaviour', or the result of teachers' unconscious bias. Although this study did not include any CYP with an official diagnosis of autism, it is possible that the behaviour of the child could change based on the context. Whatever the reason, this highlights some of the issues in accessing support and services for CYP from minority ethnic communities. If there is a difference in how parents and professionals are interpreting the child's behaviour, it is likely that the parents will feel that their concerns are being ignored (as Venessa felt with her daughters) or that they are facing discrimination because of their ethnicity, as found in a study by Dababnah et al. (2018).

It is also important to understand what is considered an effective outcome of a support or an intervention scheme from the perspective of the CYP. Young people in Ruphrect-Smith et al.'s (2023) study commented that they particularly valued empowerment as a positive outcome, but this was not always shared by professionals as an effective measurement of success. If there is a mismatch between the professional and CYP's perceptions, then it is likely that the CYP will be less satisfied with the outcome of the support and/ or intervention plan. It could be argued that this mismatch is similar to what Milton (2012) describes as the double-empathy problem when explaining the differences in perceptions of autistic people and neurotypical people (as mentioned earlier in Chapter 1). When it comes to CYP on the autism spectrum from minority ethnic communities, there can also be the additional barrier that professionals from a White majority community may not understand the experiences and aspirations of someone from a different ethnic community.

Key points for clinicians to consider

The above discussion highlights the importance of considering a CYP's socio-cultural background and how it impacts their experience of autism and any associated mental health difficulties when providing a diagnosis or considering appropriate services and support for them and their families. This is especially important as some research suggests that CYP from collectivist societies may benefit from the protective effects that their family and community provide. Neblett et al. (2012) evaluated this in relation to the racial discrimination that young people from minority ethnic communities experience and concluded that positive messages around the child's culture, which was provided by their parents and wider family, could counteract the negative impact that discrimination could have on their mental health. It is hard to know how relevant this is for autistic CYP. However, studies such as this should encourage all professionals to provide opportunities for CYP to develop their autistic as well as their ethnic identities. It is possible that focusing only on one of these identities may not meet the specific issues that these CYP face due to their dual marginalisation status.

As culture plays a role in interpreting behaviours associated with autism and mental health difficulties, it is important to engage with the CYP and their families to understand what they are experiencing. Spending time to understand this in an empathetic way would help in providing an intervention or support pathway that is acceptable for the child and their family. This approach can reduce the potential bias within the construction of mental health assessment tools. It is also necessary to raise the awareness of different communities to reduce the likelihood of stigma experienced by some CYP and their families.

Finally, it is important that clinicians and professionals working in the mental health sector are aware of their own biases and how these could impact their practice. Being conscious of our own biases would help us to challenge ourselves and address the potential impact such biases could have on our professional judgments.

Cultural awareness training and cross-cultural communication should be an integral part of professional training in this field. These principles can be further explored in Davis et al.'s (2018) multi-cultural orientation framework and Perepa's (2019) work, combined with an experience-sensitive approach (McGreevy et al., 2024; Table 7.1).

Table 7.1 Principles for culturally inclusive practice

Insiderness	Consider that each CYP on the autism spectrum with mental health issues from minority ethnic communities will be experiences these multiple identities in an individual way.
Agency	Allow the CYP to embrace the identity they prefer at any given time and provide them opportunities to engage in decision making about their lives.
Uniqueness	Recognise the other identities that the individual has in addition to their autism, mental health, and ethnicity. For example, their gender, sexuality, and religion, and how these shape their individual experiences.
Sense making	Acknowledge your own lack of cultural understanding and show cultural humility by trying to make sense of the experiences of someone who has a different cultural experience to your own. Reflect on the appropriateness of the tools and procedures used in your setting for someone from a different ethnic background.
Personal journey	It is important to acknowledge and affirm the multiple levels of discrimination that some CYP on the autism spectrum from minority ethnic communities would have experienced.
Sense of place	Ensure that wherever you are meeting the family or/and CYP provides them a sense of belonging and does not alienate them.
Embodiment	Provide opportunities for the CYP to explore their multiple identities without demeaning or belittling any of them.
Togetherness	Work in collaboration with the family members and the CYP to understand what their priorities and needs are and incorporate these within your service.

Venessa's family experiences reimagined

There were so many difficulties with my second daughter when it came to school, when out in the community, and when being at home. She was a happy-go-lucky child, full of energy and very confident. Once she moved into secondary school, she changed drastically. When I raised my concerns with the teacher, the school staff invited me to a meeting and listened to my concerns. The SENCO discussed with my daughter what her experiences at school were like. Following this she suggested to me that I should seek a diagnosis of autism.

During the assessment process for her autism, the paediatrician suggested that there might be additional issues that we may need to explore. After discussing these with us, a CAMHS referral was made. Professionals believed me and provided me with opportunities to share what has worked in the past as well as our family makes sense of presenting issues.

We were seen by a White middle-class professional who acknowledged that he did not understand our life experiences and spent time understanding how being Black, female, autistic, and with anxiety influenced my daughter's life. He specifically focused on understanding what makes my daughter sleepless at night – her sensory comfort, her social worries and sense of belonging, her routines, and struggles. This professional was genuinely interested in listening to us and working with us with humility and curiosity. In addition, both my daughter and I received counselling to help us overcome the cultural and psychological trauma that we have been through. We were given a healing space to process our frustrations and fears. Following the diagnosis, the same professional asked whether my daughter would like to meet an older Black autistic woman. When my daughter said she would like this, a meeting was arranged with this woman. My daughter feels a bit more confident now, although she did not feel it was useful to meet the older autistic woman (after three meetings, she felt there was a generational gap in understanding). Instead, a local autism charity facilitated an autistic girls' network which she now attends on a regular basis.

Note

1 Global majority is used to explain that while an ethnic group or culture is a minority within a given context, they could be a majority when considered globally. Therefore, they are only experiencing a minority status within the given context. However, the term global majority does not always consider White minorities, and therefore we are using the terms ethnic minorities and global majority as alternatives in this chapter.

References

Bernard, D. L., Calhoun, C. D., Banks, D. E., Halliday, C. A., Hughes-Halbert, C., & Danielson, C. K. (2021). Making the "C-ACE" for a culturally-informed adverse childhood experiences framework to understand the pervasive mental health impact of racism on Black youth. *Journal of Child & Adolescent Trauma*, *14*, 233–247. https://doi.org/10.1007/s40653-020-00319-9

Berry, J. W. (2005). Acculturation: Living successfully in two cultures. *International Journal of Intercultural Relations*, *29*(6), 697–712. https://doi.org/10.1016/j.ijintrel.2005.07.013

Corrigan, P. W., Kerr, A., & Knudsen, L. (2005). The stigma of mental illness: Explanatory models and methods for change. *Applied and Preventive Psychology*, *11*(3), 179–190. https://doi.org/10.1016/j.appsy.2005.07.001

Cummings, J. R., & Druss, B. G. (2011). Racial/ethnic differences in mental health service use among adolescents with major depression. *Journal of the American Academy of Child & Adolescent Psychiatry*, *50*(2), 160–170. https://doi.org/10.1016/j.jaac.2010.11.004

Dababnah, S., Shaia, W. E., Campion, K., & Nichols, H. M. (2018). "We had to keep pushing": Caregivers' perspectives on autism screening and referral practices of black children in primary care. *Intellectual and Developmental Disabilities*, *56*(5), 321–336. https://doi.org/10.1352/1934-9556-56.5.321

Davis, D. E., DeBlaere, C., Owen, J., Hook, J. N., Rivera, D. P., Choe, E., … Placeres, V. (2018). The multicultural orientation framework: A narrative review. *Psychotherapy*, *55*(1), 89. https://psycnet.apa.org/doi/10.1037/pst0000160

Duarte, C. S., Bird, H. R., Shrout, P. E., Wu, P., Lewis-Fernandéz, R., Shen, S., & Canino, G. (2008). Culture and psychiatric symptoms in Puerto Rican children: Longitudinal results from one ethnic group in two contexts. *Journal of Child Psychology and Psychiatry*, *49*(5), 563–572. https://doi.org/10.1111/j.1469-7610.2007.01863.x

Edbrooke-Childs, J., & Patalay, P. (2019). Ethnic differences in referral routes to youth mental health services. *Journal of the American Academy of Child & Adolescent Psychiatry*, *58*(3), 368–375. https://doi.org/10.1016/j.jaac.2018.07.906

Erikson, E. H. (1959). *Identity and the life cycle*. New York: Norton.

Hardy, K. (2013). Healing the hidden wounds of racial trauma. *Reclaiming Children and Youth*, *22*(1), 24–28.

Hussein, A. M., Pellicano, E., & Crane, L. (2019). Understanding and awareness of autism among Somali parents living in the United Kingdom. *Autism*, *23*(6), 1408–1418. https://doi.org/10.1177/1362361318813996

Liang, J., Matheson, B. E., & Douglas, J. M. (2016). Mental health diagnostic considerations in racial/ethnic minority youth. *Journal of Child and Family Studies*, *25*, 1926–1940. https://doi.org/10.1007/s10826-015-0351-z

Link, B. G., Phelan, J. C., & Hatzenbuehler, M. L. (2014). Stigma and social inequality. *Handbook of the Social Psychology of Inequality*, 49–64. https://doi.org/10.1007/978-94-017-9002-4_3

Mackin, P., Targum, S. D., Kalali, A., Rom, D., & Young, A. H. (2006). Culture and assessment of manic symptoms. *The British Journal of Psychiatry*, *189*(4), 379–380. https://doi.org/10.1192/bjp.bp.105.013920

Mandell, D. S., Ittenbach, R. F., Levy, S. E., & Pinto-Martin, J. A. (2007). Disparities in diagnoses received prior to a diagnosis of autism spectrum disorder. *Journal of Autism and Developmental Disorders*, *37*(9), 1795–1802. https://doi.org/10.1007/s10803-006-0314-8

Marcia, J. E. (1980). Identity in adolescence. *Handbook of Adolescent Psychology*, *9*(11), 159–187.

McGreevy, E., Quinn, A., Law, R., Botha, M., Evans, M., Rose, K., ... & Pavlopoulou, G. (2024). An Experience Sensitive Approach to Care with and for Autistic Children and Young People in Clinical Services. *Journal of Humanistic Psychology*, *1*, 27. https://doi.org/10.1177/00221678241232442

Milton, D. (2012). On the ontological status of autism: The 'double-empathy problem'. *Disability and Society*, *27*(6), 883–887. https://doi.org/10.1080/09687599.2012. 710008

Minsky, S., Petti, T., Gara, M., Vega, W., Lu, W., & Kiely, G. (2006). Ethnicity and clinical psychiatric diagnosis in childhood. *Administration and Policy in Mental Health & Mental Health Services Research*, *33*, 558–567. https://doi.org/10.1007/ s10488-006-0069-8

Neblett, E. W., Rivas-Drake, D., & Umaña-Taylor, A. J. (2012). The promise of racial and ethnic protective factors in promoting ethnic minority youth development. *Child Development Perspectives*, *6*, 295–303. https://doi.org/10.1111/j.1750–8606. 2012.00239.x

NHS CAMHS Benchmarking. (2019). Retrieved from: https://digital.nhs.uk/data-and-information/publications/statistical/mental-health-of-children-and-young-people-in-england/2020-wave-1-follow-up/data-sets [Accessed 21st December 2022]

NHS Digital. (2020). Mental health of children and young people in England, 2020. Retrieved from: https://www.nhsbenchmarking.nhs.uk/news/2019-child-and-adolescent-mental-health-services-project-results-published [Accessed 20th December 2022]

Obeid, R., Daou, N., DeNigris, D., Shane-Simpson, C., Brooks, P. J., & Gillespie-Lynch, K. (2015). A cross-cultural comparison of knowledge and stigma associated with autism spectrum disorder among college students in Lebanon and the United States. *Journal of Autism and Developmental Disorders*, *45*, 3520–3536. https://doi. org/10.1007/s10803-015-2499-1

Perepa, P. (2019). *Autism, ethnicity and culture: Working with children and families from minority communities*. London: Jessica Kingsley Publishers.

Perepa, P., Wallace, S., & Guldberg, K. (2023). *The experiences of marginalised families with autistic children*. Birmingham: University of Birmingham.

Pottick, K. J., Kirk, S. A., Hsieh, D. K., & Tian, X. (2007). Judging mental disorder in youths: Effects of client, clinician, and contextual differences. *Journal of Consulting and Clinical Psychology*, *75*, 1–8. https://psycnet.apa.org/doi/10.1037/0022-006X.75.1.1

Roman-Urrestarazu, A., van Kessel, R., Allison, C., Matthews, F., Brayne, C., & Baron-Cohen, S. (2021). Association of race/ethnicity and social disadvantage with autism prevalence in 7 million school children in England. *JAMA Pediatrics*, *175*(6), e210054. https://doi.org/10.1001/jamapediatrics.2021.0054

Ruphrect-Smith, H., Davies, S., Jacob, J., & Edbrooke-Childs, J. (2023). Ethnic differences in treatment outcome for children and young people accessing mental health support. *European Child & Adolescent Psychiatry*, *33*, 1–11. https://doi.org/10.1007/ s00787-023-02233-5

Smith, J., Sulek, R., Abdullahi, I., Green, C. C., Bent, C. A., Dissanayake, C., & Hudry, K. (2021). Comparison of mental health, well-being and parenting sense of competency among Australian and South-East Asian parents of autistic children accessing early intervention in Australia. *Autism*, *25*(6), 1784–1796. https://doi.org/ 10.1177/13623613211010006

Chapter 8

Gender, sexuality, and autism in the therapy room

Lucy Matthews

Introduction

Just like everybody else, autistic people have more than one identity. This book has spoken a lot about adopting an experience-sensitive approach, whereby a therapist learns from their clients, avoids making assumptions, and investigates different dimensions of their clients' lives and their environments: their sense of belonging and meaning and so on. In order to fully capture their sense of self, you need to understand how they identify with their gender identity and sexuality as well.

Gender identity is a person's internal sense of their own gender. People who identify as the sex they were assigned at birth are called cisgender, or cis, whereas those who do not may use terms such as transgender, nonbinary, or gender-fluid. Researchers and practitioners may often use the phrase 'gender diverse' as an umbrella term for different gender identities, similar to the way some people use 'neurodiverse' to describe variations in cognitive style.

The world is a very heteronormative place, and it's so often assumed that we are all heterosexual as well as cis-gendered. We know that gender nonconformity and different sexual identities are highly co-occurring within the autistic population. There is a growing body of evidence which demonstrates this correlation. Both gender identity and sexuality are more likely to be divergent from societal norms among autistic people than in the general population. Similarly, autism appears to be more prevalent among gender-diverse people than it is in the general population – three to six times as common, according to Warrier et al. (2020). Some experts estimate that between 6 and 25.5% of gender-diverse people are autistic.

It is therefore vitally important that this is considered and integrated into practice when clinicians are working with autistic individuals. For instance, Strang et al. (2018) found that 22.5% of young people who had been diagnosed as autistic were transgender, compared with 2.5% of the overall general population.

DOI: 10.4324/9781003352327-12

Double marginalisation

Those with multiple minority identities are likely to face an excess amount of marginalisation. This intersectionality means that not only can autistic individuals experience disadvantage within society due to not being the dominant neurotype, but they are also likely to face discrimination based on their alternative gender identity and/or sexuality. Gender identity and sexuality can also, of course, both be atypical – causing an additional likelihood of discrimination. Someone could be transgender and gay – thus experiencing challenges from stigma and negativity from both of those angles separately. Because of the high levels of autism within the gender-diverse and queer communities, and vice versa, it is impossible to claim to be neurodivergent affirming without being LGBTQIA+ affirming as well. Recognising and acting upon intersectionality is vital.

Living within such a neuro-normative society is difficult enough for autistic people. Living within a double minority – being both autistic and LGBTQIA+ – is not easy. As a result, LGBTQIA+ autistic people may have a greater risk of developing mental health problems (Snapp et al., 2015). It is incredibly difficult to feel as though you are constantly being told that the way you are, fundamentally, as a human being isn't right. That who you are isn't acceptable, and that you need to change. Now imagine coupling that with messages that tell you, in a heteronormative and cisnormative society, that you are also wrong in that regard. It can be a huge challenge, and a risk, to open up about your different identities within the world in which we currently live. If, partially due to all of this, you end up seeking help from mental health services and they end up complying with this narrative, it can feel scary, lonely, and ultimately traumatising – or re-traumatising.

Let's consider this case study:

Aoife (they/them) is a 19-year-old non-binary autistic person who is pansexual. Aoife is from a strict Catholic family and has felt unable to come out to their family about their sexuality or gender identity. They would like to start experimenting with alternative, less gendered names in the near future, and feel able to be authentic and open about their different identities. After experiencing thoughts of self-harm and suicide, they are referred for therapy by their GP. They look up the service which they are referred to in advance, due to anxiety about acceptance and judgement. They do not see anything on the website that indicates LGBTQIA+ inclusivity. On the day of their first appointment, Aoife arrives at Reception and is asked to complete a personal information form. One of the first questions asks them whether they are male or female, with no alternative option.

How do you think this might make Aoife feel on entry to the service? How might this influence their relationship and initial openness with their therapist?

Representation is really important. Seeing yourself reflected in the world around you is vital to make you feel valid and acceptable for who you are. When you enter a service for the first time, you feel very vulnerable. Something as simple as including alternative gender options on a form might feel like a small thing but could instantly increase someone's trust in the service – and subsequently the therapist they are about to encounter. How many times might someone like Aoife have experienced being misgendered, or have had people commenting on their appearance through a gendered lens, using gendered language? When you introduce yourself to a client, do you include your pronouns? Simple considerations of things like this by the therapist can be monumental in creating a safe space for those who may be gender non-conforming and set the therapeutic relationship off on the right foot from the moment your client sets foot in the door.

Examine your biases and expectations

Aoife is living in a very religious family. They have experienced negative views from those around them in relation to people who align with their identity for their entire lives – imagine the impact that could have on someone. Now imagine this has led them to feel as though they are better off dead, they finally reach out for help whilst in a desperate mind frame and then get to the place which is supposed to be helping them only to find that they don't feel safe there either. Working with non-binary and gender-diverse individuals needs to be done without judgment and expectation.

Someone who is non-binary might present more traditionally feminine to some sessions, more traditionally masculine to others, and androgynously at other points. Making a big deal of this might actually alienate your client further – accept them however they are presenting. If they want to discuss their gender presentation that day, then having the space for them to feel comfortable to do so, and showing them that this is safe, is brilliant – but this should be on their say so, not yours. Avoiding gendered words such as 'pretty', 'handsome', etc. is also advisable. Don't assume anything from someone's presentation on a given day. This is similar to autism – do not assume that the way someone is presenting is a true reflection of how they are. Masking plays a huge role in the external facade you might see with an autistic person and their appearing to be vivacious and positive might not mean what it would appear to on the surface. This is also true in written correspondence; be careful about the comments you make based on appearance and use correct pronouns in any assessment letters which are sent out. You could end up in the unfortunate position where you are doing quite well within the session of creating a suitable environment for the person, but then being clumsy with wording in your letters which then diminishes the trust that person has in you.

The experiences within the case studies in this chapter might be fictitious, but they represent common occurrences of those within the

LGBTQIA+ community. People might even be having these experiences in your therapy room, and you're not even aware of it because they don't feel safe enough to discuss it with you.

Let's consider another case:

Adedayo (he/him) is a 15-year-old autistic boy who identifies as queer. He has been referred to CAMHS because he is struggling with depression, the symptoms of which were recognised by a trusted teacher at his school. He has not yet disclosed his sexuality to anyone. Adedayo notices, when arriving for his initial appointment, that there are no posters in the reception area which represent him in terms of his neurotype, ethnicity or sexuality. Adedayo is assigned a male therapist who he sees as being traditionally masculine; he feels wary after observing some similar traits in his therapist as in some of the boys who have bullied him at school. During his therapy sessions, his therapist makes very heteronormative statements on a regular basis, as well as repeatedly using idioms which Adedayo finds difficult to interpret. Although Adedayo would like to be able to talk to somebody about his sexuality for the first time ever, he feels as though he needs to mask his different identities and does not feel safe emotionally with his therapist.

Do you think Adedayo would be able to come out to his therapist and discuss his sexuality? What could his therapist and the service have done differently to ensure that he felt safe to be his authentic self and address his underlying difficulties?

As with Aoife above, immediately upon entering the service, Adedayo is wary as he does not feel as though he sees himself represented within the building. Is inclusivity visible in your service? Do you have posters that represent different gender identities, sexualities, ethnicities, and types of families? How about your website – does this offer the same impression of inclusivity?

Being proactive about addressing masking in the therapy room

By now, you should hopefully know a bit about autistic masking. Think about when you are personally in a situation which is unfamiliar to you, in a new setting and with new people – would you feel happy to open up to people there straight away about sensitive parts of yourself (especially those which have been stigmatised throughout your life)? Of course not, most people wouldn't – and that's okay. But within the therapy setting, the trust to do this needs to be built up over time in order for the therapy to be effective, and to have a strong therapeutic relationship. Everyone masks parts of themselves sometimes and puts on a slightly different face depending on what situation they are in and with whom, but autistic people mask a fundamental part of who they are on a regular basis, and it is *exhausting*.

There is evidence to suggest that autistic people who mask experience higher levels of suicidality (Cassidy et al., 2020), as well as burnout and general mental health issues (Pearson & Rose, 2021). Added to that, LGBTQIA+ young people are more than twice as likely to experience suicidal thoughts as non-LGBTQIA+ youth, with more than two-thirds (68%) of those surveyed in a study published by Just Like Us (2021) stating that they have had suicidal thoughts. Masking within society is tiring enough, and on its own can lead to these outcomes, but imagine that your client is coming to sessions and feeling as though they are obligated to heavily mask with you as well. Where is the let-up? Where is the place of safety where they feel able to be themselves? If they don't feel as though they can do this with you, having a chance at truly impactful therapy overall is likely to be low.

Adedayo clearly doesn't feel safe with his therapist to drop this mask or discuss issues around his sexuality. The use of certain types of language (e.g. idioms, metaphors) might be a challenge for some (not all) autistic people, and this has already made him feel alienated. On top of that, his therapist has used language which is very heteronormative on multiple occasions. For someone who is struggling with their sexuality and has not opened up about it to *anyone* in their life so far, this type of language is not facilitating a safe space for them to do so. As a result, Adedayo might feel as though he needs to follow the therapist's agenda – a retreat from what he was hoping to discuss and deal with in his therapy sessions, and work on other, safer, things instead. Not feeling able to talk about this in therapy could have devastating consequences for Adedayo, as we can see from the statistics above.

How could you, if you were his therapist, ensure that he felt safe to drop the various masks and speak freely with you? Do you use examples of different types of relationships and family structures in discussions with clients? For example, not asking a (self-identified) male client if he has a girlfriend – instead either asking whether he has a partner, or partners, or even better: asking if he has a boyfriend, girlfriend, or partner so that he knows that you'd be okay with him telling you that he had, or wanted, a boyfriend. Additionally, not making these sorts of assumptions about their family (immediate and wider) or friends in conversation would emphasise this openness.

To move beyond 'scripted' responses, you can talk about masking with the young person. It is essential to be curious about why how, and in which ways and situations, autistic LGBTQIA+ CYP may be masking and hiding parts of themselves. Consider the ways in which this may impact their sense of self, mood, and well-being, and what this may look like in different contexts.

Each child or young person will have individual and unique ways of communicating strong feelings – both positive and negative. It is important to recognise, accept, and validate these ways of expressing feelings, and ensure that the child or young person feels safe to do so in the therapy room.

The self you bring to the therapy room

Which self will you bring to the therapy room, regardless of your own ideologies, to create a safe space for young people like Adedayo to express their feelings? Have you reflected on your own views around gender and sexuality? What are your thoughts and feelings? What has influenced your views on these things (e.g. colleagues, family, the media)? Might this have an impact on the way you present yourself within the therapy room?

Here is a final case study to consider:

Jamilla (she/her) is an autistic and ADHD transgender 21-year-old. Jamilla has very high anxiety after being physically attacked due to her gender identity, having had multiple challenging situations with peers following miscommunications, and having been briefly homeless after moving away from her family - who would not accept her new identity. She self-refers for therapy when her anxiety becomes too much for her to manage. Initially, sessions with her therapist go well and she starts feeling able to be open with her therapist, however when conversations about her gender identity present themselves, and Jamilla uses terms which the therapist is unfamiliar with, the therapist decides that she is unable to work with Jamilla because she is 'too complex' for the service, despite her largely wanting help with strategies for her anxiety. The therapist informs Jamilla of this, stops seeing her and refers her to another service, who decides that she does not reach their threshold - Jamilla then loses her support.

What could have been done differently in this scenario? Do you think that training and additional knowledge could have made a difference to the support which Jamilla was offered? Did her sexuality and neurodivergence genuinely make her a complex case, or was the therapist simply feeling out of their depth?

Your clients largely do not care about your qualifications, or whether you are up to date on acronyms around their identities – they just want someone who is going to see them for who they are, listen, and accept them. It's the small things which are the most vital in shaping relationships and creating change for people. Notice that it wasn't Jamilla who was uncomfortable in this situation – in fact, she was starting to feel comfortable within the therapeutic relationship and open up. It was her *therapist* who was uncomfortable here. Instead of sitting with that discomfort or educating herself about the terms and challenges which she didn't have experience, the therapist decided that it wasn't possible for her to work with Jamilla. I would imagine that this therapist had plenty of experience working with people who needed help with their anxiety – and this is fundamentally what Jamilla needed. Her different identities were important to her and would come up alongside this, but she predominantly wanted support with anxiety after traumatic incidents – which is a common area for therapists to support their clients with.

Educating yourself is important, however, it is also crucial that you are educating yourself *outside* the therapy room. Staying curious about what is happening for the young person and how they feel should remain the focus of sessions – not probing with questions purely to learn from the person. The therapist should be willing to learn, listen, and grow from working with the client, but should not want their client to be the one to educate them. If this happens naturally, great – but it shouldn't be the therapist's goal.

Therapists will likely be working with both diagnosed and undiagnosed autistic people, and these clients will all be on their own journeys when it comes to their gender and sexuality. For some, this might not have much, or any, influence (if they are heterosexual and cis-gendered), but for others this may be a significant feature in their lives – and everything else in between. Do you feel as though you can create a safe space for individuals throughout this journey? If so, how? If not, why not? What could you do to change and improve this?

Your client might want to explore their different identities with you but be able to sense your discomfort around these topics. This could cause them to avoid discussing these things with you – is that then a real safe space for them to be in? Jamilla will have clearly known that her therapist was uncomfortable – if not during the sessions, then certainly upon being deemed 'too complex' and discharged. As a result of her therapist's discomfort, she lost the relationship in which she'd started to feel able to be authentic, as well as further help for the mental health difficulties she was facing. This could actually add to the trauma which Jamilla has experienced and feel like an additional form of rejection.

Treading carefully: discussions about the past

Another consideration when working with transgender clients is that they might not feel able to discuss their past in the same way as other clients might. Depending on the modality of the therapy, it is common for therapists to want to make links to the past and discuss someone's childhood. For some transgender people, this might be actively triggering for them. It might be the case that an individual finds it painful to acknowledge that they even existed prior to their transition, seeing this point as a kind of rebirth. Keeping this in mind would be advisable – treading carefully around discussions of situations which will have occurred pre-transition and working out how they feel about this as an individual so as not to add to their difficulties.

What the individuals here predominantly need, alongside other autistic and LGBTQIA+ people, is tolerance, acceptance, and understanding. They need you to be supportive and authentic, and to provide them with some-where in the world where they can unmask and feel as though they are truly seen, emotionally held, and accepted. The type of therapy you're delivering is almost secondary to this – the relationship is the foundation of everything in that room. Give these young people the safe environment that they often so desperately need.

Conclusion

Creating a feeling of safety within the therapy room is essential if you are to create a productive therapeutic relationship and become an ally for that young person. Simple actions can be taken to increase trust and provide this safe space, both with someone's initial contact with services and during therapy sessions. Working without judgement and expectation regarding someone's gender identity and presentation and being aware of and tackling heteronormativity and masking can make a big difference.

Therapists should educate themselves (without expecting their clients to educate them) about areas of their clients' identities which they lack experience within order to be able to work effectively with a diverse range of individuals. This might mean facing your own discomfort and challenging the way you have previously worked, and your service operates.

Whilst the author can speak from their perspective, using case studies to make you think about this important topic, it is essential for you to take this information out into the world with you and develop it further. Do not consider this to be all you need to read on the topic – continue to educate yourself and grow in this area of understanding. If that can be by learning from people with lived experience – even better! Have conversations in your day-to-day life and connect with service users and others to ensure that those who are already in higher risk groups, and who are contending with issues surrounding intersectionality, have a safe space with you – even if they struggle to find this in the world outside the therapy room.

References

Cassidy, S. A., Gould, K., Townsend, E., Pelton, M., Robertson, A. E., & Rodgers, J. (2020). Is camouflaging autistic traits associated with suicidal thoughts and behaviours? Expanding the interpersonal psychological theory of suicide in an undergraduate student sample. *Journal of Autism and Developmental Disorders*, *50*(10), 3638–3648. https://doi.org/10.1007/s10803-019-04323-3

Milsom, R. (2021). *Growing up LGBT+*. Just Like Us. Retrieved from: https://www.justlikeus.org/wp-content/uploads/2021/11/Just-Like-Us-2021-report-Growing-Up-LGBT.pdf

Pearson, A., & Rose, K. (2021). A conceptual analysis of autistic masking: Understanding the narrative of stigma and the illusion of choice. *Autism in Adulthood*, *3*(1), 52–60. https://doi.org/10.1089/aut.2020.0043

Strang, J. F., Powers, M. D., Knauss, M., Sibarium, E., Leibowitz, S. F., Kenworthy, L., … Anthony, L. G. (2018). "They thought it was an obsession": Trajectories and perspectives of autistic transgender and gender-diverse adolescents. *Journal of*

Autism and Developmental Disorders, *48*, 4039–4055. https://doi.org/10.1007/s10803-018-3723-6

Warrier, V., Greenberg, D. M., Weir, E., Buckingham, C., Smith, P., Lai, M. C., Allison, C., & Baron-Cohen, S. (2020). Elevated rates of autism, other neurodevelopmental and psychiatric diagnoses, and autistic traits in transgender and gender-diverse individuals. *Nature Communications*, *11*(1), 3959. https://doi.org/10.1038/s41467-020-17794-1

Working in partnership with autistic CYP and their families

Chapter 9

Working with parents and carers

An empathic Low arousal approach to distressed behaviour

Andy McDonnell

A low arousal approach is an empathic stress support

Autistic CYPs with and without learning disabilities often displays distressed behaviour. Traditional behavioural models interpret this as a deficit within the child and focus on addressing the behaviour and its functions. Alternative approaches often involve deeper analysis, interpretations that go 'beyond behaviour' (Delahooke, 2019), and a focus on generalised well-being and stress management (McDonnell et al., 2019). One such approach is the Low Arousal Approach (McDonnell, 2010) developed by Studio 3, a non-confrontational approach which places emphasis on how practitioners, carers and family members behave and respond to crisis situations, as opposed to traditional medicalised models which focus instead on changing or managing the distressed individual. The central idea of the approach assumes that if some behaviours of concern are mediated by a heightened state of physiological arousal, the reduction of this arousal state should reduce distressed behaviours, at least in the short term (McDonnell et al., 2019). Thus, arousal and stress regulation are the aim of the approach, whereby practitioners attempt to co-regulate and de-escalate during distressing situations and/or model this for parents and carers.

Whilst reactive strategies for managing behaviour are necessary, they are not sufficient to achieve behavioural change (McDonnell, 2010). Changing behaviours requires a collaborative approach, where individuals can focus on providing support at times of 'meltdowns' in the context of the elements which contribute to crisis situations (Lipsky, 2011). The Low Arousal Approach is a crisis management strategy that focuses on how we support individuals through these meltdowns in a humanistic and empathic manner. This approach has also been described as Empathic Stress Support (McDonnell, 2020), which has been offered as a framework for humanising behavioural methodology. The Low Arousal Approach has been

DOI: 10.4324/9781003352327-14

implemented in care and educational settings within a stress and well-being framework (McCreadie et al., 2019), as well as by families supporting individuals at home, following coaching and support from the Studio 3 team of expert trainers and practitioners. This chapter seeks to demonstrate, using anonymised case examples, how the Low Arousal Approach to behaviour management can be used with autistic CYPs and their families to promote overall well-being and stress management, leading to a reduction in distressed behaviour.

Definition of the low arousal approach

The Low Arousal Approach is a collection of non-aversive behaviour management strategies which focus on reducing physiological arousal as well as internal and external environmental stressors in order to avoid or de-escalate crisis situations (Elvén, 2010; McDonnell, 2019, 2022; McDonnell et al., 1994; Woodcock & Page, 2010). Essentially, applying a Low Arousal Approach means that supporters focus on what they can do to reduce their own physiological arousal in order to help regulate the arousal of others, in addition to identifying stress, trauma, and other triggers that could be contributing to aggressive or distressed behaviour.

McDonnell, McCreadie, and Dickinson identified four key elements of the Low Arousal Approach (2019, pp. 458–459):

First, decreasing staff demands and requests, to reduce potential points of conflict around an individual. Second, avoidance of potentially arousing triggers (e.g. direct eye contact, and touch and removal of spectators to the incident). Third, the avoidance of non-verbal behaviours that may lead to conflict (e.g. aggressive postures and stances). Fourth, challenging staff/carer beliefs about short-term management of behaviours of concern.

The approach relies on people around the autistic person in distress reflecting on incidents and identifying areas where their own behaviour may have contributed to an incident. This means encouraging supporters to focus on their own stress management and arousal regulation. The aim is to create a system of support that fosters a calm and regulated environment; after all, how can we help someone to calm down when we ourselves are highly stressed? Whilst it is distressing to witness individuals in highly charged emotional moments and not intervene, taking a moment to collect yourself and take a step back can make a huge difference when managing meltdowns in the moment. Low Arousal does not mean 'no arousal' whatsoever, but it does mean looking at these incidents in a different way. Once a calm situation has been restored, there is an opportunity for all participants to reflect and learn from the incident.

A low arousal approach is a trauma-informed approach

In order to support autistic CYPs and their families, it is essential to view the world from their perspective and attempt to understand their experiences. Many autistic young people often experience stress and trauma, especially in adolescence, as they can feel as though they are trying to understand a world that is chaotic and confusing (Vermeulen, 2012). Helping and supporting individuals to try and make sense of a predominantly neurotypical world not adapted to accommodate their needs is central to a Low Arousal Approach and an essential part of the role of supporters. The following example demonstrates an anonymised case example of a young man who struggled with his autistic identity:

> John was a sixteen-year-old autistic young man who in adolescence became increasingly isolated and aggressive towards his family members. This led to a crisis admission to a specialist service, where John did not fit in, and would isolate himself and not engage with his supporters. John became curious about the behaviour of his frontline staff, often describing them as behaving 'a little weird.' John discovered that his staff team had had training in the Low Arousal Approach. As a consequence of this training, his support staff tried to reduce demands and requests and understand his stress and sensory issues. John ultimately discovered his 'own voice' and began a journey of independence that was self-directed. John is now supported to live independently, and fifteen years on has an important community job advocating for the rights of people with disabilities. He is an advocate for the Low Arousal Approach and his relationship with his family continues to thrive.

Understanding stress responses in others requires supporters to manage their own stress and arousal first

Vermeulen (2022) has argued that individuals often make 'prediction errors' which leads them to misjudge social situations, making it easier to self-isolate than to attempt to navigate confusing situations. By calming John's environment down and reducing the need for social interaction, his staff team were able to make him more comfortable to be himself, and ultimately support him to understand and regulate his internal and external world.

In terms of the Low Arousal Approach, it is particularly important to understand that in times of extreme distress, individuals may misinterpret sensory feedback from their own bodies (Mahler, 2016). Self-harm is a behaviour of concern that often helps an individual to tune out from the world around them.

Helping an individual to understand why they feel the need to self-injure is part of the journey, as shown in the example below:

> Jennifer was a nineteen-year-old autistic woman who became 'overwhelmed' in her mid-adolescence. She began to isolate herself and engage in deliberate self-harm which led to her being detained in a specialist service. Jennifer now lives at home with her family who are practitioners of the Low Arousal Approach. Jennifer's journey has involved helping her to understand why she becomes stressed from a sensory and environmental perspective, and how this impacts her behaviour. She is now able to understand that when she self-harmed, it temporarily blocked out distressing thoughts and feelings. There is now a shared understanding between Jennifer and her parents that when she engaged in self-harm, which took the form of cutting her forearms and repeatedly banging her head, these were 'maladaptive coping strategies.' It has been a three-year process, but Jennifer is now able to regulate her behaviour without the need to engage in deliberate self-harm.

Jennifer is able to discuss how her parents support her and has read copious amounts of literature and materials about the Low Arousal Approach to managing behaviours. Her family describe her as having a fantastic sense of humour. Jennifer herself has told them that she is an expert on understanding Low Arousal Approaches. She has described that, when people around her are calm, she feels calm. Witnessing individuals interact with her in a calm and regulated manner has arguably made Jennifer herself less 'hypervigilant.' It is really important that young people with lived experience be provided with a sense of safety.

McDonnell (2019) described the 'battle for control' that can often be created between autistic people and their supporters. This applies to battles with family members, people who work in care settings, and other professionals. In these circumstances, individuals often are not malicious in their intentions, but they attempt to take control of the autistic young person by imposing more rules and boundaries. Many individuals tend to resist excessive rules and boundaries, and often this can lead to elicited aggression. Low Arousal Approaches do not encourage completely boundaryless and structureless engagement, but sometimes it is necessary to reduce the number of rules and demands around a young person. Autistic young people need to be given a sense of control over their world, or it can become a frightening and unmanageable place:

> Sunita was a fourteen-year-old autistic young person who engaged in behaviours of concern, including self-injurious behaviour. Sunita and her family lost all confidence in their ability to manage her meltdowns alone. Sunita isolated herself in her bedroom as a coping response to being

overwhelmed by even the most basic day-to-day activities. Sunita's family adopted a low demand crisis intervention approach which avoided the necessity of Sunita engaging with her family in the short term. Sunita was also encouraged to focus on cardiac exercise to help reduce her biological stress. Finally, Sunita began a journey that involved understanding her own identity and in particular, her identity as an autistic adolescent woman.

The process of change took nearly two years. In that time, Sunita became 'nocturnal,' developing an 'autistic sleep pattern' (Pavlopoulou, 2021). Sunita reported that nighttime felt quiet and safe to her, and so cocooned herself in this world that provided a sense of safety and security to her. It was only after her stress levels appeared to reduce that her sleep pattern began to change. It is important to note that it is very easy for autistic young people to become disempowered and helpless in these circumstances. Sunita needed time to help her regulate her own behaviour and give her the confidence to take back control.

Supporting families to understand stress and trauma

Understanding stress and trauma is essential for parents, carers, and family members working in an empathic framework. Psychologist Mona Delahooke's recent book *Beyond Behaviour* (2019) is full of empathic examples of how practitioners and family members alike can overcome their negative thoughts and biases about behaviour and see the person within. A key component of the Low Arousal Approach is to 'manage the stress first, and the behaviour second' when supporting autistic CYPs and individuals with a wide range of additional support needs.

In 2003, a research paper described an approach to working with families that included providing de-escalation strategies and some limited physical interventions taught within the Studio 3 syllabus (Shinnick & McDonnell, 2003). This study demonstrated that families needed to be equipped with crisis management skills in order to prevent the admission of an individual to a hospital setting. De-escalation skills are a necessity for families supporting distressed young people, including practical applications of Low Arousal Approaches (Elvén, 2010; Woodcock & Page, 2010).

In a recent qualitative study, parents who applied the Low Arousal Approach provided feedback on what they found helpful (McDonnell et al., 2022). One of the major themes family members discussed was that training in the Low Arousal Approach had affirmed some of their beliefs about behaviour, and in some ways empowered them to engage with professionals outside of the traditional behavioural methodology. Providing advice and support to families about navigating care and educational environments involves empowering families to make decisions in partnership with staff.

Collaboration also involves a shared understanding that stress and trauma are major factors in behaviours of concern in children with autism (Elley & Morewood, 2022).

Implications for practice (for practitioners and families)

Low-arousal approaches to supporting young people and their families require professionals to be highly reflective individuals. It could be argued that such approaches to arousal regulation are, to a certain extent, 'transdiagnostic' in nature (McDermott, 2022; *personal communication*). This means that, regardless of a person's diagnostic label, Low Arousal Approaches represent a 'way of being' with individuals who are in distress, be it for a variety of different reasons.

There are considerable heated debates in the autism field about the efficacy of various interventions that are behaviour-based, with some authors being critical (Delahooke, 2019; Kohn, 1999; Milton, 2018), and others espousing the virtues (Gore et al., 2022). Regardless of the philosophical stance of practitioners, families and/or community members need to be able to manage crisis situations. The examples outlined in this chapter have a number of implications for practice. The following list is not exhaustive, but may help people to understand that Low Arousal Approaches are reflective in nature (McDonnell, 2019):

Understanding behaviours

Enter the person's world and try to understand their distress from their perspective. Even when we struggle to understand why someone may meltdown (ranging from physical aggression to severe self-injury) distressed behaviours are a form of communication. It is important to analyse and understand why that person is distressed.

Compassion

Try to resist the urge to 'fix' people who are not broken, but see the world differently (Sinclair, 1993). The challenge for families is to use the tools and technology of behaviour change in a manner that helps them support the people at home. There are elements of a range of approaches that may be helpful, but this should be tempered with a realistic approach.

Co-production

Professionals often provide practical advice, but the reality is that they are not as present as family members. Education is equally important for family members as well as professionals. Having conversations about managing behaviours may challenge all people's thinking.

Stress reduction

Stress reduction is central to the entire approach. It is important that we focus on the transactional nature of stress and, in particular, our own responses to crisis situations. Parents and family members should construct their own stress support plans and include within them stress reduction strategies which they personally find helpful. Consider evidence-based approaches such as cardiac exercise, mindfulness, or flow activities that help supporters to tune out, rather than 'tune in' (McCreadie & McDermott, 2014).

Control

Providing a sense of safety and control often requires reductions of demands and requests in the short term. It is important to view this as a negotiation process and to think about the nature of the demands and requests, and whether at times they really are as important as you think them to be. We should avoid language like 'giving in' and change it to more positive statements such as 'strategic capitulation' or 'tactical withdrawal' (McDonnell, 2019).

Keep calm

Be mindful and 'in the moment' when experiencing increased arousal and distress. We can often feel helpless in these situations, but it is important to remind yourself to manage situations rather than change behaviours (McDonnell, 2019).

Emotional contagion

It is important to be aware of emotional contagion (Elvén, 2010). Negative and positive emotions alike can be transmitted between people, changing the dynamic and potentially escalating a situation. It is important to reflect and emotionally debrief with friends or colleagues after experiencing behaviours of concern.

Reflection

Avoid over-analysis at the moment. This is especially important for people who have had some training in behaviour analysis methods. People are often expected to 'jump into the chaos of things' (Pitonyak, 2008). It is better to spend time with the individual and develop a relationship first, and then to try and understand the meaning of their behaviours once a situation has calmed down.

Beliefs about behaviour

Families must be encouraged to view distressed behaviour as a coping response to a confusing and unpredictable world. For example, avoiding certain people and places can be a coping strategy for some distressed people – one that cannot be easily replaced. Taking away a person's coping strategy may lead to more distressed behaviour, so try to understand why a person may need to engage in that behaviour.

Reduce demands

Be 'in the moment' and try to avoid too many situations that involve introducing goals and activities. Always remember that to be person-centred you must develop goals that are meaningful to the individual.

Provide context

Try to create predictable situations where an individual can feel safe and secure. Providing context for what will happen now and next, and having consistent and predictable daily routines will help to reduce stress (Vermeulen, 2012). Do not discourage avoidance of situations if the alternative is a meltdown.

Empathy

Autistic adolescents often struggle with understanding situations that require emotional empathy (Trimmer et al., 2016). However, empathy and compassion are also essential for supporters when managing extreme and distressed behaviours. Practitioners must be aware that to support an individual they need to try and understand and empathise with the individual's distress, which can be difficult as this is a two-way street (Milton, 2021). It is perhaps best to think of the mantra, 'See the person, see the stress, see the trauma - not just their behaviours.'

Conclusion

Supporting families and young people using the Low Arousal Approach to managing behaviours often requires a different mindset. For family members who often experience intense emotional situations, achieving a sense of calm is not easy. Similarly, for autistic CYPs, trying to make sense of a world which can be chaotic for them is difficult. The Low Arousal Approach requires people to go on a journey of self-discovery, and to enter these chaotic worlds rather than being passive observers. This means that stress reduction is sine qua non; stress management for the individual, their families, and other supporters has to drive day-to-day practice. We need to allow individuals to achieve their own self-determination and self-regulation, but to do this requires co-regulation. To quote Shakespeare, 'to thine own self be true.' We can only begin to manage crises by changing our own behaviour first, which is the core principle of the Low Arousal Approach.

Useful resources

There are a range of resources available on the Studio 3 website at www. studio3.org.

Below is a selection of videos we think would be useful for practitioners starting their Low Arousal journey:

- Gareth Morewood on Behaviour is in the Eye of the Perceiver – https://youtu.be/sagZ9J7AEXo
- Damian Milton discusses the Double Empathy Problem – https://youtu.be/3-zq8r-igAo
- Bo Hejlskov Elvén on Affect is Contagious – https://www.youtube.com/watch?v=jTSsT8ixdrw
- Professor Andrew McDonnell on Being a Reflective Low Arousal Practitioner – https://youtu.be/ibqR7QRBrJg
- Professor Andrew McDonnell on Catastrophising Incidents – https://youtu.be/ubdkK8QuNGo
- Inclusion using the Low Arousal Approach – Pooky Knightsmith talks to Gareth Morewood https://www.youtube.com/watch?v=V_pUsTQpYjc

References

Crompton, C. J., DeBrabander, K., Heasman, B., Milton, D., & Sasson, N. J. (2021). Double empathy: Why autistic people are often misunderstood. *Frontiers for Young Minds* [Online]. Retrieved from: https://kids.frontiersin.org/articles/10.3389/frym.2021.554875

Delahooke, M. (2019). *Beyond behaviours: Using brain science and compassion to understand and solve children's behavioral challenges.* London: John Murray Press.

Elly, D., & Morewood, G. (2022). *Championing your autistic teen at secondary school: Getting the best from mainstream settings.* London: Jessica Kingsley Publishers.

Elvén, B. H. (2010). *No fighting, no biting, no screaming: How to make behaving positively possible for people with autism and other developmental disabilities.* London: Jessica Kingsley Publishers.

Gore, N. J., Sapiets, S. J., Denne, L. D., Hastings, R. P., Toogood, S., MacDonald, A., ... Williams, D. (2022). Positive behavioural support in the UK: A state of the nation report. *International Journal of Positive Behavioural Support, 12*(1), i–46.

Kohn, A. (1999). *Punished by rewards: The trouble with gold stars, incentive plans, A's, praise, and other bribes.* Boston, MA: Houghton Mifflin.

Lipsky, D. (2011). *From anxiety to meltdown: How individuals on the autism spectrum deal with anxiety, experience meltdowns, manifest tantrums, and how you can intervene effectively*. London: Jessica Kingsley Publishers.

Mahler, K. (2016). *Interoception: The eighth sensory system*. Shawnee, KS: AAPC Publishing.

McCreadie, M., & McDermott, J. (2014). 'Tuning in' client practitioner stress transactions in autism. In G. Jones & E. Hurley (Eds.), *GAP: Autism, happiness and wellbeing* (pp. 24–31). Birmingham: BILD.

McDonnell, A., McCreadie, M., & Dickinson, P. (2019). Behavioural issues and supports. In R. Jordan, J. M. Roberts, & K. Hume (Eds.), *The SAGE handbook of autism and education*. Thousand Oaks, CA: SAGE Publishing.

McDonnell, A., McEvoy, J. & Dearden, R. L. (1994). Coping with violent situations in the caring environment. In T. Wykes (Ed.), *Violence and health care professionals* (pp. 189–206). Boston, MA: Springer.

McDonnell, A. A., Page, A., Bews-Pugh, S., Morgalla, K. A., Kaur-Johal, T., & Maher, M. (2024). Families' experiences of the Low Arousal Approach: a qualitative study. *Frontiers in Psychology, 15*, 1328825.

McDonnell, A. A. (2010). *Managing aggressive behaviour in care settings: Understanding and applying low arousal approaches*. Oxford: Wiley-Blackwell.

McDonnell, A. A. (2019). *The reflective journey: A practitioner's guide to the low arousal approach*. Peterborough: Studio 3 Publications.

McDonnell, A. A. (2020). *Empathic stress support*. Studio 3 Publications [Online]. Retrieved from: www.studio3.org/practitioner-articles.

McDonnell, A. A. (2022). *Freedom from restraint and seclusion: The Studio 3 approach*. Peterborough: Studio 3 Publications.

Milton, D. E. (2017). *A mismatch of salience: Explorations of the nature of autism from theory to practice*. East Sussex: Pavilion Publishing and Media Ltd.

Pavlopoulou G. (2021). Corrigendum: A good night's sleep: Learning about sleep from autistic adolescents' personal accounts. *Frontiers in Psychology, 11*. https://doi.org/10.3389/fpsyg.2021.657385.

Pitonyak, D. (2008). Jumping into the chaos of things. *www.dimagine.com* [Online]. Retrieved from http://dimagine.com/wp-content/uploads/2018/03/Jumping.pdf.

Shinnick, A., & McDonnell, A. (2003). Training family members in behaviour management methods. *Learning Disability Practice, 6*(2), 16–20. https://doi.org/10.7748/ldp.6.2.16.s16.

Sinclair, J. (1993). Don't mourn for us. *Our Voice, 1*(3) [Online]. Retrieved from: https://philosophy.ucsc.edu/SinclairDontMournForUs.pdf.

Trimmer, E., McDonald, S., & Rushby, J. A. (2016). Not knowing what I feel: Emotional empathy in autism spectrum disorders. *Autism, 21*(4) [Online]. Retrieved from: https://journals.sagepub.com/doi/abs/10.1177/1362361316648520.

Vermeulen, P. (2012). *Autism as context blindness*. Shawnee, KS: AAPC Publishing.

Vermeulen, P. (2022). *Autism and the predictive brain: Absolute thinking in a relative world*. Oxfordshire: Taylor & Francis.

Woodcock, L., & Page, A. (2010). *Managing family meltdown: The low arousal approach and autism*. London: Jessica Kingsley Publishers.

Chapter 10

Working with siblings of autistic CYP

Nikita K. Hayden and Clare Kassa

Siblings matter

Sibling relationships are an important and unique relationship. Our sibling relationships have the potential to be life's longest-lasting relationships, potentially lasting from birth or early childhood, into old age. In the general sibling literature, poorer sibling relationship quality has been associated with poorer mental health outcomes, such as depression, in both childhood and adulthood (Feinberg et al., 2012; Waldinger et al., 2007). Siblings spend a significant amount of their free time together (Dunifon et al., 2017). We develop into the people we are, in many respects, through our social interactions with others. It stands to reason, therefore, that our earliest, most intense, and enduring relationships, such as our relationships with our siblings, will have an important influence on who we are, and on our future relationships beyond the family home. For example, children can learn how to manage conflict and ways of communicating their feelings, needs, and boundaries in their sibling relationships. For sibling relationships where one sibling is autistic, siblings have the potential to offer support, advocacy, and friendship, whereas elsewhere in society, autistic people continue to face discrimination and exclusion. Therefore, sibling relationships can be important for autistic and non-autistic siblings. Throughout this chapter, to ease clarity, we write about siblings as a pair, with one autistic sibling, and one non-autistic sibling. In doing so, we acknowledge that many siblings have multiple siblings, including families with two or more autistic children. This chapter is in three parts. First, we consider structural and conceptual questions related to siblings and families of autistic children. Second, we consider empirical research about siblings' psychological outcomes and sibling relationships. Third, we provide practical suggestions for practitioners supporting siblings and families of autistic children drawing on our experience of working for Sibs, a UK charity dedicated to supporting siblings of disabled children and adults.

DOI: 10.4324/9781003352327-15

Structural and conceptual context around siblings' lives

Family theories are useful in helping us to further conceptualise why siblings are important to consider when thinking about the lives and experiences of disabled CYP (Hayden & Hastings, 2022). For example, family systems perspectives rest on the assumption that family members are interrelated. Therefore, we would expect that siblings would have a reciprocal effect on one another. Family stress theories help us to consider the ways that issues often associated with a child's autism diagnosis, such as stresses related to getting appropriate support in school, may have reverberations throughout the family system, with parents and siblings also being affected. Therefore, family theories can help us to consider the importance of recognising and understanding the whole family system, including siblings, in our practice (cf. Hayden & Hastings, 2022).

We know that families of autistic children experience poverty and socio-economic deprivation at higher levels than other families (Blackwell, 2022; Cidav et al., 2011; Roddy & O'Neill, 2019). This is a significant problem because, as stated by Hayden and Hastings (2022) 'poverty is a highly stressful experience ... having lower socio-economic status and experiencing deprivation is a consistent and considerable risk factor for worse outcomes'. UK population-level data[1] also tells us that some siblings of children with intellectual disabilities experience elevated behavioural and emotional problems compared to other children. Yet, experiencing socio-economic deprivation is a more important variable for understanding siblings' behavioural and emotional problems than the mere presence of a disabled brother or sister (Hayden et al., 2019a). Considered together in relation to siblings, we know that: (1) some siblings experience worse outcomes and require more support; (2) this is likely related to indirect structural factors, such as socio-economic position; (3) these siblings are more likely to be living in a household experiencing poverty; and that, (4) put simply, poverty is very bad for us.

It is important to resist negative stereotypes about autistic people, to challenge harmful stereotypes about autistic people, whilst also acknowledging that some autistic people and some family members of autistic people may need support. These support needs do not stem *merely* from the presence of a disabled family member, but because these support needs are being exacerbated by a society where ableism, exclusion, and poverty are rife and where our welfare system is underfunded. Underfunding services such as schools, social services, mental health services, and disability services will disproportionately disadvantage the most vulnerable in society, such as the needs of disabled people. The ideology of the UK (and much of the northern hemisphere) is often described as neoliberal, a form of governance that favours privatisation of public services, reductions in taxes and therefore welfare services, and the reduction of government control on the market. What this means in a social sense, is a process of individualisation, whereby we are seen as each responsible for ourselves as individuals, where nuclear families are dominant, and where we rely less on community and society now than at any other point in human history (Hayden & Hastings, 2022). In the UK context, this problem is becoming more pronounced, with care services increasingly privatised for-profit.

Most of the sibling disability literature is positioned in the field of psychology. However, given the importance of these structural and social aspects affecting disabled people and their families, it is important to consider what the field of disability studies, along with sociology and the humanities, has to teach the field of sibling disability research. Disability studies draw on a multitude of interdisciplinary ideas to explore disability as a social and cultural phenomenon, and to challenge ableism. Ariella Meltzer, in particular, has sought to bring together sibling disability research and disability studies (see Meltzer, 2018; Meltzer & Kramer, 2016). This work has included an important critique of individualisation in sibling disability research, and an exploration of feminist perspectives in relation to sibling disability research (Meltzer & Kramer, 2016). Meltzer (2018) extended these critiques around the individualisation of siblings by drawing on the concepts of embodiment and enactment. Meltzer (2018) explained that:

> ...the concept of embodiment has been used to highlight that the body is not a static, isolated or individualised entity, but rather, aspects of the body are absorbed into one's sense of self or identity and then performed or enacted in how an individual conducts themselves in their everyday relations with others.

> (2018, p. 5)

For Meltzer (2018), these psychosocial concepts allow us to consider how disability is experienced both internally and socially without medicalising or individualising disabled people or their families. Shaquinta L. L. Richardson (2018) has also considered siblings and disability studies and has brought into conversation sibling disability research with broader ideas around oppression, marginalisation, inclusion, empowerment, and transformation (see Richardson & Jordan, 2017; Richardson & Stoneman, 2019). For practitioners interested in siblings, these works would encourage us to find ways of fostering and centring the sibling relationship, to include both siblings in our work, and to de-individualise our approaches and assumptions.

Disrupting this societal structure and culture of individualisation often feels impossible, however, with disability activists are working tirelessly to challenge these ableist ideologies. Meltzer and Muir (2021) emphasise, when seeking to support siblings, that we need to examine not only individual factors surrounding the sibling but also wider societal influences. So, what can we do as practitioners and researchers to disrupt this dominant individualising ideology and seek to change things at a broader societal level? We think there are two main things. First, we can be reflexive. We can reflect on ways of challenging and resisting ableism, exclusion, and individualisation, and then incorporate these ideas into our praxis.[2] This praxis might look like supporting, including, and championing autistic people or challenging colleagues' assumptions and language. It might look like a thoughtful and critical peer review. It could involve donating money to charities or becoming an active member of a community, such as a mutual aid community. It may look more explicitly political too, such as campaigning for specific causes and issues or supporting politicians who would work to properly fund and enhance social welfare. Second, you can support policy changes and challenge institutional cultures at your workplace so that they are more person-centred and are inclusive and respectful of the views of autistic people and their family members. For example, you may offer more flexibility and accommodations for employees and colleagues who are disabled or who are carers. You may also be able to find ways of supporting families to access the extra support that they need or funding that they may be entitled to. For siblings specifically, at the institutional level, you might create a working group at your institution to (1) consider what knowledge and expertise siblings have and how you might be able to incorporate their expertise in the support you give their autistic siblings; and (2) whether there are ways that your organisations can provide support or community for non-autistic siblings. For example, this could look like planning family days for siblings to meet one another. What all these structural and societal problems mean in practice, however, is that autistic people and their families will have unmet support needs. As practitioners, you will already be aware of this and may find the story in our vignette familiar (see Vignette for Mo's story below). To support parents, Sibs offers parent training to help them support siblings.[3]

Mo's story: a vignette

Mo is 11 and he has an autistic brother. Mo recently got very upset at break time in school. He spoke to a teacher about how difficult he was finding things at home. Mo's brother had been finding things hard and had started lashing out at Mo and sometimes Mo's belongings would get broken.

The school called a meeting with Mo's parents to find out more about Mo's life at home. Mo's school told his parents about Sibs and Mo's parents showed Mo Young Sibs – the online service provided by Sibs for siblings aged seven to 17 years. Together, Mo and his parents wrote a message to Sibs via the website asking for help. Sibs were able to write back to Mo to help with some of his questions about autism and acknowledge how Mo was feeling. Sibs also let Mo know about a young sibling support group that he could join to meet other young people. Mo was also told that he could come back and ask questions at any time.

Mo's Mum and Dad have also been in touch with Sibs for some advice on how they can support Mo, especially around giving more attention to Mo and helping Mo to stay safe. Sibs was able to share some tips on spending regular time together and making a plan with Mo when he was finding things at home hard. Sibs also gave ideas on ways to build a positive relationship between their two sons. This included helping Mo and his brother to learn to recognize when either of them was not enjoying an activity – through identifying facial expressions, sounds, or gestures. Sibs also invited Mo's parents to a workshop for parents to support siblings.

Sibs also explained to Mo's parents that it is important to sometimes let Mo come first. Coming first might look like Mo being allowed to sometimes choose the film, to choose what food to have for dinner, or to choose where to sit in the car. It is important that all children in a family feel like their needs are met.

Thinking more structurally again, many parents are overextended with little outside support from their wider family, the community, and society. Receiving state support for their autistic child (which they are fully entitled to) is often described as a never-ending 'battle' by parents. Services are significantly under-resourced and are not able to provide all children with all of the support that they need, hence why these barriers to accessing services are inherent in many support systems, where aggressive cost-cutting techniques are often employed. With parents of autistic children stretched thin, fighting stressful battles with support services, and experiencing poverty at higher rates, we can see how there are structural reasons that siblings may not be getting the support they need, making it wholly inappropriate to simply blame the individual autistic child for their behaviours. Seen through a structural lens, we can have more understanding when parents are not able to intervene early in conflict. A structural lens also makes it easier to have compassion for parents who may not have the energy or skills yet to support each time an incident occurs between their children, and parents may not always have the time to reflect on and enact changes to support their children as often as they would like to. We can see that indirect reasons are being exacerbated by societal inequalities that are driving many sibling support needs. These structural factors, however, do not negate the reality that some parents and siblings of autistic children are experiencing mental health problems. Siblings and parents are unlikely to position the difficulties that they experience as being related to unmet support needs due to an unequal and ableist society and are instead more likely to see these issues as individual and familial. As practitioners, you may have the opportunity to support individuals and families but are less able to affect things structurally. For this reason, once we have considered the empirical sibling literature in further detail, the remainder of this chapter considers individual and relational aspects of siblings' experiences which we hope will support practitioners to support families.

Psychological context: are siblings an 'at risk' group?

An important question that perhaps over-dominates the sibling disability literature is: Are siblings of disabled children at risk of experiencing worse psychological outcomes compared to other children? The reason for the dominance of this question is likely due to a 'negative narrative' described by Hastings (2016), whereby researchers and practitioners potentially have negative assumptions about the experiences and outcomes of family members of disabled people. We have identified several studies that draw on population-level data to examine how siblings of disabled children fare compared to siblings of non-disabled children. Stark et al. (2022), drawing on data from one population-level dataset (Stockholm Youth Cohort), found that siblings of young autistic people (aged 10–27 years) had a higher risk of self-harm compared to the general population. This risk was slightly greater for siblings of autistic young people without an intellectual disability. This finding may be related to structural factors too. For example, an autistic person without an intellectual disability may have been diagnosed later, may have received less support, or may have had a more 'hidden' disability that meant they received less understanding in the community when problems arose. As highlighted by Roddy and O'Neill (2019), autistic children's support needs are disproportionately met by families rather than wider society or services, and this may have had an indirect effect on siblings' mental health outcomes.

Studies by Marquis et al. (2019, 2020) used population-level data from the Ministry of Health in British Columbia, Canada. They found that siblings of children with developmental disabilities (including autism) had higher odds of depression and other mental health conditions compared to siblings of children without developmental disabilities (Marquis et al., 2019). Drawing on the same data, Marquis et al. (2020) also found that siblings of autistic children had greater odds of mental health problems compared to siblings of children with Down syndrome. This finding is at times described as the 'Down syndrome advantage', a disputed effect, whereby data suggests that family members of people with Down syndrome have better outcomes compared to family members of people with other developmental disabilities. Some writers have suggested that these differences are due to the relatively high levels of prosocial behaviours displayed by people with Down syndrome. There are likely to be more societal explanations too. People with Down syndrome are diagnosed very early, increasingly during gestation, so their families can access early intervention and support and have more time and clearer resources to understand and process the diagnosis. People with Down syndrome and their families are also part of a large developmental disability community who are particularly politically and socially active, creating grassroots activity groups, raising awareness of Down syndrome, and successfully passing major UK legislation to further support people with Down syndrome (i.e., the Down

Syndrome Act, 2022). Down syndrome is also a visibly identifiable disability, and this literal visibility, along with increased awareness of Down syndrome through grassroots campaigning, means that people with Down syndrome are likely to have a very different experience in the community and society compared to autistic people. For example, parents of an autistic child having a meltdown in the park, or the cinema, may be treated with more judgement, less sympathy, and less support or compassion than parents of a child with Down syndrome behaving in a similar way. Siblings sometimes describe a range of negative feelings and outcomes in these types of situations, including feeling anger at the people they encounter, shame and embarrassment about their family (which is common among all young people, whether or not they have a disabled family member), and then, as a consequence, their family going out into the community less frequently. Drawing on family systems perspectives, this social isolation and lack of social support is likely to influence the entire family system and the outcomes of each member of the family system.

As discussed, we need to resist a 'negative narrative' (Hastings, 2016) or a 'tragedy narrative', whereby families are assumed to have negative experiences based on their relationships with disabled people. For example, the population data we have discussed highlights that although there are some siblings in need of support, not all siblings experience mental health and behavioural problems. Population data from Hayden et al. (2019a) suggest that there are structural, family, and individual-level reasons why some siblings have worse outcomes; these reasons include experiencing socio-economic deprivation, maternal mental health support needs, being from a single-parent household, and disabled siblings having an elevated score on the Strengths and Difficulties Questionnaire, a measure of behavioural and emotional symptoms in young people.

Siblings are not necessarily on the radar of professionals, however. For the sub-group of siblings experiencing elevated mental health and behavioural problems themselves, this may be a problem. Even for siblings who do not need to access support services for their own mental health and well-being, siblings are likely to need support accessing information. Siblings will need age-appropriate information about autism and any co-occurring conditions that go beyond medicalised definitions of autism but also consider social and systemic considerations of autism. This could include information on how non-autistic siblings can be allies to their autistic siblings. Siblings may also need resources on how they can talk to their parents about their feelings and experiences, and about where they can go for support for both sibling and non-sibling related issues. Adult siblings who decide to take on support and care roles for their disabled siblings who have high support needs will need appropriate and clear information, provided at the right time, on a range of areas, including wills and trusts, financial deputyship, finding high-quality care services, hiring, and paying carers, and about talking to parents about taking over care roles. Siblings may also need help accessing a community of informal support, for example being directed to join a sibling support group. Meeting these needs is important for sibling relationships, as non-autistic and autistic siblings with unmet support needs are unlikely to be able to provide consistent love, support, and care for one another. Siblings are often important people in one another's lives, and the relationship should be better recognised and understood by universal services.

Services seeking to support siblings should be aware that siblings of disabled children may also be providing care and support for their disabled brothers and sisters. A group that has received relatively more attention from children's support services in the UK are young carers. A recent report specifically about young carers caring for a sibling with a long-term illness or disability (including autism) recommended that more work was needed by support services to raise awareness of, and to recognise, sibling young carers (Miller, 2021). Therefore, professionals should consider how these caring roles may affect sibling and family functioning. Siblings may have brothers and sisters with high support needs that they care for, and this caring role may be lifelong. But siblings may also be providing support to their parents, for example, by providing emotional and practical support to parents or by being a 'third parent'. This 'third parent' role can be described as parentification, whereby children take on an inappropriate carer role for parents or siblings. Pavlopoulou and Dimitriou (2019) found in their qualitative study that non-autistic sisters showed an appreciation for all their parents did for them whilst also acknowledging that their parents often asked for too much support from non-autistic siblings. Overall, non-autistic siblings are an important group to consider when working with autistic children and their families.

Sibling relationships

Studies that have examined sibling relationships where one sibling is autistic have tended to focus on how the autistic sibling's behaviours and support needs impact the non-autistic sibling or their sibling relationship. Hayden et al. (2023) examined sibling relationships in 500 sibling pairs where one sibling had an intellectual disability (50.6% were autistic) and one sibling did not have an intellectual or developmental disability. They found that both siblings' 'positive' and 'negative' behaviours were associated with both 'negative' and 'positive' aspects of their sibling relationships. This finding is important because it disrupts an assumption in the disability sibling research field that it is the disabled sibling who is negatively impacting the relationship, rather than the effect being both positive *and* negative, for *both* siblings (i.e., a reciprocal, bidirectional effect).

In a rare study that included data directly from autistic siblings on their sibling relationships, Petalas et al. (2015) identified two broad themes in their qualitative interviews with autistic adolescents. First, there was a sense that their sibling experiences were 'typical' and like sibling relationships where neither sibling was autistic, with the presence of conflict, positive regard, enjoyment, acceptance, and social comparisons. Second, the autistic adolescents highlighted ways in which they perceived that their autism was present in their sibling relationships, describing how autism affected their social interactions, emotional control, impulsivity, and comparisons. One autistic adolescent 'reported a sense of reduced emotional and behavioural control … [and] the use of excessive force with his sister' (Petalas et al., 2015, p. 44). In cases of sibling violence, adults should intervene promptly to prevent harm. Unlike conflicts between unrelated peers, familial relationships can complicate the dynamics and require immediate attention to ensure the safety of all involved. It is important to highlight that in population studies of siblings where one is autistic, autistic siblings are more likely to be bullied by their non-autistic siblings (rather than the other way around; Toseeb et al., 2018, 2020). Of course, not all negative interactions between siblings can be classified as bullying. Therefore, one sibling hurting another sibling because they were overwhelmed and distressed would be unlikely to be classified as sibling bullying.

Involving and supporting siblings

There are various contexts where professionals may be able to involve or offer support to siblings. Support can be offered in the family home, in schools (an example of sibling support from Sibs Talk can be found in Hayden et al., 2019b), by child and adolescent mental health services, healthcare systems, social workers, and by community or voluntary sector organisations. The following topic areas are relevant across these services and systems: Listening to siblings, Inclusion, Talking about disability, and Sibling relationships. Below we consider each area in turn.

An example of sibling support: Sibs Talk

Sibs Talk is a one-to-one, manualised support intervention developed by the UK charity Sibs for pupils aged seven to 11 years who have a brother or sister with a special educational need, disability, or chronic health condition. Sibs Talk focuses on acknowledging siblings' feelings and experiences first and foremost, before facilitating discussions around coping strategies. Sessions are facilitated by a school staff member, and full training is provided by Sibs. The training includes content on Sibs' F.R.A.M.E model, which is based on work with siblings being Fun, Relieving isolation, Acknowledging feelings, Modelling coping strategies, and Enhancing knowledge.

A simple pre- and post-evaluation of Sibs Talk has been conducted (Hayden et al., 2019b). The sample included 55 siblings with disabled brothers and sisters from 11 schools. Almost half of these siblings (49.1%) had an autistic brother or sister. The findings from the evaluation were positive and showed a statistically significant improvement in siblings' hyperactivity, prosocial behaviours, total behavioural difficulties, and emotional problems. Effect sizes were small to medium. Siblings also provided written comments about their experiences of Sibs Talk:

> 'I know a lot about my sister. I learnt that people do listen to what I have to say. I learnt to be more open-minded'.
> 'To learn about my feelings when I'm angry, sad, jealous, lonely, guilty, worried, embarrassed'.
> 'I have a sister who's autistic and who makes me proud'.
> 'I don't have to keep things to myself. That it is not my brother's fault he is how he is. I have learnt that I can share things with you'.
>
> (Hayden et al., 2019b, pp. 414–415)

Sibs continues to offer Sibs Talk and Sibs Talk training to schools and has since delivered Sibs Talk training to child and adolescent mental health services and young carers services.

Listening to feelings

One of the most important things that parents and practitioners can do to support siblings is to acknowledge non-autistic siblings' feelings about their autistic siblings. Siblings will often share both positive and negative feelings, however, families and professionals disproportionately seek support from Sibs on ways to respond to siblings sharing negative feelings, so we focus our advice on responding to these negative feelings here. Siblings may feel angry, worried, sad, or embarrassed about their sibling's experiences, and siblings should be able to express these feelings and feel listened to. It is important to avoid blaming, solving, or explaining when listening to siblings express their feelings. The UK charity Sibs focuses on three key areas when working with siblings:

1 Listen to the feelings behind the words – pay attention to tone of voice and body language as well as what the sibling is telling you.
2 Name the feeling – check with the sibling that what you think they are feeling is correct.
3 Acknowledge the feeling – provide an understanding and empathetic response.

For example, a sibling comes into school and tells you she hates her autistic brother. Her autistic brother had a bad day at school, and he scribbled on her homework. Sophie is in tears. We may respond to Sophie as follows:

> Sophie, you sound very upset. I am sorry to hear your brother scribbled on your homework. That would make other people feel sad or angry too. What happened?

There are also things that you should avoid in your response:

- 'You should have put your homework in a safe place' (blaming).
- 'Your brother can't help it, he is autistic' (explaining).
- 'Never mind you can do your homework again in school time' (solving).

The focus of these initial conversations is on acknowledging the non-autistic sibling's needs at that moment, rather than centring their autistic sibling. There are of course times when it is important to talk about autism and help a sibling understand autism. However, when a sibling is upset or distressed is probably not the best time for a big discussion about autism. Problem-solving and talking about autism are of course important conversations to have with siblings, but this initial discussion, when siblings are upset, should be primarily understood as an opportunity to acknowledge and validate the sibling's experiences and feelings. It is also important to adapt what you say to a sibling based on their age and understanding.

Siblings of autistic children may feel worried about their autistic brother or sister's health and well-being, particularly if they have co-occurring health problems or high support needs. Siblings may also worry about school or about bringing friends home. One thing that Sibs suggests is making a worry box, where siblings can write down their worries. The worry box can then be used by siblings to talk about their worries with their parents. Once the feelings have been acknowledged as described above, these worries can be sorted into things that can change, and things that cannot change. For things that cannot change, a discussion may need to be had about *why* things are the way they are for the sibling to be able to begin to accept circumstances that cannot be changed. For things that can change, the sibling and parent will discuss who will take action: the sibling themselves, the parents, or a practitioner, such as a teacher. For example, a parent may need to talk to the sibling's class teacher if the sibling is often tired in school, perhaps because they share a bedroom with their autistic brother or sister who has sleep difficulties. Overall, siblings should be encouraged to share both their positive and negative experiences as siblings.

Many young siblings also worry about what will happen to their brother or sister in the future. It is helpful for siblings as they grow up to know that they do not necessarily have to take on full-time carer roles and that there are other options, with siblings having a choice about the role that they play in their brothers' or sisters' lives in the future. Siblings must have the opportunity to live their own lives and have their own futures. Therefore, siblings should be supported to take breaks from their sibling role and pursue their interests. We also sometimes hear from adult siblings about the opposite situation occurring, where they wanted to initiate the conversation about taking over care from their parents or planning for the future, but their parents were reluctant to have the conversation. Allowing siblings to talk about the future, as well as the present, is important to understand whether siblings have any concerns about future care and support.

This focus on acknowledging feelings is part of Sibs' F.R.A.M.E. model which emphasises that sibling support should be Fun, Relieving isolation, Acknowledging feelings, Modelling coping strategies, and Enhancing knowledge. Sibs' F.R.A.M.E. model was developed in practice and has not been empirically tested. However, this model of listening to and acknowledging siblings' feelings is also seen in the sibling literature, where a recent realist review highlighted the importance of a mechanism that validates siblings' feelings and experiences in interventions that support siblings, and a mechanism that increases the communication between siblings and their parents (Marquis et al., 2022). Marquis et al. (2022) suggested that this validation can be achieved by: parents listening to siblings; siblings learning that their relationship with their disabled brother or sister is similar or shared with other people; and listening to other siblings talk about their experiences. Therefore, sibling groups can be a useful way for siblings to feel listened to, feel less alone in their experiences, and feel more included.

Sibling inclusion

Professionals should consider whether there are ways to include siblings in meetings and planning, where appropriate. This can have benefits for the sibling and the family system, such as improving the sibling's understanding, reducing jealousy if the sibling feels that they are getting less attention than their autistic brother or sister, and allowing siblings to have a say in things that will affect them. Sibs highlights several ways that siblings could be included. For example, siblings could be introduced to professionals, and be given an opportunity to learn about what they do, as well as ask any questions that they may have. There may also be ways to involve siblings in therapy or in meetings, such as involving siblings in parts of a session, or by asking siblings about how things could be improved for their family or their autistic brother or sister. Siblings who are adolescents may also be included in meetings and reviews, as siblings often have relevant knowledge and experience that would be useful to include in the meeting. For example, siblings who share a bedroom with their autistic siblings may know more about their autistic sibling's sleep habits as well as their morning and evening routines than their parents.

Talking about disability

It is important for siblings to be provided with opportunities to talk and learn about disability and autism. A consistent support need for siblings is the access to appropriate information at the right time. Supporting siblings to learn about their autistic siblings' diagnoses and experiences is important for fostering understanding, and acceptance, and reducing worries. There is a lot of misinformation about autism, so it is important that siblings receive accurate information. A problem that many families can experience is the need to provide differential parenting to children, and then children perceive this as unequal and unfair treatment. This happens in all families. Older children often get more responsibilities and opportunities whereas younger children often get more support but also more monitoring and restrictions. However, families of autistic children may have different conventions that siblings may perceive as unfair. Differential treatment might include allowing different mealtime and food rules, such as the autistic brother or sister being allowed to eat another food option, to sit away from the dining table, or being able to eat with their hands, whereas the sibling might be expected to use a knife and fork and to eat the main meal prepared. Another example is the convention in most families that older siblings have later bedtimes than younger siblings. Many autistic children and adolescents experience sleep problems and therefore, a younger autistic child or adolescent may be allowed to stay up later than an older non-disabled sibling (with or without restrictions).

Having conversations with non-autistic siblings about disability and the needs of their autistic siblings can therefore be important in helping siblings to learn that unequal treatment is different from unfair treatment. This development of understanding is important, because non-autistic siblings may potentially perceive that their autistic brother or sister getting more attention from parents as meaning that their parents love their autistic sibling more than them. Helping siblings to understand their siblings' disabilities is also important for fostering sibling relationships and for building trust and openness in the family. When talking to siblings about autism, it is important to be open and honest and to answer any questions as they come up. Siblings should be provided with age-appropriate information allowing for more details or specifics to be added as they get older and keeping them up to date as things change and develop. This sharing and modelling of information can support siblings who may get asked about their siblings' autism at school or by peers. Therefore, it can help siblings to develop a one-sentence answer to frequently asked questions so that siblings can feel more confident talking about their family and their experiences.

Supporting sibling relationships

Throughout this chapter, we hope that we have effectively communicated the importance of sibling relationships in the lives of children and adults. Parents often ask for suggestions from Sibs about how they can help support this important sibling relationship when one of their children is autistic. Both autistic and non-autistic siblings often have a great deal of love and affection for one another. An important theme from Pavlopoulou and Dimitriou was formed around the following quote: 'I don't live with autism, I live with my sister' (2019, p. 7). This theme highlighted how non-autistic siblings can have a 'myriad of feelings ... [feel] a sense of togetherness at home ... [and have] a positive view on differences' (Pavlopoulou and Dimitriou, 2019, p. 7). However, both autistic and non-autistic siblings can also get frustrated with, and distressed by, one another and so they may need support with their sibling relationship. This is a common sibling experience – whether one, both, or neither sibling is autistic. For example, non-autistic and autistic siblings may learn that they need to communicate more clearly and be patient with one another, and siblings may begin to understand why it may be necessary for their parents to treat them and their autistic siblings differently. Siblings may also learn that if their autistic brother or sister has difficulties playing in the way that the non-autistic sibling expects or desires, this does not mean that their autistic sibling does not like or love them. Autistic siblings may also need support understanding that their siblings may not always want to do the same thing as them. For example, if the autistic child's sibling does not share their interests, they may be encouraged, along with their sibling, to take turns doing one another's favourite activities.

It may be helpful if both siblings are taught how to interact with one another. For example, if the autistic brother or sister is using augmentative and alternative communication and/or Makaton signs, then non-autistic siblings could also be included and taught how to use these resources to communicate with their autistic siblings. Both siblings may need help to be taught ways to understand when one another are no longer enjoying an activity or an interaction, this could be through facial expressions, sounds, and gestures, as well as through verbal communication and signs. Parents and professionals may also learn from how both autistic and non-autistic siblings navigate their sibling relationships and interactions with one another. Parents are often working to find specific activities that all their children can enjoy. Professionals should consider how they can support parents in coming up with new ideas for activities that both siblings may enjoy doing together (and apart). Autistic siblings may need some extra support to try new things, for example, families could attend autism-friendly events, particularly when first visiting a new venue, and professionals could support parents to produce visual plans to help prepare their autistic children for new activities in new places.

Conclusion

In this chapter, we have highlighted the importance of sibling relationships and the needs of non-autistic siblings. Overall, we suggest the following recommendations for practitioners seeking to involve or support siblings:

1 **Listen:** First, when interacting with siblings, professionals should listen to siblings and acknowledge their feelings and expertise.
2 **Include:** Professionals should consider ways that they can include siblings, such as by involving siblings in therapies and activities where

appropriate or asking siblings to share their views about matters that affect the family.

3 **Learn:** Siblings need support to access information. Siblings should get the opportunity to talk about and learn more about autism. Professionals can support this by explaining their role and letting the sibling ask any questions that they may have.

4 **Ask:** Siblings have expertise that may help you support their autistic sibling and their family better. Consider whether there are appropriate ways of asking and incorporating siblings' views in your work.

5 **Involve:** Sibling relationships are important for both siblings so professionals should consider how they can help to foster the sibling relationship. For example, an activity service for autistic children and adolescents may consider organising a sibling or family day. This activity would not only help to support sibling dyads to play and interact with one another, but it would also give siblings opportunities to meet other siblings, and autistic children the opportunity to meet other autistic children. Community is important given the structural problems we have discussed in this chapter. It is important to help autistic children and their siblings to meet people who share similarities with them and who may understand them, particularly when this group of children and their families may experience social isolation related to discrimination and exclusion in other social contexts.

6 **Develop:** Talk to your colleagues and consider setting up a working group in your service to find ways that your service can include and/or support siblings in your work, either directly or indirectly. Support by practitioners will vary based on your service but may include signposting, helping family members to navigate unfamiliar services, including siblings' expertise in your usual work, indirectly supporting siblings via parents, or developing and providing direct support to siblings.

7 **Support:** Many professionals will not work directly with siblings themselves. Therefore, part of your role will be about supporting parents to support siblings. This may involve professionals encouraging parents to spend time alone with their siblings (and providing support so this can happen) and helping parents to come up with shared activities that all of their children can enjoy together.

Throughout this chapter, we have highlighted how non-autistic siblings are important in the lives of their families and their autistic siblings, and what practitioners can do to help support non-autistic siblings. There are structural problems at a societal level that both limit the resources available for this group of children and potentially exacerbate their support needs. We hope that you will be able to incorporate some of these ideas into your practice to further support autistic children, their non-autistic siblings, and their wider families.

Notes

1 Population data is often high-quality, more representative, less biased, and larger scale than other data, making these datasets ideal for answering questions about how the outcomes of siblings of disabled children compare to the outcomes of siblings of non-disabled children.
2 Praxis refers to a process of reflection and action. Paulo Freire defined praxis as 'reflection and action upon the world in order to transform it' (1970, p. 33).
3 https://www.sibs.org.uk/sibs-workshops-and-training/.

References

Blackwell, C. (2022). *The needs of children on the autism spectrum and their families: Exploring household costs and factors impacting access to resources.* Loughborough University. https://doi.org/10.17028/rd.lboro.20489139.v1

Cidav, Z., Marcus, A. C., & Mandell., D. S. (2011). Implications of childhood autism for parental employment and earnings. *Pediatrics, 129*(4), 617–623. https://doi.org/10.1542/peds.2011-2700

Dunifon, R., Fomby, P., & Musick, K. (2017). Siblings and children's time use in the United States. *Demographic Research, 37,* 1611–1624. https://doi.org/10.0.15.214/DemRes.2017.37.49

Feinberg, M. E., Solmeyer, A. R., & McHale, S. M. (2012). The third rail of family systems: Sibling relationships, mental and behavioral health, and preventive intervention in childhood and adolescence. *Clinical Child and Family Psychology Review, 15,* 43–57. https://doi.org/10.1007/s10567-011-0104-5

Freire, P. (1970). *Pedagogy of the oppressed.* Penguin.

Hastings, R. P. (2016). Do children with intellectual and developmental disabilities have a negative impact on other family members? The case for rejecting a negative narrative. *International Review of Research in Developmental Disabilities, 50,* 165–194. https://doi.org/10.1016/bs.irrdd.2016.05.002

Hayden, N. K., & Hastings, R. P. (2022). Family theories and siblings of people with intellectual and developmental disabilities. *International Review of Research in Developmental Disabilities, 63,* 1–49. https://doi.org/10.1016/bs.irrdd.2022.09.001

Hayden, N. K., Hastings, R. P., & Bailey, T. (2023). Behavioural adjustment of children with intellectual disability and their sibling is associated with their sibling relationship quality. *Journal of Intellectual Disability Research.* https://doi.org/10.1111/jir.13006

Hayden, N. K., Hastings, R. P., Totsika, V., & Langley, E. (2019a). A population-based study of the behavioral and emotional adjustment of older siblings of children with and without intellectual disability. *Journal of Abnormal Child Psychology, 47*(8), 1409–1419. https://doi.org/10.1007/s10802-018-00510-5

Hayden, N. K., McCaffrey, M., Fraser-Lim, C., & Hastings, R. P. (2019b). Supporting siblings of children with a special educational need or disability: An evaluation of Sibs Talk, a one-to-one intervention delivered by staff in mainstream schools. *Support for Learning, 34*(4), 404–420. https://doi.org/10.1111/1467-9604.12275

Marquis, S., McGrail, K., & Hayes, M. V. (2020). Using administrative data to examine variables affecting the mental health of siblings of children who have a developmental disability. *Research in Developmental Disabilities, 96*(November 2018), 103516. https://doi.org/10.1016/j.ridd.2019.103516

Marquis, S., O'Leary, R., Hayden, N. K., & Baumbusch, J. (2022). A realist review of programs for siblings of children who have an intellectual/developmental disability. *Family Relations, December 2021*, 1–20. https://doi.org/10.1111/fare.12789

Marquis, S. M., McGrail, K., & Hayes, M. V. (2019). A population-level study of the mental health of siblings of children who have a developmental disability. *SSM – Population Health, 8*(February), 100441. https://doi.org/10.1016/j.ssmph.2019.100441

Meltzer, A. (2018). Embodying and enacting disability as siblings: Experiencing disability in relationships between young adult siblings with and without disabilities. *Disability and Society, 33*(8), 1212–1233. https://doi.org/10.1080/09687599.2018.1481016

Meltzer, A., & Kramer, J. (2016). Siblinghood through disability studies perspectives: Diversifying discourse and knowledge about siblings with and without disabilities. *Disability and Society, 31*(1), 17–32. https://doi.org/10.1080/09687599.2015.1127212

Meltzer, A., & Muir, K. (2021). An ecological and systems thinking approach for support to siblings with and without disabilities. *Social Theory and Health, 20*, 246–362. https://doi.org/10.1057/s41285-020-00158-6

Miller, E. (2021). As me – I'm here too!: A research and evaluation project into the lived experiences of young carers providing care for siblings with a long-term illness or disability. Edinburgh Young Carers. https://www.youngcarers.org.uk/wp-content/uploads/2021/06/Ask-Me-Im-Here-Too.pdf

Pavlopoulou, G., & Dimitriou, D. (2019). 'I don't live with autism; I live with my sister'. Sisters' accounts on growing up with their preverbal autistic siblings. *Research in Developmental Disabilities, 88*(March 2018), 1–15. https://doi.org/10.1016/j.ridd.2019.01.013

Petalas, M. A., Hastings, R. P., Nash, S., & Duff, S. (2015). Typicality and subtle difference in sibling relationships: Experiences of adolescents with autism. *Journal of Child and Family Studies, 24*, 38–49. https://doi.org/10.1007/s10826-013-9811-5

Richardson, S. L. L. (2018). I am my sister's keeper: A critical case analysis of sisterhood, Black womanhood, and Asperger's syndrome in a black family (Doctoral dissertation, University of Georgia).

Richardson, S. L. L., & Jordan, L. S. (2017). Qualitative inquiry of sibling relationships: Reinforcement of disability devaluation through the exclusion of voices. *Disability and Society, 32*(10), 1534–1554. https://doi.org/10.1080/09687599.2017.1351330

Richardson, S. L. L., & Stoneman, Z. (2019). It takes a sister: Sisterhood and Black womanhood in families of people with intellectual and developmental disabilities. *Disability and Society, 34*(4), 607–628. https://doi.org/10.1080/09687599.2018.1555451

Roddy, A., & O'Neill, C. (2019). The economic costs and its predictors for childhood autism spectrum disorders in Ireland: How is the burden distributed? *Autism, 23*(5), 1106–1118. https://doi.org/10.1177/1362361318801

Stark, I., Rai, D., Lundberg, M., Culpin, I., Nordström, S. I., Ohlis, A., & Magnusson, C. (2022). Autism and self-harm: A population-based and discordant sibling study of young individuals. *Acta Psychiatrica Scandinavica, 146*(5), 468–477. https://doi.org/10.1111/acps.13479

Toseeb, U., McChesney, G., & Wolke, D. (2018). The prevalence and psychopathological correlates of sibling bullying in children with and without autism spectrum disorder. *Journal of Autism and Developmental Disorders, 48*(7), 2308–2318. https://doi.org/10.1007/s10803-018-3484-2

Toseeb, U., McChesney, G., Oldfield, J., & Wolke, D. (2020). Sibling bullying in middle childhood is associated with psychosocial difficulties in early adolescence: The case of individuals with autism spectrum disorder. *Journal of Autism and Developmental Disorders*, *50*(5), 1457–1469. https://doi.org/10.1007/s10803-019-04116-8

Waldinger, R. J., Vaillant, G. E., & Orav, E. J. (2007). Childhood sibling relationships as a predictor of major depression in adulthood: A 30-year prospective study. *American Journal of Psychiatry*, *164*(6), 949–954. https://doi.org/10.1176/ajp.2007.164.6.949

Chapter 11

Working with schools

A synergy approach

Richard Mills

The importance of framing and self-reflection when working with CYP at risk of exclusion

During our time with the National Autistic Society, my colleague Dr Michael McCreadie and I were asked by a residential school in England to see and give advice on a student.

> 'Jamie' was described as 'powerfully built', 'severely autistic', 'non-verbal' and presenting with 'severe challenging behaviour', specifically, 'non-compliant', 'aggressive', 'dangerous', and 'violent'. It was said he represented a 'high risk' to staff and other students. Prior to our visit, we read reports, which repeated these statements. Yet, when we visited the school, we were greeted by the head of the school's residential unit where 'Jamie' lived and were presented with a very different perspective. Here, no one was afraid of 'Jamie'. Staff said they enjoyed his company – as he did theirs. With them, he was not 'terrifying' or 'dangerous', but an energetic young man of good humour, and mischief. He was interesting. They told us of his preferred activities and his strong dislike of the confines of the classroom. Here the narrative was one of affection, empathy, and warmth. Staff had a connection with him, and liked and respected him. They expressed frustration at how he was seen by some teachers, who were with 'Jamie' in the classroom, where he was described as 'unpredictable' and 'complex'. Here, he had few redeeming features. In their words, 'something had to be done'.

We wondered why the same young person was perceived so differently by two distinct groups at the same school, and importantly, what could be done about it.

We concluded that any intervention should be with staff and not with 'Jamie'. The focus was not 'Jamie' or his 'behaviour' but on how staff experienced and perceived these and their responses. How staff character, stress, their influences, and the narrative around 'Jamie' combined to shape school culture and responses.

DOI: 10.4324/9781003352327-16

This involved exploring self-reflection: how emotional perceptions of 'Jamie' generated anxiety and stress, how these, in turn, affected responses, individually and collectively, and how they might change these. How could they switch from this emotional 'frame' to one that was more considered and rational? To become calmer, less prone to impulse, more empathic, and kinder. How they might develop a plan for challenging their perceptions of how they thought about 'Jamie' and how they would work with him.

A further example of how such 'framing' occurs came to us from a family support programme, which catered for families where a child presented with 'behaviours of concern'.

At the start of the six-month programme, parents were asked to identify all the issues where they needed help. One family had only one. That they could attend church as a family. The family worker asked what was preventing this. Their answer, pointing to their child, 'Eric' and 'his "problem" behaviour'.

A summary of events follows.

The worker asked them 'What does Eric do?'

Parents	'He makes noises and runs up and down the church – you see he's autistic and can't keep still, he spoils it for others (churchgoers) and although we love him and really want to be together at church, it is embarrassing for us'.
Worker	'So you think the others disapprove?'
Parents	yes – we get looks'.
Worker	'and you think those looks are disapproving?'
Parents	yes – of course'
Worker	'do you mind if I check on this with the priest to see how he feels about this?'
Parents	'OK, but not sure it will help'.

The worker subsequently met with the priest. He expressed dismay that the parents should feel this way and said that all were welcome at his church. He said that with the parents' permission, he would raise the issue with his congregation. This he did. The congregation expressed sadness and surprise that these parents should feel this way. They wanted the priest to ensure the family knew their feelings and that they were welcome, however, their child behaved. Some said they had autistic family members themselves and were desperate for him to convey their feelings.

The priest shared this news with the family, and it was agreed they would attend church the following Sunday. They were greeted warmly. Eric behaved as he usually did, making noises and periodically leaving his seat to run into the aisle. When he did this the family received reassuring gestures of acceptance and support from the congregation. Following the service, they were further reassured and warmly welcomed.

Thereafter they attended regularly. Eric had not changed but they had. They had achieved their goal of attending church as a family, not through changing Eric's behaviour, but by changing how they thought about it and how they responded. They had reframed' the issue.

In an interesting subsequent development, the parents reported that over time Eric's behaviour did in fact change, in that he remained in his seat. They reflected that this may have been a result of them no longer transmitting their stress to Eric and that church became a more familiar and relaxed experience for all of them, but in any event, they felt it didn't matter as their goal had been accomplished.

The synergy approach

Developed by AT-Autism, a UK non-profit organisation and the Laskaridis Foundation, Piraeus, Greece, Synergy was a response to a need for Greek schools to be more inclusive of children displaying 'challenging behaviours' (Bagkakis & Koulis, 2023). Our initial meetings with teachers there were revealing. We found dedicated professionals struggling to manage their workloads and often reporting having to endure criticism and blame. They were experiencing multiple stressors, which included resources, the intake of traumatised refugee children, colleague attitudes, leadership, and the effects of austerity. Some teachers had not been paid for months. They were asking for support, and guidance and for their voices to be heard. This was an early lesson for us on the importance of listening. For us to understand the experiences of teachers it was necessary to listen, develop a dialogue and reflect, not judge.

Teachers advised they had received training in a range of what they described as 'traditional' approaches around the management of behaviour based on rewards and sanctions. They felt the approaches were often unethical, simplistic, 'formulaic', and did not address trauma. Some said they were unable to apply the techniques they were taught in their settings. Even where they had, the children had not responded, or their behaviour worsened. Teachers said they often felt isolated, stressed, and unable to cope in such situations. Some said they felt blamed and exhausted.

Due to the restrictions of time and budget, training was practical, short, and self-sustaining. Peer mentoring was set up and remains a vital component in reducing teachers' isolation and stress. Offering support, not blame or instruction, actively listening, and asking questions. To support them to arrive at their own solutions by examining and addressing their influences. This, in turn, influenced the design of the training, which became two workshops, one concerning practice, and one on the training of mentors. The model was also sensitive to local culture and conditions and based on sound theoretical and ethical principles. With hindsight, this brevity is a strength as it enhances consistency and fidelity but must be supported by peer mentoring to embed key principles.

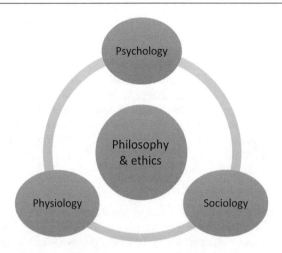

Figure 11.1 Summary of theoretical and ethical framework.

The need to consider how our responses are formed

We first consider how our responses are formed. How emotional responses differ from rational judgements, how narratives form, how people and situations are 'framed', and how they influence our thinking and responses. The philosopher Epictetus (55 AD–135 AD) (Evans, 2013), observed, 'Men are disturbed not by things but by their opinions about them'. One of the founders of cognitive behavioural therapy, Albert Ellis, credits the influence of Epictetus with how 'framing' is critical in how we make sense of our experience and our resulting actions, and a key driver of human behaviour: 'people are not disturbed by things, but rather by their view of things' (Ellis, 1980a,b). More recently, psychologists Daniel Kahneman and Amos Tversky, on judgements, narratives, and risk, emphasise the relevance of emotional factors on our beliefs and behaviour (Tversky & Kahneman, 1974).

Synergy draws on established interconnected classic scientific theories and ethical principles. These concern psychology, sociology, physiology, and philosophy (Figure 11.1).

- Psychology:
  Understanding the emotional versus the rational 'brain'. How 'framing' and narrative influence beliefs, actions, and culture (Ellis, 1980a,b, 1992; Tversky & Kahneman, 1974); Epictetus (in Evans, 2011). Understanding biases and influences. (Asch, 1951; Bandura,1977, 1982;Milgram 1963). The importance of listening and dialogue (Rogers, 1959).

- Sociology:
  Deep understanding (verstehen) reflects empathy for lived experience.
  'The double empathy problem' (Milton, 2012). Rejection of simplistic
  or reductionist theory. Understanding stigma and identity and how these
  impact narratives and cultures (Weber [in Platt, 1985]; Dilthey [in Rick-
  man, 2015]; Goffman, 1961; Wolfensberger, 1983).
- Stress and physiological arousal:
  The effects of stress and arousal on human thoughts and behaviour
  (McDonnell, 2019; Mobbs et al., 2007; Pfaff et al., 2007).
- Philosophy and ethics:
  Reduce harm. Increase tolerance, connection, and understanding. Focus on
  worker character, influences, virtue, and the limitations of control (Epictetus, Seneca (in Evans, 2011)). The importance of acceptance, of not rush-
  ing to judgement (Ellis, 1992; Rogers, 1959; Tversky & Kahneman, 1974,
  2011).

Kahneman describes the brain as comprising two 'systems': our 'emotional
brain', *System One*, and our 'rational brain', *System Two* (Kahneman, 2011).
This is aligned to the philosophical and therapeutic traditions described earlier, and central to the Synergy approach.

Easy and instinctive, *System One* is our constant companion. We don't
have to think. *System One* is essential for our survival. It provides protection
from hazards and danger. Our first and most natural response to dealing with
a stressful event is emotional. When acute, it may be summarised as 'flight,
fight or freeze' (Mobbs et al., 2007; Pfaff et al., 2007; Roelofs, 2017). This
alters our physiology, thinking and behaviour. In this state, our mind and
body are highly alert. We react immediately and impulsively (McDonnell
et al., 2015; McDonnell, 2019). But although natural and important this
impulsivity is potentially problematic and harmful. It can cause us to make
the wrong call. It is strongly associated with trauma (Shepherd & Wild,
2014). We see *System One* at work in rage, anger, shutdown, and panic.
System One also stores our prejudices and biases, where we instinctively
frame and categorise people and events. *System One* will influence how
attitudes, narratives and cultures develop (Hozak & Olsen, 2015; Kahneman, 2011). Seneca encourages us to reflect and 'examine our impressions'
(Veyne, 2002).

Tversky and Kahneman (1974) describe how our first impressions are
powerful and enduring, influencing how we think and what we do. The effect
is difficult to reverse. It forms part of our subconscious. It can create stigma
and prejudice. The 'othering' and demonisation of people and groups are
examples (Figure 11.2).

System Two is more rational and reflective. It is where our thoughts and
judgements are more mindful, considered, and deliberate. In *System Two* we
become self-aware. We are more in control of our beliefs and actions. We can

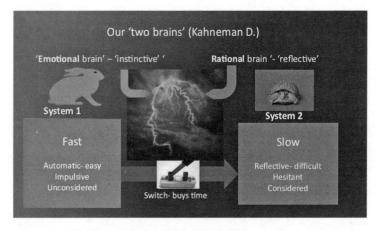

Figure 11.2 Two brains. Adapted from Kahneman (2011).

weigh the pros and cons. Biases, or groupthink are examined and challenged. We can develop a plan and carry it out (Gooderham, 2009; Kabat-Zinn, 2003; Mailoo, 2015; McDonnell et al., 2015)

But *System Two* requires effort and practice. It does not come easily. And although it is less likely to produce bad judgements, *System Two* is not free of error. But being in touch with, and in control of one's own emotions in this way, can help to prevent harmful stress and produce better judgements, actions, and outcomes.

We need to consciously *make the switch* from *System One* to *System Two*. From our emotional to our rational 'brain' and do this before biological effects on the body and mind related to *System One* take hold. This is particularly so in crises. This demands a focus on self-awareness and reflection. Eventualities are anticipated. Biases and errors are thought through and challenged, resulting in a plan for what *we* will do. This plan is rehearsed.

The factors influencing the behaviour of others are multiple and mysterious. The concept of *verstehen* described by both Weber and Dilthey is a reminder that deep understanding based on empathy for the experience of the other is laudable, but not without risk. Often, we cannot know what this experience is. We may make educated guesses or assumptions, and act influenced by our heuristics or biases (Kahneman, 2011; Walker, 2011). Being aware of these factors is important.

It is here that a switch from *System One* to *System Two* is helpful. Awareness and preparedness are key. Teachers have found it of huge practical value to ask themselves 'Am I in *System One* or *System Two*?' In this, regardless of other factors; *a plan* is developed to ensure *we* gain and retain control of ourselves and our actions. Once stressed, if we lose control of ourselves, calm reflection and action become much more difficult. (Ellis, 1980a,b; Kabat-Zinn, 2003; McDonnell, 2019).

The control of our emotions and actions as professionals

There are several ways we can make the switch from *System One* to *System Two* when working with people described as displaying 'behaviours of concern'. We can plan for us to always be calm, accepting and kind. We can change our thinking to explore and build a more positive story about the person. We can be careful and respectful in our descriptions, avoiding damaging or demeaning language or terminology. We can raise and discuss our feelings and concerns with a mentor, who can listen to our thoughts and feelings without judgement. We can connect and do enjoyable things with the young person (McDonnell, 2019). These actions help us to make the switch to *System Two* and in deciding our plan. We are mindful yet alert to the dangers of how our thinking and actions are affected in *System One*. In our minds, we run through dealing with potential problems, including our own psychological triggers or fears (Kabat-Zinn, 2003).

This offers protection on several levels, to both supporters and to the person receiving support. We focus on the control of our emotions and actions as professionals. We practise being self-aware, calm, kind, respectful. We are alert and rational. Over time, with practice and support, this becomes more natural, or our second nature – a 'way of life'.

It is also important to be aware of other influences on how our behaviours are shaped and maintained. Bandura (1977, 2006) emphasises the importance of role models. How we learn from observing others, rather than being under explicit instruction. Leadership and teamwork therefore involve modelling the right behaviours, attitudes, and narratives. We are likely to influence attitudes, narratives, practice, and culture by what we do and by providing an example for others to emulate and follow.

We have seen how people may be consciously or unconsciously coerced, individually or as a part of a team or group. Asch (1951) showed how unconscious factors influenced groups and led to conformity or compliance with group norms. Milgram (1963) and Zimbardo (1971) both illustrated the dangers of authority and how easily ordinary people could commit unspeakable acts. These classic experiments have since been replicated in part with similar results (Burger, 2009; Miller, 1999). The effects can be seen in the recurring scandals in modern services, such as Winterbourne View Hospital and how 'whistle-blowers' who speak out are demonised (Bubb, 2014). These experiments have also shown how access to external influences can diminish the effects of group-think on practice and behaviour (Janis, 2008; Turner & Pratkanis, 1998). We believe it is here that external mentoring can play a significant and critical role.

Interventions that change the behaviour of another human being are elusive and locating the 'causes' of behaviour, problematic. This is evident from the host of unsuccessful approaches and the continuing growth of 'specialised' services for autistic CYP regarded as presenting with 'behaviours of concern'. But how far are these a continuing part of the problem? In the UK, the narrative that segregates people in this way is regarded by some as having done more harm than good, as evidenced by the serial scandals of the 'Assessment and Treatment Units' and the lack of progress in improving these conditions or reducing admissions (Bubb, 2014; Care Quality Commission 2020; Panel, 2021).

This chapter suggests that approaches based on calm and rational responses, greater self-awareness, and being prepared mentally and emotionally, can reduce stress, avoid confrontation, and produce better outcomes. Having a plan that switches us from *System One* to *System Two*. The focus is always on what *we* will do.

Knowing, reflecting, and acting

Workers in a range of services, such as schools, often report a high level of stress linked to 'behaviours of concern' or 'risk'. The reasons for such behaviours may be difficult to comprehend and change. They may relate to how a child is experiencing the world and involve fear, trauma, stress, frustration, anger, boredom, or illness. Some behaviours may have no purpose or meaning that is obvious or accessible to us. We may struggle to empathise (Milton, 2012). One agreed characteristic is that the behaviour of others is not within our control. What *is* within our control is what *we* think and do. Our character, our ability to be self-aware, to remain calm, patient, and kind, to reflect, empathise and focus on what *we can* control. Namely, our thoughts and actions, our beliefs, self-awareness, and how we gain and maintain control of ourselves to be with others. This forms the basis of Synergy (Figure 11.3).

- **Know** what is within *our* control and what is not: We can control only what *we* do. Our thoughts, beliefs, and actions. Our character, values, and virtues are important. It's what *we* do that counts. Switch from *System One* to *System Two* – from our 'emotional' to our 'rational' brain.
- **Reflect** and 'examine our impressions' (our thoughts and beliefs, influences, biases, and actions). Develop empathy based on a deeper understanding of the experience of the other. We *can* control only what *we* do. We don't rush to judgement.

Figure 11.3 Synergy components.

- **Plan** (for what *we* will do) We anticipate. We remain calm, kind, and in control of *our* actions. Apply our knowledge and skills proactively. We pay attention to what we do and how we speak of others. We recognise we are a model for others. We have a plan for what *we* will do.

An example concerns Josephina, a teacher working with secondary school-age children in a mainstream school. One of the children in her class, 'Karl', is autistic. Josephina had little experience with autistic children and had found working with 'Karl' stressful. With the support of her mentor, Josephina was able to identify those factors within herself that she felt affected her confidence, stress, and capability. These included arriving at school in a stressed state, often because of heavy traffic, worrying about what would happen if 'Karl' had a 'bad day'. And how she would deal with this. The mentor was able to explore each of these feelings in turn.

Using this approach Josephina was able to reflect on what was and was not within her control. e.g., Her self-awareness of her stressors and her approach. She would remain calm. She was able to reflect on those factors that caused her to respond as she did by examining her impressions. How she framed 'Karl' and how he experienced his day.

Finally, she planned what she would do to work effectively with 'Karl'. To manage herself effectively even if a crisis was to occur. She would model calm kindness to her colleagues and other children.

The outcome was 'a plan for Josephina'. This involved a checklist of events that covered what Josephina would do to prepare for the day and throughout. At her suggestion, this started with arriving at school a little earlier to recover from the stress of travel. The focus was on those things she could do.

Plan for Josephina

- *I am relaxed and calm.*
- *The room is prepared for 'Karl'.*
- *The daily schedule is available and accessible to 'Karl'.*
- *Room check is complete for sensory intrusions.*
- *Materials are ready for 'Karl' to use.*
- *The equipment and materials we need for 'Karl' are in place.*
- *I am ready to greet 'Karl' calmly.*
- *The team is in place and ready to greet 'Karl' calmly.*
- *The team understands the plan should 'Karl' become distressed.*
- *Plan B is also understood (Plan B involved taking children out of class but was never needed)*

Josephina reported that having this plan for herself and the support of the mentor increased her confidence, reduced her stress, and encouraged her to address systemic policy issues within the school.

Rather than wait for a problem to arise and then deal with it reactively, the proactive plan gave clear guidance so that everyone knew what they should do. It was not rigidly prescriptive and allowed time for reflection. This plan also reduced the stress of other members of the team and replaced a negative 'risk' narrative and culture with one that was more relaxed and positive. This also allowed her to challenge some of the school policies that she felt created the risk narrative and added to staff stress.

This was a common finding of the report of the independent evaluation by the University of the Peloponnese, which is currently being prepared for publication.

Conclusion

The aim of Synergy is to offer a method for thinking about 'behaviours of concern' that focuses primarily on teacher character, mindset, well-being, influences, and actions. Supporting teachers and other school staff, individually and in groups to understand and focus on what is within their control, to reflect and to examine impressions and narratives, and to make realistic plans for responding. To switch from emotional to rational responses. Synergy is not intended to be exclusively autism-specific or to offer specific techniques in the management of behaviour, but to pave the way for reflective approaches that are effective and ethical. Independent evaluation (currently in prep by the University of Peloponnese) suggests Synergy reduces staff stress and improves confidence and school capacity.

Acknowledgements

The author would like to note that elements of the Synergy programme described in this chapter continue to be evaluated by the University of the Peloponnese led by Professor George Bagakis.

The author sincerely thanks their colleagues from the Laskaridis Foundation, Piraeus, Greece for their practical hard work, ideas, and support, and to the late Dr Michael McCreadie of AT-Autism and Studio 3, who continues to inspire and influence.

Further reading

Bubb, S. (2014). *Winterbourne view – Time for change: Transforming the commissioning of services for people with learning disabilities and/or autism.* London: NHS England.

Dunne, J. (1986). Sense of community in l'Arche and in the writings of Jean Vanier. *Journal of Community Psychology, 14*(1), 41–54. https://doi.org/10.1002/1520-6629 (198601)14:1%3C41::AID-JCOP2290140105%3E3.0.CO;2-T

Eaton, W. W. (1994). Social facts and the sociological imagination: The contributions of sociology to psychiatric epidemiology. *Acta Psychiatrica Scandinavica, 90*, 25–38. https://doi.org/10.1111/j.1600-0447.1994.tb05911.x

Goffman, E. (1961). *Asylums: Essays on the social situation of mental patients and other inmates*. Piscataway, NJ: AldineTransaction.

Jetten, J., & Hornsey, M. J. (2014). Deviance and dissent in groups. *Annual Review of Psychology, 65*, 461–485. https://doi.org/10.1146/annurev-psych-010213-115151

Milton, D., Mills, R., & Pellicano, E. (2014). Ethics and autism: Where is the autistic voice? Commentary on Post et al. *Journal of Autism and Developmental Disorders, 44*, 2650–2651. https://doi.org/10.1007/s10803-012-1739-x

Milton, D., Gurbuz, E., & López, B. (2022). The 'double empathy problem': Ten years on. *Autism, 26*(8), 1901–1903. https://doi.org/10.1177/13623613221129123

Milton, D. E. (2012). On the ontological status of autism: The 'double empathy problem'. *Disability & Society, 27*(6), 883–887. https://doi.org/10.1080/09687599.2012.710008

Palys, T. S. (2003). *Research decisions: Quantitative and qualitative perspectives*. Scarborough, ON: Thomson Nelson.

Panel, O. (2021). Monitoring mental health care. *The Lancet Psychiatry.* https://doi.org/10.1016/S2215-0366(22)00006-2

Rosenhan, D. L. (1973). On being sane in insane places. *Science, 179*(4070), 250–258. https://doi.org/10.1126/science.179.4070.250

Rosenstock, I. M., Strecher, V. J., & Becker, M. H. (1988). Social learning theory and the health belief model. *Health Education Quarterly, 15*(2), 175–183. https://doi.org/10.1177/109019818801500203

Scheff, T. J. (2017). *Being mentally ill: A sociological study*. New York: Routledge.

Schwitzgebel, E. (2006). Belief. In: E. Zalta. (Ed.) *The Stanford encyclopaedia of philosophy*. Stanford: Stanford University.

Sherif, C. W., Sherif, M., & Nebergall, R. E. (1965). *Attitude and attitude change: The social judgment-involvement approach* (pp. 127–167). Philadelphia: Saunders.

Sherif, M. (1956). Experiments in group conflict. *Scientific American, 195*(5), 54–59.

Smith, J. K. (1983). Quantitative versus qualitative research: An attempt to clarify the issue. *Educational Researcher, 12*(3), 6–13. https://doi.org/10.3102/0013189X012003006

Traustadottir, R. (2009). Disability studies, the social model and legal developments. The UN Convention on the Rights of Persons with Disabilities: *European and Scandinavian Perspectives. 100.* 3-16. https://doi.org/10.1163/ej.9789004169715.i-320.7

Tucker, W. T. (1965). Max Weber's verstehen. *The Sociological Quarterly, 6*(2), 157–165. https://doi.org/10.1111/j.1533-8525.1965.tb01649.x

References

Asch, S. E. (1951). Effects of group pressure on the modification and distortion of judgments. In H. Guetzknow (Ed.), *Groups, leadership and men* (pp. 177–190). Pittsburgh, PA: Carnegie Press.

Bagkakis, P., & Koulis, T. (2023). A preliminary report on the evaluation of the Synergy programme in Greek schools from the University of the Peloponnese. (*Under review*).

Bandura, A. (1977). *Social learning theory*. Prentice Hall, NJ: Englewood Cliffs.

Bandura, A. (1982). Self-efficacy mechanism in human agency. *American Psychologist, 37*(2), 122. https://psycnet.apa.org/doi/10.1037/0003-066X.37.2.122

Bandura, A. (2006). Toward a psychology of human agency. *Perspectives on Psychological Science, 1*(2), 164–180.

Burger, J. M. (2009). Replicating Milgram: Would people still obey today?. *American Psychologist, 64*(1), 1.

Care Quality Commission. (2020). Out of sight–who cares?: Restraint, segregation and seclusion review. Retrieved from: https://www.cqc.org.uk/sites/default/files/20201023_rssreview_report.pdf

Dilthey, W., & Rickman, H. P. (2015). *Pattern and meaning in history: Wilhelm Dilthey's thoughts on history and society*. Harper.

Ellis, A. (1980a). Discomfort anxiety: A new cognitive behavioural construct. *Rational Living, 15*(1), 25–30.

Ellis, A. (1980b). Rational-emotive therapy and cognitive behaviour therapy: Similarities and differences. *Cognitive Therapy and Research, 4*, 325–340. https://doi.org/10.1007/BF01178210

Ellis, A. (1992). Group rational-emotive and cognitive-behavioural therapy. *International Journal of Group Psychotherapy, 42*(1), 63–80. https://doi.org/10.1080/00207284.1992.11732580

Evans, J. (2013). *Philosophy for life and other dangerous situations: Ancient philosophy for modern problems*. Novato, CA: New World Library.

Gooderham, P. (2009). Changing the face of whistleblowing. *BMJ, 338.* https://doi.org/10.1136/bmj.b2090

Hozak, K., & Olsen, E. O. (2015). Lean psychology and the theories of "Thinking, Fast and Slow". *International Journal of Lean Six Sigma, 6*(3), 206–225.

Janis, I. L. (2008). Groupthink. *IEEE Engineering Management Review, 36*(1), 36.

Kabat-Zinn, J. (2003). Mindfulness-based interventions in context: Past, present, and future. *Clinical Psychology: Science and Practice, 10*(2), 144–156. https://psycnet.apa.org/doi/10.1093/clipsy.bpg016

Kahneman, D. (2011). *Thinking, fast and slow: Farrar, Straus and Giroux*. New York.

Mailoo, V. (2015). Common sense or cognitive bias and groupthink: Does it belong in our clinical reasoning? *British Journal of General Practice, 65*(630), 27–27. https://doi.org/10.3399/bjgp15X683173

McDonnell, A. (2019). *The reflective journey: A practitioner's guide to the low arousal approach*. Alcester, UK: Studio 3.

McDonnell, A., McCreadie, M., Mills, R., Deveau, R., Anker, R., & Hayden, J. (2015). The role of physiological arousal in the management of challenging behaviours in individuals with autistic spectrum disorders. *Research in Developmental Disabilities, 36*, 311–322. https://doi.org/10.1016/j.ridd.2014.09.012

Miller, A. G. (2009). Reflections on Replicating Milgram (Burger, 2009). *The American psychologist, 64*(1), 20–27.

Milgram, S. (1963). Behavioural study of obedience. *The Journal of Abnormal and Social Psychology, 67*(4), 371. https://psycnet.apa.org/doi/10.1037/h0040525

Milton, D. E. (2012). On the ontological status of autism: The 'double empathy problem'. *Disability & Society, 27*(6), 883–887. https://doi.org/10.1080/09687599.2012.710008

Mobbs, D., Petrovic, P., Marchant, J. L., Hassabis, D., Weiskopf, N., Seymour, B., … Frith, C. D. (2007). When fear is near: Threat imminence elicits prefrontal-periaqueductal gray shifts in humans. *Science, 317*(5841), 1079–1083. https://doi.org/10.1126/science.1144298

Pfaff, D. W., Martin, E. M., & Ribeiro, A. C. (2007). Relations between mechanisms of CNS arousal and mechanisms of stress. *Stress, 10*(4), 316–325. https://doi.org/10.1080/10253890701638030

Platt, J. (1985). Weber's verstehen and the history of qualitative research: The missing link. *British Journal of Sociology, 36*(3), 448–466. https://doi.org/10.2307/590460

Roelofs, K. (2017). Freeze for action: Neurobiological mechanisms in animal and human freezing. *Philosophical Transactions of the Royal Society B: Biological Sciences, 372*(1718), 20160206. https://doi.org/10.1098/rstb.2016.0206

Rogers, C. (1959). *A theory of therapy, personality, and interpersonal relationships: As developed in the client-centered framework* (Volume 3). New York: McGraw-Hill.

Shepherd, L., & Wild, J. (2014). Emotion regulation, physiological arousal and PTSD symptoms in trauma-exposed individuals. *Journal of Behavior Therapy and Experimental Psychiatry, 45*(3), 360–367. https://doi.org/10.1016/j.jbtep.2014.03.002

Turner, M. E., & Pratkanis, A. R. (1998). Twenty-five years of groupthink theory and research: Lessons from the evaluation of a theory. *Organizational Behavior and Human Decision Processes, 73*(2–3), 105–115. https://doi.org/10.1006/obhd.1998.2756

Tversky, A., & Kahneman, D. (1973). Availability: A heuristic for judging frequency and probability. *Cognitive Psychology, 5*(2), 207–232. https://doi.org/10.1016/0010-0285(73)90033-9

Tversky, A., & Kahneman, D. (1974). Judgement under uncertainty: Heuristics and biases. Biases in judgments reveal some heuristics of thinking under uncertainty. *Science, 185*(4157), 1124–1131. https://doi.org/10.1126/science.185.4157.1124

Veyne, P. (2002). *Seneca: The life of a stoic.* New York: Routledge.

Walker, K. (2011). Weber: Antipositivism & Verstehen. *Early Theorists & the Science of Society, 123.*

Weber, M. (2017). *Methodology of social sciences.* New York: Routledge.

Wolfensberger, W. (1983). Social role valorization: A proposed new term for the principle of normalization. *Mental Retardation, 21*(6), 234.

Zimbardo, P. G. (1971). The power and pathology of imprisonment. (*Congressional Record.*) (Serial No 15, October 25, 1971). Hearings before Subcommittee No. 3, of the Committee on the Judiciary, House of Representatives, Ninety-Second Congress, (*First session on Corrections, Part II, Prisons, Prison Reform and Prisoner's Rights: California.*) Washington, DC: U.S. Government Printing Office.

Developing curiosity in-service delivery and service transformation

Chapter 12

When the helping professions hurt – the need to build trust and make sense of each other in the therapy room

Kieran Rose and Roslyn Law

Setting the scene

The Sociologist Erving Goffman used the imagery of theatre to portray the nuances and significance of face-to-face social interaction (Goffman, 1959). He put forth a theory of social interaction that he refers to as the dramaturgical model of social life. He describes stigma, impression management, and the importance of working to ensure that all parties have the same 'definition of the situation', meaning that all understand what is meant to happen in that situation, what to expect from the others involved, and thus how they themselves should behave.

The importance of reflecting on this as therapists working with Neurodivergent people (Walker, 2022), is vital.

Scene 1: How we met

Roslyn

During a therapy session, someone I had been working with for over a year asked me, 'Are you good enough at what you do to work with me? Do you know enough to help me?' These questions didn't come entirely out of the blue, although they felt like they did at the time. The young person who posed the questions had recently received the results of an assessment, which identified Autism and ADHD, in addition to Dyspraxia, which had been identified several years earlier. Despite what looks, in hindsight, like an embarrassing array of signals, I had not anticipated this outcome and when asked, had said as much. Suddenly we found ourselves in a position where my qualifications and potential to help were rightly being questioned.

In this moment of discomfort, it was tempting to reassure and set aside the worries, to hide behind qualifications and models, or to turn the tables and explore the painful experience of anxiety, frustration, or irritation as the

DOI: 10.4324/9781003352327-18

problems to be addressed. Instead, I stayed with the discomfort to give as honest an answer as I could, 'I don't think I am, but I want to be and, if you are willing, I will do what it takes to do better'. That moment, and the young person's generosity, proved transformative.

In the hours and days that followed, I felt a mix of panic and excitement. The option of looking the other way and staying uninformed was no longer available and the opportunity to learn and 'do better' had just been handed to me. I am convinced that growth is truthfully only possible when we are open to corrective feedback, however painful and challenging. This experience was unequivocally both, but it was also as though I had discovered a new path, previously unseen, or perhaps ignored, and I was taking it for the first time. This daunting prospect was made much easier by knowing I had people around me who knew much more than me and who I trusted to guide me.

I realised that if I had missed these signals because I was lacking contextual awareness, I needed to learn from someone who was immersed in the context I was blind to. I wrote to a neurodivergent colleague who was well connected with other neurodivergent (particularly autistic) people and said: 'I now know what I don't know – please help!'.

I was pointed in Kieran's direction, to his writing, his presentations, and crucially his email address. I read, listened, and tried to remain honest. In my first email, I told him,

> I recently had the good fortune to be told in no uncertain terms to raise my game by a young person I am working with… We, and more specifically I, have unknowingly colluded with the internal and external demand to mask.
> (Pearson & Rose, 2021, 2023)

Without taking time to inform myself, I wouldn't have been able to say even that. I was beginning to discover what it really meant to know what I didn't know, and it sharply raised my anxieties. Not only did it reveal example after example, running back over years of clinical practice, where I recognised the same potential to do harm, but I realised that they had all happened when I thought I was doing my job well and teaching others to do the same. My first invitation to Kieran was not to teach me and my colleagues, but to help us to risk-assess what we were doing.

Kieran

When a professional arrives in my email inbox with words to the effect of 'I'm realising I don't know enough…', which tends to happen increasingly frequently; I mentally both sigh and cheer in equal measure.

There are a good many professionals who either have, or are, making the realisation that something fundamental needs to change in their practice, that their knowledge and interpretation of context is lacking, and that the application of their professional practice, despite best intentions, is causing significant, (mostly) unwitting harm. It is difficult to understand and accept that despite years of training and practice, of both convincing yourself that you are, and being held by others to the standard of being the 'expert', all that may be based on a foundation of sand, and only result in an end product of professionally contributing to a cycle of stigma and trauma; and the compounding of poor mental health and early death (Rose, 2022) in the population you have trained to support.

All professionals working with autistic people should be sitting incredibly uncomfortably (you probably are after that last statement). As a professional, I truly believe that sitting uncomfortably within your professional practice is the best place to be, because discomfort is an indication of paying attention and active reflection: it is an opportunity to learn, broaden the scope of your practice and do better.

Within mental health specifically, from psychiatry, through to psychology and therapeutic practice, the lack of informed knowledge, the prevalence of normative bias and the reliance on 'off the shelf' models of support created by, framed around, and intended for people who exist and identify through a normative lens, is staggering; the lack of non-biased and unflawed 'evidence' for this practice, along with the lack of critical reflection for it, is shocking; making the de-construction and rebuilding of these narratives through a cultural, de-colonised, de-ableist, and trauma-based formulation, imperative.

The accumulation of trauma over the lifespan of an autistic person is something that seldom gets identified and more rarely, even if identified, validated. Most autistic people, diagnosed or not, are pathologised through many different lenses including their behaviour, diet, communication style, social motivations, play, movement, emotions, interests, attention, learning style, self-regulation, and even sleep; and are often misperceived and stigmatised via informal cultural labels with negative connotations such as 'weird', 'quirky', 'geeky' and so on, which both misrepresent and mask neurodivergence to both the observer and the experiencer.

Scene 2: Professional biases

Roslyn

As my awareness and understanding developed, I noticed that talking directly and simply about neurodivergence became a routine part of many clinical conversations. It proved enormously helpful when working with a man, whose ADHD was recognised in his early twenties, that we could distinguish between the impact of mood changes and his 'ADHD brain'. He knew the difference and taught me to do the same. New metaphors became a shared language as we considered where the torchlight beam of his ADHD mind was shining and what might be in the surrounding shadows. We counted the 'spoons' he had used on a particular day and how that might help us to understand his fluctuating energy and enthusiasm for the demands and opportunities that he had faced and what remained to be done, or as was often the case, not done. Spoons were used as a metaphor to quantify the energy and attention or 'spoons' he had available each day. Each daily activity, from deciding what to wear to having an emotionally in-depth conversation, used a different number of his daily allocation of spoons. This concept allowed us to acknowledge the many moment-to-moment decisions involved in getting through the day without becoming overwhelmed. The tone shifted from self and anticipated judgement to one of shared understanding, and from regret and shame to informed planning.

He described having his ADHD recognised as a moment when the scattered pieces of so many years fell into place. There was now a way to think about his experience that didn't inevitably lead to the conclusion that he was a failure or deficient in some way. He simply processed information differently and at times needed ideas and help to work around the implications of that. Crucially, we adjusted the focus of our work from his recurring battle to shape up and sort himself out to helping those around him to use the same insights he had shared with me – how to invite his family to step into his shoes rather than asking him to take this leap of imagination.

These conversations also allowed us to look at the impact of professional bias from a novel perspective. As I have discovered often happens, when this young man's ADHD was recognised, the framework prompted those around him to consider its fit for other family members. On this occasion, it was his dad, who had so often been the person he felt most acutely concerned about letting down, who became the focus of attention. The new idea was taken up with some enthusiasm by his mother and siblings who were keen to persuade a somewhat beleaguered dad that he had to admit his own unrecognised ADHD. At first, he was not keen, until his previously 'troublesome' son gently explained some of his day-to-day experiences, each of which turned on a lightbulb of recognition in his father. Previously antagonistic relationships began to run more smoothly until his father took his insight to his own therapist only to be told that the therapist didn't think that he had ADHD at all, and his experience was much better explained by the anxiety and depression they had already identified and were treating. 'That wasn't helpful', was his son's conclusion as some of the dividing lines they had lived with for so long began to reappear.

In another example, a young woman I had worked with periodically since she was a child started to come into focus in my mind in a way that hadn't characterised our work previously. Her agonising struggle to focus her attention on exam revision and tendency to 'zone out' mid-session threw up signals that I began to attend to differently. No longer satisfied with anxiety and depression as the catch-all explanations, I began to pause, notice when we disconnected and ask about those moments. I listened as example after example poured out. When I tentatively raised the possibility of ADHD as something for us to think about, I discovered this had been raised at school but not pursued by her parents who understood her distractibility in terms of lack of effort and application. Again, and again, I have started to notice how readily we lean into explanations that do a good enough job of satisfying our curiosity and permit us to avoid the inconvenient shadows around the edges. Taking up this discussion with her mother, I was initially met with a blunt rejection of the idea. Mum explained that her daughter was not like her vision of the classic hyperactive boy who runs around a classroom and cannot concentrate, so the idea had no relevance. Asking her to bear with me, we walked through the criteria that would be used for a diagnosis and mum confirmed everyone, not only for her daughter but also for herself.

Kieran

An uninformed practitioner not understanding of the narratives that surround neurodivergent people might not recognise neurodivergence, or any of what is substantial trauma.

If mental health practitioners have no or little recognition of the level of the lifelong invalidation and stigma experienced by autistic people; nor the occurrence of other co-occurring conditions and the trauma that develops from all these intersections, then they will continue to centre neurodivergent poor mental health as part of the neurodivergent experience, all based on a poor interpretation of what neurodivergence is. The outcome of this is a continuation of what has happened historically: a compounding of mental health issues and encouragement of further self-blame and internalised ableism within the client.

The recognition of this compounding of internalised ableism occurring, and the change of culture and practice around these biases can lead to a multitude of new dawns and understandings and validation not only for clients and their families but also for practitioners.

With deeper and contextual knowledge comes greater empathy and understanding. Unfortunately, though, while learning the skills to support, we too often focus so strongly on our tools and our belief systems, that we often detach from the humanitarian recognition that we are working with people who exist within contexts we might not even be able to begin to imagine.

Scene 3: Reflective discussions

Roslyn

If we are lucky, we are sometimes invited into worlds we didn't know existed or were needed. As I stumbled around with new, exciting, and sometimes alarming awareness, I felt an increasing need to talk about it. I don't think especially well in isolation, but in conversation, ideas come to life. Where then could I take my fledgling awareness to be nurtured and take flight? Standard supervision offered support but also revealed that most of us tend to hold on to what we were first taught and interpret new things through that lens.

As John Kenneth Galbraith once said, 'Faced with the choice between changing one's mind and proving that there is no need to do so, almost everybody gets busy on the proof' (Galbraith, 1965). In fast-moving fields like autism specifically, and neurodivergence more broadly, understanding is rapidly out of date, so what hope is there if that understanding was last updated years, if not decades ago, as was the case for me? I needed to find people with a different lens.

Damian Milton's description of the double empathy problem became not only an elegant description of the challenge of understanding different worldviews but also a lived reality for me (Milton, 2012). I realised that I couldn't develop by looking in from the outside, I had to find people who could help me to look out from the inside.

Kieran once again became my anchor point. I spent weeks quietly listening to the discussions he and his community of colleagues, practitioners, parents, and peers have had. At first, I literally didn't have the confidence to show my face, sitting behind a blank Zoom screen and scrambling to keep up. I read the papers he frequently sent my way, worked my way through recommended reading lists, listened to person after person speaking from the inside and invited me to step alongside to see.

All the while Kieran and I kept talking. I could learn on my own, but we could think together. Joint teaching sessions began when we invited my students into our conversations. We raised questions, offered few answers, and intentionally did nothing to reassure the discomfort this generated. Therein we hope lies growth. Inspired, I shared what was emerging from our conversations across training with therapists and supervisors and tried to gently pause and redirect them as Kieran has so often done for me. Getting it wrong isn't the problem, I realised What's truly dangerous is the choice to do nothing to improve and prevent similar mistakes in the future, which could have severe consequences.

Recently in 'Supervision of Supervision' I heard about a trainee therapist working with a young person who found it difficult to process the information shared in the session. The trainee was described as working creatively, e.g., providing more visual prompts rather than relying on verbal communication to support learning and discussion. The possibility that the young person was autistic had been discussed in their supervision and the supervisor brought it to our discussions. The young person's experience and the emotional significance of her relationship with her autistic brother both supported this as a possibility to explore. It therefore came as a surprise to me when the draft formulation and treatment plan proposed by the trainee made no reference to autism at all. Was I mistaking this young person for someone else? No, it was simply that the adults had talked about this amongst themselves but had not included the young person in the discussion. The emotional elephant in the room had not been named and consequently, they were in danger of embarking on clinical work that at best ran the risk of being unhelpful and at worst damaging. In supervision, we paused to think about what had happened and why. We sat with the discomfort and the opportunity it created. We agreed to suspend the usual timetable for the manualised therapy and go back to reopen the conversation, this time with the young person as a part of it, inviting discussion of all parts of themself they thought might be relevant to understanding their current distress.

This type of deliberate practice, where aspects of an individual's practice are specifically targeted for careful and repeated attention because they are more challenging or uncomfortable, has become a common currency in Interpersonal Therapy training and supervision. I am endlessly impressed by how openly my students have embraced this opportunity. Through repeated practice with corrective feedback, change is gradually achieved. In supervision, I have come to think of the target of this practice as identifying, 'oops moments'. Where didn't I know what to say or how to say it? When was I flooded with tension, felt self-conscious and became more concerned about avoiding an error or causing offence than making a deeper connection? When did I ignore my gut instinct that something was missing and carry on regardless? Here, Kieran and I have found fruitful common ground in believing in the necessity of pursuing the opportunity offered when we sit uncomfortably with our professional practice.

Kieran and Roslyn

The beginnings of our coming together were framed around what made us different. Our definitions of situations came from very mismatched places, a non-autistic professional and an autistic professional both with unalike ideas and distinct experiences. There was a willingness to bridge what was effectively a gap in cultural comprehension. A gap obscured for Roslyn by her privilege and unwitting inclination towards normative bias. A bridge was framed around Kieran's knowledge and curation of learning but was only completed with Roslyn's need to learn.

Kieran's generosity and patience with that education enabled us to walk alongside each other. Roslyn's lack of knowledge, while not irrelevant, was less important to Kieran than her curiosity and openness to learning, and the need for both of us to humanise experience, which ultimately supported Roslyn to embrace the transition from a *diagnosis and deficit model* to a *neurodiversity and trauma understanding model* (see Chapter 15 for more). This evolved into a mutual recognition of similarity: both of us have a compulsion to go out of our safety zones to be of use to someone else.

This allowed us to continuously be uncomfortable with each other's situations. From Kieran's point of view, his discomfort in being personally vulnerable to someone who by her own admittance and hindsight, has unwittingly committed professional harm to his community; and Roslyn's discomfort in openly admitting that her professional knowledge was limited and that she had committed harm.

Our collective willingness to sit with that discomfort and the recognition of our mutual similarities created a space where moving forward, we can be safely vulnerable with each other in mutually uncharted territory.

Stage directions

- Seek similarities over differences, and employ a strengths, needs, and aspirations framework rather than a deficits framework.
- Pay specific attention to the environment, context, and sensory experience. Positive physical and interpersonal environments can help neurodivergent young people to flourish just like everyone else. When difficulties emerge, consider changes in the environment as much as the young person.
- Anxiety and overwhelm are not inevitable. They are expressions of distress when the environmental demands become too much or prevent the use of adaptive strategies.
- Consider what unconscious othering leads you to do – refuse requests for help, impose normative expectations without consultation, treat differently.
- Recognise the unconscious bias and microaggressions in the language we use and their cumulative and reinforcing effect – 'managing', 'too much', 'so rude', 'too sensitive', 'fitting in', 'challenging behaviour'.
- At every moment ask yourself, how is what I am doing and saying perpetuating the subjective disconnection that autistic people experience throughout their lives? Would I come to the same conclusion if using a trauma-informed lens?
- Recognise when you are teaching someone to mask and thereby increase their subjective distress and risk. Ask yourself, am I contributing to the imposition of normative ideals, where someone fits in rather than making room for them to flourish?
- Recognise the risk of asking the young person to split their attentional resources e.g., look at me and listen, concentrate, and ignore the background noise. Have you considered the perpetual interplay between internal experience (feelings), external influence (environment and context), and implicit and explicit expectations (values, norms, standards)?
- Ensure supervision forces you to reframe and consider what you could be doing differently and what you might be missing.
- Seek out valuable and challenging sources of knowledge.

References

Galbraith, K. J. (1965). New York Times, Book review of 'CAME THE REVOLUTION; THE GENERAL THEORY OF EMPLOYMENT, INTEREST, AND MONEY. By John Maynard Keynes'.

Goffman, E. (1959). *The presentation of self in everyday life*. New York: Bantam.
Milton, D. E. (2012). On the ontological status of autism: The 'double empathy problem'. *Disability & Society, 27*(6), 883–887. https://doi.org/10.1080/09687599.2012.710008
Pearson, A., & Rose, K. (2021). A conceptual analysis of autistic masking: Understanding the narrative of stigma and the illusion of choice. *Autism in Adulthood, 3*(1), 52–60. http://doi.org/10.1089/aut.2020.0043
Pearson, A., & Rose, K. (2023). *Autistic masking: Understanding identity management and the role of stigma.* West Sussex: Pavilion Press.
Rose, K. The Inside of autism. Online training accessed 2022, Retrieved from: www.theautisticadvocate.com
Walker, N. (2022). *Neuroqueer Heresies*. Autonomous Press. Retrieved from: https://neuroqueer.com/neuroqueer-heresies/

Chapter 13

Supporting autistic children to thrive – it's everybody's business

Mairi Evans

Introduction

Sarah just managed to get to the CAMHS appointment on time. It had been yet another difficult morning. Her eldest, now 16, had been self-harming again – something Sarah had become aware of that morning when she had picked up some plates from her daughter's room and found the tell-tale bloodstained tissues, and then the offending sharpener blades hidden behind the drawers. Then, Sarah's youngest daughter, aged 11, nearly didn't make it to school. Her old socks were in the wash and despite the claim they were 'soft touch' the new pairs apparently had seams that were like barbed wire. This situation led to a frantic 10 minutes of searching for the old pair in the washing basket, a lot of deep breathing, and what felt like a small miracle to get her to leave for school at all.

Sarah felt flustered as she sat in the chair in the CAMHS clinic room. She looked at the smartly dressed woman in front of her. She took a slow breath to contain and centre herself.

'Good morning' Sarah said. 'How have things been for you this week, and what is important for us to talk about today....' The woman looked at her in tears and began to tell her what a difficult morning she had just had and how her daughter had refused to attend the appointment with her...

Sarah's story is not unique. She is one of a growing number of clinicians and health professionals working in children and adult mental health services who are either parents to neurodivergent children, are neurodivergent themselves, or both.

In this chapter, I write as a clinician with nearly 25 years of CAMHS experience and who, like Sarah, am a parent to two children (a boy and a girl) who are neurodivergent. I explore the changes in awareness of autism in CAMHS over time and the increase in the 'known' numbers of autistic children accessing specialist CAMHS services. I also invite readers to consider current CAMHS commissioning structures and how they could develop to best serve autistic children. I share some practice examples along the way and ask readers working in CAMHS to be mindful of your colleagues, who like

DOI: 10.4324/9781003352327-19

Sarah, will be both working within CAMHS as clinicians alongside accessing CAMHS support for their families.

Then (my early CAMHS experience)

In 1999, after five years of working as a children's social worker, I began work as a Child Guidance Social worker in a North London Clinic. I was training as a Family Therapist at the time and my passion was to work therapeutically with and alongside people to support change, rather than to carry out the social policing role that I was increasingly being asked to take in social care. My early Child Guidance 'caseload' included young people with encopresis (soiling), children with anxiety and low mood, children described as having behavioural problems, as well as young people who self-harmed.

Two years later I worked as a family therapist in an adult mental health hospital alongside another child guidance post. This role enabled me to work with children and families where the children and parents were both accessing mental health services. This included children who had seen their parents attempt suicide, children and mothers who had been sexually abused by the same family members, children or adults with varying mental health disorders, trauma, and multigenerational suicide attempts. Working with children, young people, and families with complex social and mental health needs, I appreciated the importance of enabling people to be heard, understood, and supported to change their lives. If I hadn't encountered something before, I would learn about it. I read, I spoke to those who knew more about things than I did, and I would use the skills I had as a therapist and adapt them to engage whoever I was supporting, whatever I was supporting them with. My work was varied, including with children who were high risk and whose therapeutic needs were complex, and those with less risk or less complex therapeutic needs.

Whilst I worked with children with ADHD, autism was rarely talked about. Autism was something that 'other people' worked with. If I am honest, I was probably informed, as were many, by the stereotypes of autism as something rare, that affected boys, that involved learning difficulties and observable communication difficulties, or that was associated with savant skills. ADHD was also seen as something which was more likely to affect boys, and the approach taken by many therapists, especially social constructionists, was that ADHD was a social construct and relational rather than anything medical or neurological.

In hindsight, the lack of knowledge about autism and girls was highlighted to me in or around 2002. I was working with a girl of about 12/13 who was socially very isolated. She always attended appointments with her favourite book, a children's story about a forest. There was concern that she was putting herself at risk by travelling for hours on the bus. She used limited language, reduced reciprocal communication, and avoided eye contact. I adopted a variety of creative methods to engage her in communicating about her relationships and emotions. I had limited knowledge of autism at that time but suspected that she was autistic and referred her to a consultant colleague for an assessment. However, I was told that she could not be autistic. I am not sure she even got as far as an assessment. At that time, I saw similar presentations in my adult mental health role with people, often women, labelled as having personality disorders or undefinable mental health disorders. Autistic people were most likely to have been missed, or mis-diagnosed, and knowledge of autism was limited, especially any understanding of autism in adulthood or for women and girls.

Now (CAMHS today)

Fast forward to the present and much has changed for clinicians working in CAMHS. Most services are separated into defined pathways; and complexity and risk, which once presented as the exception, have now become the norm. Additionally, case management has become intrinsic to managing the complex professional systems that surround the children and families we work with, all managing increased demand with reduced resources. The increase in referrals to CAMHS was high prior to the COVID-19 pandemic. Since 2019, NHS data and clinical experience, have both shown a stark rise in referrals to CAMHS and in the number of CYP with a 'probable' mental health disorder. Added to this, the workforce for CAMHS is an increasing challenge with services running with vacancies, relying on agency staff, and having to think creatively about how they will continue to meet demand. Anyone starting out as a clinician in CAMHS now will have a very different experience to the one I had 20 years ago. The need is high, the risks are greater, and capacity is far outstripped by demand. I am increasingly impressed by anyone new to the profession who can stay and manage the risks, demands, and growing criticism.

Alongside an increase in demand for CAMHS, and predating the COVID-19 lockdown, has been the increased prevalence of diagnosed, or suspected, autism for children accessing all child mental health services, including T4 CYP's mental health inpatient services. This backdrop is coupled with the pre-existing and increasing wait for autism and ADHD assessments. There has been debate about the reason for this increase: whether there has been an 'actual' increase in autism and/or ADHD rather than an increase in knowledge and identification, or if there is an over-diagnosis of neurodevelopmental conditions (Evans-Wickens, 2021). Whatever the reasons behind it, experience has shown that the prevalence of autism among CYP accessing mental health services exceeds the percentage of autistic people believed to be in the general population, for CYP's inpatient services, and in particular with autistic girls. This was highlighted to me again recently when a family therapy colleague of mine, who works in a specialist community CAMHS team commented to me that every one of the children on her caseload was autistic.

In 2019/2020 I interviewed twelve mothers of autistic girls about the diagnostic journey of their daughters (Evans-Wickens, 2021). All of the mothers highlighted emotional and mental health difficulties for their daughter's pre-assessment, ranging from behavioural difficulties and anxiety to severe OCD, self-harm, and attempted suicide. Their hope for the diagnosis of their daughters, as well as having a better understanding of their needs, was to access the right support for them. However, as highlighted in other studies (Sheerman, 2021) whilst the diagnosis brought many benefits, a theme throughout the interviews was that even with a diagnosis support was hard to come by. In one case the diagnosis was even seen as a barrier.

> ...the fact that she has a diagnosis of ADHD and autism meant that she didn't qualify (.) So, we weren't able to access that help because she's, quotes 'not broken enough' to get there. So, yes, it has been a block but that was a very specific block. I think it has more to do with the fact that there isn't anything (Barbara).
>
> (Evans-Wickens, 2021)

Despite the challenges described by Barbara, there are increasing numbers of autistic children accessing specialist CAMHS. But, why the increase?

In 1990, Freeston Wilson, an autistic adult, made a reference to autism being "a miner's canary" and a "prophetic warning to us all about what our way of life is doing to our bodies" (Murray, 2022; Wilson, 2014). Canaries were brought to the mines as 'exceptional risk detectors' and 'early indicators' (Bonney, 2020) due to their sensitivity to carbon monoxide. The connection made by Freeston, and expanded by others (Murray, 2022), was that autistic people are more susceptible to the increasing demands, environmental changes, and sensory overload of modern society in much the same way canaries were more susceptible to carbon monoxide in the mines. Could increasing numbers of autistic children be accessing CAMHS because they are exceptional risk detectors warning of the potential harms from daily life? There are increasing news reports about poverty, global warming, and political unrest. Are our autistic children forewarning us about increasing risk in the same way a canary falling to the bottom of the cage was a warning sign to miners?

If so, the response to autistic children has differed from that of the canaries. When the canaries fell from their perch this was seen because of the unsafe environment. An 'early indicator' that things were not right 'out there' due to poisonous gases, rather than an internal problem with the canary. As Murray (2022) states in her discussion on eugenics, "When the air in the mine is poisoned, we do not prevent canaries being born in case they suffer from the poison and upset us: we clean the air or close the mine". However, as a clinician I have often seen an autistic child's high anxiety or distress described as 'anxiety in the context of autism', suggesting the problem is an internal one and not due to external factors. Could this framing be the equivalent to saying, 'asphyxiation in the context of being a canary'?

THRIVE – a whole system approach

Whilst the pandemic has seen an increase in demand for CAMHS, for both autistic and neurotypical CYP, concerns about the ability of CAMHS to meet the needs of CYP pre-date the spread of COVID-19. In 2014, following a Health Committee spotlight on child mental health describing CAMH Services as 'dysfunctional' and 'ingrained' with problems, Wolpert et al. (2014) responded with the THRIVE framework. THRIVE offered a shift in how CAMHS was 'conceptualised' and 'potentially delivered' and made suggestions as to how services could be reviewed, improved, and commissioned. Even in 2014, the identified increase in mental disorders and self-harm in young people evidenced that something had to be done, and it had to be done differently. The ethos of THRIVE was that it offered a whole system approach to improve the challenges created by "differences in language and philosophy between the wider systems (health, education, social care)" which made "cross-agency working hard and agreement on coordinating policies challenging" (Wolpert et al., 2014). This approach included an increase in school-based intervention, and a better focus on the best practice standards, data, and outcome measures that the Health Committee had described as lacking. The framework, refreshed and updated in 2017 and 2019, promoted cross-agency, and cross-professional working and needs led support ensuring "a high level of respect for colleagues in other sectors" (Wolpert et al., 2019). This approach is also taken by the SEND code of practice which states that 'local education, health and social care should work together' to ensure that CYP with SEN or disabilities achieve the best possible outcomes (SEN code of practice 1.22).

The THRIVE approach is now utilised by Integrated Care Boards (ICBs) (https://www.england.nhs.uk/publication/integrated-care-boards-in-england/ and services across the country) and services across the country when reviewing, designing, and commissioning new or existing services. The framework describes different levels of support, advice, or intervention based on need, ranging from universal services (Thriving/Getting Advice) to more specialist services (Getting More Help, Getting Risk Support), (See Figure 13.1)

Thriving

The desire is for all our young people to thrive and reach their potential. Support required, and provided, includes prevention, health promotion, and awareness raising not targeting specific children or young people.

Getting advice

It is acknowledged that a percentage of CYP and/or their carers, will at times need advice due to changes in life circumstances, mild transitional difficulties, or due to chronic difficulties which they can manage with information and advice. Support in this quadrant is education-led, with a 'language of wellness'.

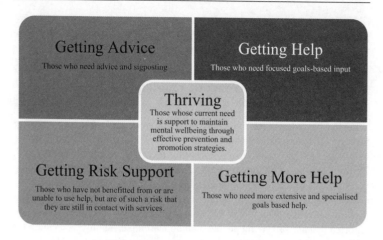

Figure 13.1 THRIVE framework (Wolpert et al., 2019).

Getting help

For some CYP, additional support will be required via focused and evidence-based treatments with clear aims, and criteria for assessing that those aims have been achieved. Whilst the provision may be schools-based, delivery is health-led and will require appropriately trained staff.

Getting more help

The framework observes that there will be a smaller percentage of CYP who have mental health conditions, such as eating disorders or psychosis, which won't respond to short-term targeted interventions, and where longer more specialist interventions are required. Provision here is health-based and health-led by specialists and skilled clinicians.

Getting risk support

Whilst the aim of the framework is to identify the best support and treatment based on goals and outcomes, it acknowledges that there are some CYP who will not respond to evidence-based treatments and who remain a significant risk and concern. For these young people joint agency working is vital. Wolpert et al. (2014) suggested that these young people are not provided with health treatment, due to the lack of evidence base, however, health and social care will have a role in managing risk and safety. Collaboration across agencies is vital for successful risk support and a lack of collaboration has been highlighted as a potential barrier to the successful implementation of THRIVE

(Farr et al., 2021). In my clinical experience, young people in the 'risk support' group include an increasing number of neurodivergent CYP who have not engaged, or been engaged, in getting help support earlier.

Supporting neurodivergent children to THRIVE: 'everybody's business'

What has become increasingly apparent to me in clinical and commissioning meetings is that autistic young people are over-represented in 'getting more help' and 'getting risk support', including in young people's mental health inpatient settings. One report (NHS Digital, 2021) listed figures suggesting that upwards of 25% of CYP detained at any one time between March 2017 and September 2020 were children who were autistic and/or had a learning disability. Another paper, drawing from NHS Assuring Transformation data, reported that autistic young people with no learning disability "accounted for 83% of the under 18 inpatient population on 30th September 2020" (p. 3) This statistic would make an autistic young person somewhere between 12.5 and 41 times (!) more likely to be admitted to a young person's inpatient unit than their neurotypical peers.

This over-representation of autistic CYP accessing CAMHS specialist services highlights the importance of all professionals understanding what is impacting their mental health, and how to engage and support them. It has led to the emergence of specialist services and/or training such as PEACE, a Pathway for Eating Disorders and Autism (PEACE 2020) and the CYP-IAPT (Children and Young People's[1] – Improving Access to Psychological Therapies) postgraduate programme in clinical practice with autistic CYP. PEACE and the CYP-IAPT Autism training are much needed and provide essential training or support which understands the difference of experience for autistic CYP. However, do they, along with THRIVE, also carry the risk of reinforcing the narrative of the 'specialist autism (or neurodiversity) services' or practitioners?

It is imperative that those with high risk and in high levels of distress get appropriate support, and we need clinicians within 'getting more help' and 'getting risk support' services to have the right skills and understanding of autism and neurodiversity. However, the THRIVE model promotes wellness, a shared language across professionals, and early access to advice and support. Autistic CYP should have access to CAMHS specialist services if and when they need them, but surely the idea is that we work together to prevent them from needing CAMHS in the first place. If a child needs CAMHS is this a sign that we have failed somewhere, and if more autistic children need to access CAMHS does that mean we are failing more autistic children? Are autistic children like the miner's canary, responding to environmental stressors that will eventually be harmful to all?

The ambition underpinning THRIVE is for all young people to thrive and reach their potential through prevention, health promotion, and awareness raising, as well as access to early support and advice. That should include autistic children too. With this in mind, it is vital that commissioners, service providers, and service designers, including those in education, consider accessibility and suitability of support for autistic children in all THRIVE quadrants, including universal 'getting advice' and early intervention services. Not as an 'add on' or as a specialist provision, but as a core part of all delivery.

This ambition should include the anticipatory adjustments needed for neurodivergent young people to access education, including an awareness of their individual social, sensory, and learning needs. In particular an awareness of camouflaging and that their needs may not be immediately apparent in the classroom. This goal requires close working with parents and carers, as well as with the young people themselves. This approach would include services such as MHSTs (Mental Health in School Teams) that are designed to provide and deliver evidence-based mental health interventions for mild to moderate mental health difficulties in schools as well as working with schools to bring about cultures and practices that support children's mental well-being (Ellins et al., 2023, p. 161). Unfortunately, a recent review of 23 MHST sites identified that neurodivergent children along with children with SEND and other minority groups are 'falling out of scope' for MHSTs and not 'accessing or receiving effective support' (Ellis et al., 2023, p. 104). In addition, the work on changing cultures within education has taken a backseat to the provision of low-intensity CBT which has not 'always been appropriate' or 'effective' (p. 162). Where some sites were identified as having created dedicated neurodiversity posts, this would still reinforce the narrative that autism and neurodiversity services are something separate, or as an add-on, and not (as it should be) everybody's business (Figure 13.2).

Thriving and getting advice

A neuro-inclusive approach to THRIVE requires that early support and advice, with the aim of promoting well-being, is appropriate for autistic children and their families. Early intervention in school was described as critical by Moyse (2021) if autistic young people are to be prevented from reaching crisis point. This intervention includes an understanding of sensory needs as well as informed teaching practices. The importance of this approach has been highlighted to me by a number of CYP I have worked with, like Mable.

Mable, aged 10, was referred to CAMHS due to significant risk-taking behaviour. She was running out of school, was self-harming and was exhibiting high levels of anxiety. Within CAMHS, I used a mixture of approaches

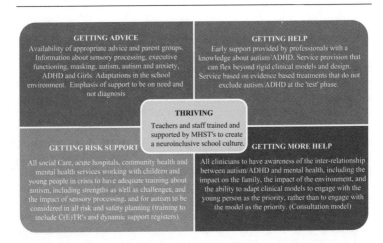

GETTING ADVICE
Availability of appropriate advice and parent groups. Information about sensory processing, executive functioning, masking, autism, autism and anxiety, ADHD and Girls. Adaptations in the school environment. Emphasis of support to be on need and not diagnosis

GETTING HELP
Early support provided by professionals with a knowledge about autism/ADHD. Service provision that can flex beyond rigid clinical models and design. Service based on evidence based treatments that do not exclude autism/ADHD at the 'test' phase.

THRIVING
Teachers and staff trained and supported by MHST's to create a neuroinclusive school culture.

GETTING RISK SUPPORT
All social Care, acute hospitals, community health and mental health services working with children and young people in crisis to have adequate training about autism, including strengths as well as challenges, and the impact of sensory processing, and for autism to be considered in all risk and safety planning (training to include C(E)TR's and dynamic support registers).

GETTING MORE HELP
All clinicians to have awareness of the inter-relationship between autism/ADHD and mental health, including the impact on the family, the impact of the environment, and the ability to adapt clinical models to engage with the young person as the priority, rather than to engage with the model as the priority. (Consultation model)

Figure 13.2 A neuro-inclusive approach to THRiVE (Evans, 2023).

to work with Mable, including flexible CBT using the Homunculi approach (Greig & McKay, 2013) and anxiety management techniques such as deep breathing. Mable engaged well but continued to exhibit significant distress before and after school. The biggest change for Mable was when I began to meet with her, her parents, and her teachers in school. I supported Mable in telling her parents, and her teachers, about how she experienced each part of her school day. Relaying this information led to a number of changes, such as going to class before the bell, a separate space for lunch due to a reaction to food smells and noise, sensory breaks, help with specific tasks, and a system for communicating when she was finding things hard. Having since sat in similar meetings to discuss my own children, I would ask professionals not to underestimate the emotional impact of such meetings on parents. Something I have reflected on with colleagues who are also parents of autistic children is that if you sit me in front of a hundred people to discuss my research, or a work-related issue, I am fine; sit me in a small meeting of supporting professionals to discuss the needs of my children and I may quickly be on the edge of tears.

Getting help

There are a number of CBT approaches adapted for autistic CYP, such as the Homunculi approach. These approaches will work with some autistic children, and not with others, the same as with any neurotypical child. Some autistic CYP may also engage well with traditional CBT approaches. Dr Stephen Shore famously said, 'If you've met one autistic person, you've met one autistic person' (Flannery & Wisner-Carlson, 2020). This can be said of all neurodivergent adults, young people, and children, and is evident in my family, my social group, my workplace, and my clinical practice. With this in mind, anything written about working with autistic CYP needs to be prefaced with a disclaimer that 'what may work for one autistic child may not work for another', in much the same way as 'what may work for one neurotypical child may not work for another'. Mable connected well with the homunculi approach, but it is not something I would recommend to everyone.

To be neuro-inclusive, Getting Help services and practitioners need to be given the freedom to flex their interventions and clinical 'toolkit' in order to engage with the child and not the clinical model. In my clinical experience this has sometimes meant working with the family system or learning support assistant, to support the work, rather than working directly with the child or young person. One example of this approach was my work with Steven and his mother.

Steven presented with high levels of anxiety. I had been unable to engage with him directly, so I worked with his mother instead. We utilised a combination of systemic therapy practice and behavioural strategies in which I acted as a consultant to his mother as she engaged Steven in the strategies at home. What was important was to be aware that this work was not easy for either Steven or his mother. Our work needed to explore the emotional and relational impact on Steven's mother as much as how Steven was responding to the interventions. Even sitting with your child to start engaging them in slow breathing techniques can be fraught with elevated levels of anxiety for both a parent and their child, something I can confirm from my own experience. So as much as Steven's mother was rewarding Steven for small steps, I too was praising her for the achievements they were both making.

Getting more help

Accessing support for your child is not easy, on an emotional or a practical level. In addition to long waits for assessment, parents can experience barriers and delays in the referral process. Particularly for children who mask and camouflage in school. Such barriers can lead to challenges in relationships with school staff and a sense that they are not believed, or even that others blame them for their child's challenges (Evans-Wickens, 2021).

When a parent reaches a specialist CAMHS clinician they may come with a history of not being heard, having to fight, feeling blamed and an experience of professionals questioning the validity of their concerns, or their ability as a parent. This was evidenced in my own research, where ten out of twelve of the mothers felt that they were being blamed for their autistic daughters' behaviours or difficulties. For example, one mother, Caroline, said:

I think there's sometimes an assumption that it's the parenting, it's the mother, it's the mother's insecurities, it's the mother's mental health.

(Evans-Wickens, 2021, p. 119)

Persistent challenges in having concerns heard can also lead to self-blame. As any form, practitioner, or therapist, it is important to be aware of how this may impact how parents or carers see you, how they think you see them, and what impact this may have on your early conversations. An awareness of past relationships with professionals was important when working with Serena and her son Nico:

> Nico tried to talk with his mum, he knew she was worried about him and worried about her too. But when he spent any time with her, he felt that she pounced on him. She would ask so many questions about his day, about his feelings, checking on if he was harming again. He found it all too much and would retreat to his room again.
>
> Serena worried so much about Nico. His last overdose had been the worst. He spent so much time in his room, and she felt she could not reach him emotionally. She felt she was failing as a parent and so alone with it all. If he showed any signs of talking to her, she jumped on the chance to engage him. She would ask about his day. Ask about his feelings and importantly, ask if he felt like harming again.

The above vignettes are adapted from clinical work I shared with a family therapy colleague in a CAMHS clinic. There had been significant concern about the escalation in Nico's (name changed) self-harming and the family were described as in crisis. There had been a number of professionals and agencies who had worked with the family and Serena came up with a story of being blamed and seen as the problem due to difficulties in their interactions and relationship. In a session, we explored the different communication styles and needs of Nico and his mother, using reflections about 'emotional credits' (adapted from an approach I was introduced to at training led by Tony Attwood). We reflected on how for some autistic people, emotional credits may be charged when they are on their own and depleted when they are around people. Whereas, for some neurotypical people emotional credits may be depleted when they are on their own but charged when they are with people (like an electricity metre or petrol tank). Serena and Nico connected with this idea. Nico was able to tell his mum that he knew she wanted company, and he was trying to spend time with her, but he found that the moment he tried she would 'pounce on him with questions'. She spoke about her worry about him, how lonely she was at home and how the moment he spoke to her she wanted to make the most of it, to connect with him and importantly to check he was okay. This had become a stuck pattern for both of them and was adding to the distress they were both feeling. The work progressed to look at how they could be together differently, creating an agreement about how they could spend time together without the need for lots of talk and questions. This compromise led to a new form of being together, reduced anxiety and enabled them to build a different relationship.

It also gave space for Serena to think about her own emotional needs away from her relationship with her son. The notion of emotional credits has been a useful one for sharing with parents, carers, and professionals. Many of our CYP (and parents) feel 'used up' at the end of the day, especially after school or big social events, and it is important for families to know what they need to do to decompress and then to 'recharge'.

Another useful approach in family therapy (which I was introduced to by David Pentecost) has been to ask family members to bring in something from home that connects with autism or ADHD, either for themselves, their sibling, or their child. This activity opens the discussion about the role autism or ADHD has in their family life and relationships. Items which have been brought in include a red T-shirt (to depict a child 'seeing red'), a packet of ADHD medication and boxes of papers and school reports. In one session a small girl brought in a packet of Haribo and told us how her brother could not eat them. We explored why, and they spoke together for the first time about how autism and ADHD impacted his life, rather than just how his behaviour impacted his family.

Getting risk support

I once attended an excellent work presented by the clinical psychologist Deborah Lee regarding a compassionate approach to PTSD. Deborah spoke about how the amygdala, wired for survival, can make it hard to think rationally when under threat, and how this can impact the hippocampus, responsible for memory and making sense of events, and the prefrontal cortex, responsible for regulating emotions which includes fear responses. Essentially the fear response, triggered by the amygdala, knocks out the thinking response, both in the moment and also after the event so it is never fully processed. There have been a number of studies connecting the functioning of the amygdala in autistic children and individuals (Amaral et al., 2003; Baron-Cohen et al., 2000; Zalla & Sperduti, 2013) and a connection has been made between autistic meltdowns and amygdala function (Deweerdt, 2020).

When someone with PTSD is asked to revisit and recount traumatic events, they can experience them as if they are there again due to the hippocampus and prefrontal cortex never having 'done their job' in the original event to tell them 'It's ok, you survived'. If this is connected to theories about autism and the amygdala, it potentially explains the difficulties experienced by a number of autistic children who have reached crisis, self-harmed and then been visited by professionals who ask them to revisit and recount events. Instead of experiencing the interaction as one intended to help and understand, it can bring back high emotion and stress as if living the event again, or the event cannot be recalled at all. In either situation, a clinician's questions can be experienced as threatening. I have witnessed this in my own practice and have been lucky enough to explore the theory with a young person I was working within a university setting who described how talking about past experiences made her feel she was reliving them again.

It is probable that a young person in crisis and needing risk support will not be available for traditional therapeutic interventions, and it is vital that anyone working with that young person, be that on an acute ward, in CAMHS, or in the local authority, has knowledge of autism. Also, an awareness that families, carers, and supporting professionals (especially families) may experience a degree of secondary trauma having witnessed repeated self-harm, meltdowns, and trauma for the young person. This is where risk support, collaborative working, and compassion for the family are of significant importance. The danger, when risks are high and resources are low, is that conversations can become focused on what services can't do or should not do. The challenge to all here is to keep the needs of the child, a young person, at the centre of the discussion and to focus on what support can be provided. This might mean sharing responsibility for a 'next best' option and exploring alternatives to traditional service interventions and requires an understanding of the framework that partner agencies have to work within.

The need for services to work effectively together to support autistic young people and their families when there is a risk of hospital admission was recognised in the NHS Long-term Plan (2019). This led to the development of Dynamic Support Registers (DSRs) and Care (Education) and Treatment reviews (C(E)TRs) [see Dynamic Support Register and Care (Education) and Treatment Review, Policy, and Guidance, 2023]. The 2023 guidance sets out an expectation that autistic people and/or people with learning disabilities should have access to a published process of how to self-refer to their local DSR. For CYP at increased risk of hospital admission, the DSR is a means of identifying and recording their needs whilst C(E)TRs are an independent meeting which will focus on their care and their treatment. The review will involve people independent of the provision of that young person's care, including experts by experience, as well as those who commission support and people working with the young person and their family. The level of risk, and related level of need, for the young person is shown using a RAG (Red/Amber/Green) rating, with red indicating an immediate risk of a hospital admission, amber identifying an immediate risk if there is not an intervention and green indicating 'some risk' if needs are not effectively managed. A separate blue rating is used to identify young people who have already been admitted to a hospital environment. Alongside the DSR, CYP identified as being at the highest risk will be allocated a key worker. A key worker is expected to have experience of working with young people identified as autistic and/or who have a learning disability. They work to help that young person, and their family, navigate the helping system, identify any barriers to them receiving support, and make sure that their voice is heard. Whilst a Key Worker brings an excellent source of support for a young person and their family, collaborative working with

CAMHS professionals and the Key Worker is essential to reduce the risk of families becoming confused about who is doing what, and why, and the potential of overburdening them with appointments and meetings.

Final thoughts, and a few requests

A lot has changed since I first began work in CAMHS, most significantly the level of demand and acuity, and the increasing numbers of autistic CYP who are requiring specialist mental health intervention due to self-harm, suicidal thoughts and behaviours, and high levels of distress. Whilst increasing awareness and diagnostic rates may account for why we are seeing more autistic children in CAMHS, as well as changes in awareness about autism and girls, this does not account for why the number of autistic young people accessing CAMHS is greater than the suspected prevalence of autism in the general population.

The increase in autistic CYP requiring mental health support requires all services across the THRIVE framework, not just those dedicated as specialist autism services, to take a neuro-inclusive approach, and for working with autistic young people to be everyone's business.

If you have read this chapter, I have a few final requests.

- Firstly, please don't see autism as somebody else's business in the same way I did 20 years ago. Autistic children, diagnosed or undiagnosed, access all services across the THRIVE framework from getting advice and getting help, to risk support.
- Learn about autism, not just specific techniques for working with autistic children, and adapt for, and with, the child that is in front of you. One approach will not suit all. Adapt and keep adapting.
- If you are commissioning or designing services, consider how early help offers include, or exclude, autistic children and their families. How can you make them inclusive so autistic children and their families can be given the early advice and support that might be needed to prevent an escalation of need or a crisis?
- Consider the journey to support for the child, young person, and their parents or carers. Have they had to fight to get to you? Have they felt blamed? Do they blame themselves? How many times have they had to tell their story before, or how many times have they felt their story was not heard?
- Work with colleagues with respect. Collaborate. Look for solutions. Be mindful of the challenges and restrictions on each of their organisations due to procedures, resources, and demand. Remember that the majority of us came into the caring professions because we care and want to help, and that the young people and families we work with need to feel that care.
- Importantly, remember that you will have colleagues, like Sarah, who have lived experience as parents, or as autistic professionals themselves. Think about the language that you use when you describe children, young people,

and their families. Autism is not just something other people work with. Autism is something that is very much a part of our lives, at home and in our families as well as with the children and families we work with.

Note

1 Now known as Children and Young People's Psychological Trainings (CYP PT).

References

Amaral, D. G., Bauman, M. D., & Mills Schumann, C. (2003). The amygdala and autism: Implications from non-human primate studies. *Genes, Brain and Behavior*, *2*(5), 295–302. https://doi.org/10.1034/j.1601-183x.2003.00043.x

Baron-Cohen, S. et al. (2000). The amygdala theory of autism. *Neuroscience & Biobehavioral Reviews*, *24*(3), 355–364. https://doi.org/10.1016/s0149-7634(00)00011-7

Bonney, A. (2020). *Canaries in the coal mine – gale*. Retrieved from: https://review.gale.com/2020/09/08/canaries-in-the-coal-mine/ (Accessed: 26 August 2023).

Ellins, J., Hocking, L., Al-Haboubi, M., Newbould, J., Fenton, S. J., Daniel, K., … Mays, N. (2023). Early evaluation of the children and young people's mental health Trailblazer programme: A rapid mixed-methods study. Retrieved from: https://pubmed.ncbi.nlm.nih.gov/37470109/ (Accessed: 26 August 2023).

Evans, M. (2023). *Culture shift in organisations part 2. The Myth of the autism specialist*. Retrieved from: https://www.youtube.com/watch?v=Abilwb17rHM

Evans-Wickens, M. (2021). *How do mothers of autistic girls perceive and experience the potential affordances and constraints of diagnosis for their daughters?* Retrieved from: https://uobrep.openrepository.com/handle/10547/625494 (Accessed: 26 August 2023).

Farr, J., Moore, A., Bruffell, H., Hayes, J., Rae, J. P., & Cooper, M. (2021). The impact of a needs-based model of care on accessibility and quality of care within children's mental health services: A qualitative investigation of the UK i-THRIVE Programme. *Child: Care, Health and Development*, *47*(4), 442–450. https://doi.org/10.1111/cch.12855

Flannery, K. A., & Wisner-Carlson, R. (2020). Autism and education. *Child and Adolescent Psychiatric Clinics*, *29*(2), 319–343. https://doi.org/10.1016/j.chc.2019.12.005

Greig, A., & MacKay, T. (2013). *The Homunculi approach to social and emotional wellbeing: A flexible CBT programme for young people on the autism spectrum or with emotional and behavioural difficulties*. London: Jessica Kingsley Publishers.

Moyse, R. (2021) *Missing: The autistic girls absent from Mainstream Secondary Schools, CentAUR*. Retrieved from: https://centaur.reading.ac.uk/97405/ (Accessed: 26 August 2023).

Murray, D. (2022) *Discussion paper on eugenics and Diversity, Monotropism*. Retrieved from: https://monotropism.org/dinah/eugenics/ (Accessed: 26 August 2023).

NHS. (2019). *The NHS long-term plan*. Retrieved from: https://www.longtermplan.nhs.uk/

NHS Digital. (2021). *Mental health of children and young people in England 2021*. Retrieved from: mhcyp_2021_rep.pdf (digital.nhs.uk)

Royal College of Paediatrics and Child Health (RCPCH). (2021). *Briefing: Children and young people's mental health*. Retrieved from: RCPCH briefing – children and young people's mental health_0.pdf

Sheerman, B. (2021). *Support surrounding diagnosis*. University of Bath. Retrieved from: https://www.bath.ac.uk/publications/resources-for-researchers-and-the-autism-community/attachments/support-surrounding-diagnosis.pdf (Accessed: 26 August 2023).

Tchanturia, K., Smith, K., Glennon, D., & Burhouse, A. (2020). Towards an improved understanding of the anorexia nervosa and autism spectrum comorbidity: PEACE pathway implementation. *Frontiers in Psychiatry*, *11*, 640. https://doi.org/10.3389/fpsyt.2020.00640

Wolpert, M., Harris, R., Hodges, S., Fuggle, P., James, R., Wiener, A., … Munk, S. (2019). *THRIVE Framework for system change*. London: CAMHS Press. Retrieved from: http://www.implementingthrive.org/wp-content/uploads/2019/03/THRIVE-Framework-for-system-change-2019.pdf

Wolpert, M., Harris, R., Jones, M., Hodges, S., Fuggle, P., James, R., Wiener, A., McKenna, C., Law, D., & Fonagy, P. (2014). *THRIVE: The AC – Tavistock Model for CAMHS*. Retrieved from: thrive-booklet_march-15.pdf (annafreud.org)

Wilson, F. (2015). Miner's Canary. *Autonomy, the Critical Journal of Interdisciplinary Autism Studies*, *1*(4).

Zalla, T., & Sperduti, M. (2013). The amygdala and the relevance detection theory of autism: An evolutionary perspective. *Frontiers in Human Neuroscience*, *7*. https://doi.org/10.3389/fnhum.2013.00894

Chapter 14

Supervisors as agents of change

Virginia Lumsden

Introduction

Supervisors have a vital role to play in developing the clinical expertise of psychological practitioners working with autistic children, young people, and their families, with the aim of ensuring psychologically informed, evidence-based, experience-sensitive care and support in a therapeutic context.

> Supervision is a joint endeavour in which a practitioner with the help of a supervisor, attends to their clients, themselves as part of their client practitioner relationships and the wider systemic context, and by doing so improves the quality of their work, transforms their client relationships, continuously develops themselves, their practice and the wider profession.
>
> Hawkins and Shohet (2012, p. 60)

It is assumed that supervisors will have a good understanding of the basic principles of clinical supervision of psychological practitioners. In particular, supervisors will be cognisant of the importance of developing psychological safety within supervision (Lee et al., 2022) as it is this belief that it is safe to take interpersonal risks (Edmondson, 1999) that creates the necessary conditions for supervision with the potential to effect meaningful change. In this chapter, several systemic concepts will be brought to life to demonstrate the way in which adopting a systemically informed approach to supervision has the potential to generate possibilities to support this process and promote the development of the '3 Cs'.

The systemic approach has its roots in family therapy (Stratton & Lask, 2013); however, adopting Burnham's (1992, p. 4) 'approach, method, technique' trichotomy presents the possibility of supervision being 'organised by systemic ideas but not designated as therapy'. This allows for the supervision of different therapeutic modalities to benefit from systemic approaches, for example, for cognitive behavioural therapy (CBT) to be offered to a child or young person in the context of understanding the system around the child, where resources may be located and how their potential may be realised.

DOI: 10.4324/9781003352327-20

Adopting a systemic approach in supervision ensures that relationships, interactions, and the wider system around the child or young person and family are integral to understanding experiences and creating opportunities for change. It allows for an understanding of problems as inherently relational (Bateson, 1972) and therefore, located in interactions between different parts of the system, or between different individuals in the system (e.g., Milton's 2012 'double-empathy' problem), rather than within an individual themselves. Ecological systems theory (Bronfenbrenner, 1979) ensures that consideration is given to the impact of wider social issues (e.g., poverty, racism, and inequality). By ensuring that 'the client is the expert' (Anderson & Goolishian, 1992), an 'experience-sensitive approach' (Pavlopoulou, 2021; Pavlopoulou & Dimitriou; 2019; Todres et al., 2009) is supported.

A systemic approach is also highly compatible with neurodiversity approaches (Dwyer, 2022) which frame the cognitive diversity that exists between individuals as natural, recognising that there are both individual strengths and challenges of neurodivergence and that challenges are not necessarily intrinsic to the individual, but created in the interaction between the individual and the environment. A systemic approach to supervision in combination with neurodiversity approaches promotes working in collaboration with the autistic child or young person, and their support network, to promote emotional well-being and mental health. Thus, the purpose of psychological therapy is not to 'address' or 'reduce' characteristics of autism; it is to collaborate in improving quality of life by identifying and building upon strengths and interests and addressing any specific difficulties that may be chosen by the child or young person. There is also explicit recognition and understanding of the way in which challenges and distress may arise out of living in a world that is predominantly governed by rules and norms created by non-autistic people. This is concordant with NICE guidelines (2013) which recommend interventions including those which 'aim to increase the parents', carers', teachers' or peers' understanding of, and sensitivity and responsiveness to, the child or young person's patterns of communication and interaction'. The role of the supervisor is, therefore, to support the supervisee to actively work to ensure that environmental adaptations and support are given as much consideration as any individual psychological approach.

The supervisor and supervisee as part of the system

It is essential that the supervisor and supervisee develop an understanding of themselves within the system/s in which they are working. A systemic approach offers up the concepts of first-order and second-order perspectives (Hoffman, 1985). From a first-order perspective, the psychological practitioner takes a position outside the family system, and from an 'expert position' conducts an assessment and then intervenes in a way which facilitates changes. This 'doing to' may be considered at odds with neurodiversity and experience-sensitive approaches because it places the child or young person and the family in a passive role, it can create a sense of powerlessness and stifles opportunities to facilitate greater understanding, particularly of lived experience.

From a second-order perspective, the psychological practitioner, and by association, the supervisor, are understood to be part of the therapeutic system and in this way working collaboratively with the child or young person and family as part of a system of both concern and mutual support. There is a recognition given to both distress and challenges at the same time as joys and strengths, and the way in which these are influenced by and have an influence upon the system within which the child or young person lives. There are multiple perspectives on problems and the system around them (Andersen, 1987) and this promotes collaboration and mutuality, with curiosity being fundamental (Cecchin, 1987). Thus, supervisors need to ensure that there is space in supervision to explore together how the practitioner may be influencing and perceiving the system, both personally and professionally, and to reflect upon power dynamics in the therapeutic process. This will support the practitioner to develop the capacity to work sensitively and meaningfully within a relational system rather than being 'outside' the system, and therefore, actively promoting collaborative ways of working with children, young people, and families.

Reflecting activity: facilitating a second-order perspective in supervision

The following types of questions may be used to elicit discussion from a second-order position in supervision. As a supervisor, you may choose to incorporate such questions as part of your ordinary supervisory practice, and/or you may choose to explicitly discuss first and second-order perspectives with a supervisee to explore in more depth some of the concepts discussed above. Either way, it will be helpful if the supervisee is encouraged to keep in mind a particular child or young person that the supervisee is currently working with.

- In the system around this child/young person, to whom do you feel closest? Why?
- What do you think the child/young person/family would say about their experience of working with you?
- During our supervision conversations, what has been most helpful/unhelpful? Has anything surprised you?

Lanes of learning: mapping your journey

A second-order perspective brings to the fore the importance of self-reflexivity (Burnham, 1986) which is the process of evaluating and observing the effects of one's therapeutic practice in the context of one's own beliefs and percep-tions. When working with autistic CYP, it is essential to understand and rec-ognise one's own beliefs, perceptions, values, and assumptions and how these might influence practice. It is recognised that there is currently a significant shift taking place in how autism is understood e.g., moving from a deficit-based approach to an approach that values neurodivergence and recognises both strengths and needs and the interrelationship between the individual and the environment. Psychological practitioners and supervisors will each have an evolving understanding of autism which will be influenced by professional experience (e.g., working therapeutically, training, organisational policy); personal experience (e.g., having an autistic family member); and social and cultural representations. These experiences will likely be in some ways con-flicting and will benefit from exploration with curiosity.

Vetere et al. (2016) write about the importance of reflecting upon your own 'professional ancestry' – that is understanding the historical sequence of the different influences on your professional development over time and including personal/professional influences such as educators and supervisors; key theoreticians; and 'general perspectives that shaped your understanding of yourself as a human being and your relationship to the world around you' (p. 4). 'Lanes of Learning' (see Table 14.1) provides a framework for mapping one's learning journey and understanding the interrelationship between differ-ent personal and professional influences over time. Inspired by Vetere et al., it has been developed to explicitly include personal lived experience (e.g., being autistic and/or having an autistic family member), professional lived experience (e.g., learning from autistic individuals in the therapy process), and social and cultural representations in the widest sense. It is intended to be completed with a specific professional focus (e.g., working with autistic CYP). It is a useful exercise for both supervisors and supervisees to develop an understanding of one's own learning, the interrelationship between learn-ing experiences, implications for practice, and hopes for future learning and practice in order to promote openness to continued learning.

Reflecting activity: lanes of learning: mapping your journey

Table 14.1 can be used as a template for mapping influences on learning over time. The template is provided as a suggested framework to facilitate a pro-cess of reflecting on learning, and in introducing this activity it is important to create a context where there are no right or wrong ways to use the template, and where the individual remains in control of what information is shared and not shared. Individuals may choose to write and/or draw, utilise different colours, to make visual representations of the relationships between different learning experiences (e.g., with lines or arrows), and annotate experiences with specific reflections.

Table 14.1 Lanes of learning: mapping your journey

Social/cultural influences	
(e.g., social media)	
People	
(e.g., colleagues, lecturers)	
Academic learning	
Professional lived experience[a]	
(e.g., working with autistic children)	
Personal lived experience	
(e.g., living with an autistic family member)	

Time

Earliest experience   Present day

[a] Professional focus: e.g., leadership, working with children, eating disorders.

Guidelines for completing the activity:

1 Populate the diagram with significant experiences that have contributed to your understanding of working with CYP with autism, using each lane as a prompt.

2 Reflect upon and discuss what has been noted so far. The following questions can be used as a prompt:

   a What have you learnt from your different experiences?
   b How do your different learning experiences relate to one another? In what ways are they complementary/contradictory?
   c Do you consider some experiences to be more valuable/more important than others? Why?

3 Consider how your learning about learning might influence your practice. The following questions can be used as a prompt:

   a What stands out to you the most in doing this activity?
   b What are the implications for your practice?
   c What was your experience of doing this activity?

You may wish to visually represent guidelines 2 and 3 on your diagram.

The supervisor has an important role to play in both promoting the psychological safety required to engage in this activity and in supporting the psychological practitioner to consider implications for practice and any additional learning that would be beneficial. It is possible that this activity may give rise to some difficult and/or uncomfortable feelings and reflections. For example, in developing a greater understanding of how autism presents in girls, a practitioner may realise that in previous work, the needs of an autistic girl were not fully recognised and understood. This is almost inevitable as one learns better ways of working, but the inevitability should not mean that the impact of this is overlooked. If supervisors are to be agents of change, then supervisors need to endeavour to co-create a supervision space where these experiences can be reflected upon in a way that promotes openness to continued learning and development, rather than defensiveness. Additionally, it may be that the practitioner is working in environments and/or with individuals whose beliefs conflict with neurodiversity approaches. For example, hearing a colleague referring to autism as a disorder or expressing an assumption that autistic children cannot show empathy. In this instance, the supervisor can support the practitioner to navigate these situations in ways that enable the practitioner to feel able to challenge the views of others but from an empathic and curious position. Hopefully, in developing an understanding of one's own 'Lanes of Learning', supervisors and supervisees can reflect upon some of the challenges in the learning journey so far and how these were overcome, at the same time as reflecting upon the times of joy, connection, and deep learning with like-minded individuals. The capacity for self-reflexivity becomes part of good reflective practice. As Socrates said, 'To know thyself is the beginning of wisdom' and implicit in this is the importance of knowing what you do not know, what you need to learn, and from whom you might learn. This is as important for supervisors as it is for supervisees, and it is hoped that as psychological practitioners themselves, supervisors will role model this for others.

Domains of supervision action

Supervisors will be familiar with the tensions between the different functions of supervision, some of which will also be influenced to a greater or lesser extent by organisational influences (e.g., the extent to which clinical supervision is valued by organisational leadership, whether managerial supervision is combined with clinical supervision and/or whether supervision is carried out by external services/agencies). With these tensions in mind, Lang et al.'s (1990) 'domains of action' is a useful concept to understand the different sorts of conversations that might take place in supervision and the different ways these conversations may influence practice. Lang et al. observe that professional roles and organisational context mean that professionals are sometimes required to adopt a particular posture as defined by professional role (e.g., responding to risk, ensuring that clinical notes meet organisational standards), and at other times, may adopt a posture of curiosity (e.g., whilst meeting with a family for therapy). Lang et al. take Maturana's (1985) domains of aesthetics, production, and explanation and apply these to professional practice (Figure 14.1).

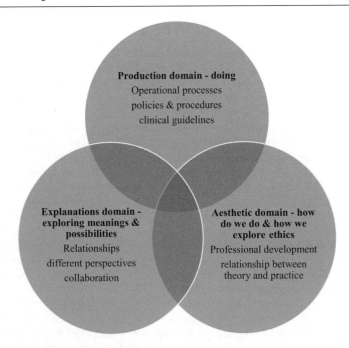

Figure 14.1 Domains of action (Lang et al., 1990).

The aesthetic domain

The aesthetic domain is concerned with the ethical dimensions of practice: "As professionals we learn, not only theory and new technologies but we also learn a form of consciousness. We learn a way of managing the relationship between, and implications for each other, of our theory, practice, and ethical position" (Lang et al., p. 44). Within this domain, there is attention to the relationship between theory and practice and recognition that "practice and theory are constantly in a process of modifying and developing each other" (p. 45) and that how a professional navigates the relationship between theory and practice will be informed by consciousness about one's own morals and ethics.

The productive domain

Within the domain of production, the professional is using professional knowledge to carry out tasks "according to the conventions which are required by the context of their profession and the agency in which they operate" (Lang et al., 1990, p. 47). This might include activities such as following organisational risk management processes, using routine outcome measures, and caseload management and audit. In the productive domain, there is a recognition of the value of "the rules that hold these things together" (Lang et al., 1990, p. 46) at the same time as an appreciation that professional creativity is required to ensure that professional conventions are enacted in a way that respects the recursive relationship between theory, practice, and ethics.

The explanations domain

The explanations domain is the domain in which there is a search for different stories, multiple perspectives, and different meanings that will facilitate change, through a position of curiosity (Cecchin, 1987). This domain is most closely related to therapy; however, working in the explanations domain and adopting a curious stance in collaboration with others is not limited to therapy and can be relevant to other activities such as organisational development, and of course, supervision. According to Lang et al. (1990) in contrast to the productive domain, where some stories are given a privileged position according to social and cultural conventions, in the explanations domain a posture (Tomm, 1984) of neutrality (Selvini et al., 1980) is adopted and this work is collaborative.

There are many ways to scaffold conversations in the explanations domain. This may be by supporting the supervisee to develop an understanding of the child or young person and family context using genograms as a visual representation of the system. Through the explanations domain, the value of extending the exercise beyond the family unit (e.g., to include places of significance and significant people outside the family unit and even pets) is recognised. Thus, it is possible to see that by working in this domain of supervision, creates possibilities for developing a greater understanding of the presenting difficulties and possible solutions. Another useful approach in this domain is the use of the "W" question: "Who wants what for whom?" (Fredman & Rapaport, 2018). These questions seek to understand different perspectives, for example, to recognise that so-called 'challenging behaviour' may not be challenging for everyone, and to ensure that the child or young person's voice is heard. Finally, the dimensions of humanising healthcare (Pavlopoulou, 2021; Todres et al., 2009) (see Table 14.2) could be used to guide experience-sensitive psychological practice and discussion in supervision.

The interrelationship of domains in a supervisory context

Lang et al. (1990, p. 51) state that "we exist in all three domains simultaneously". An understanding of the three domains and which domain may be the highest context marker for a particular episode of work can be useful in guiding a process in both therapeutic practice and supervision, with a reflection on whether the dominant domain is in the best interests of the child or young person.

Table 14.2 Dimensions of a humanising lifeworld framework adapted for psychological practitioners

Dimension	Meaning	Question/s
Insiderness	Understanding what autism means to the child or young person you are working with, from the child or young person's perspective, recognising that autism is a unique experience for each individual.	How are you developing a sense of what the child or young person's individual experience of autism is? What could support this further?
Agency	Promoting the child or young person's agency in the therapeutic process through collaboration.	How are you ensuring that the child or young person is actively involved in shaping the therapeutic process? How can the child or young person give feedback?
Uniqueness	Autistic children and young people are unique in many ways that go beyond autism.	How are you developing an understanding of the way in which the child or young person is unique? Who and what is important to this child or young person? What strengths and qualities does this young person have?
Togetherness	Relationships are important to autistic children and young people.	Who is important to the child or young person? How and why is this person/are these people important? How can this person/these people support/be included in the therapeutic process?
Sense-making	The sense that autistic children and young people make of their experiences is important.	What sense has the child or young person made of their experiences so far (e.g., of family, school)? How can the therapeutic process support sense-making?
Personal journey	Autistic children and young people's personal journeys through life are important.	What do you know about the child or young person's journey so far? How can the therapeutic process support a meaningful personal journey?

(Continued)

Table 14.2 (Continued)

Dimension	Meaning	Question/s
Sense of place	Autistic children and young people should feel safe, welcome, and at ease. They should have a sense of belonging (e.g., at home, at school).	How can you support the child or young person to feel safe, welcome, and at ease when attending sessions? What do you know about the child or young person's experience of different places? How can the therapeutic process support a sense of belonging in these places?
Embodiment	Understanding the way the mind and body work and the mind–body connection is important to autistic children and young people.	What do you know about how the child or young person experiences their mind and body? (e.g., what are their sensory preferences). How can the therapeutic process support the child or young person to understand their own mind and body?

Fredman (2014) talks about the importance of "centring the client" and highlights the ways in which pressures such as time, limited resources, recruitment and waiting lists can lead to communication about CYP that is objectifying and depersonalising. It is important to consider how the current context may lead to a risk that the production domain is focused on to the detriment of realising the potential for experience-sensitive care that exists when conversations take place in the other domains. For example, through the aesthetic domain, it is possible to explore in supervision how to understand evidence-based practice (production domain), in the context of working with autistic CYP. The aesthetic domain facilitates an understanding of how neurodiversity approaches are facilitating a changing narrative about autism and the importance of applying critical thinking to the evidence base when considering the application of theory to practice. This supports an understanding of some of the biases and assumptions that may have informed research and so-called clinical expertise, and recognition of the value of co-produced research with the neurodiversity paradigm. At the same time, the explanations domain prompts the collaborative exploration of different possibilities. Working in the explanations domain, with the evidence base in mind, is to recognise that person-centred, collaborative practice is in and of itself

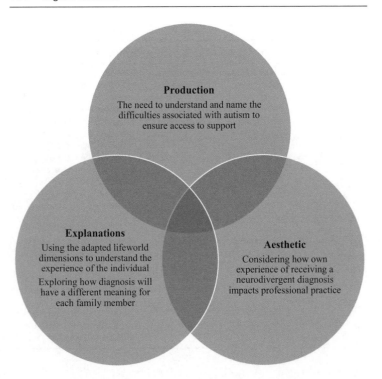

Figure 14.2 Domains of action in action: working with a family following an autism diagnosis.

evidence-based, and thus to seek to understand the individual's own experience. Indeed, conversations and decisions about which domain may be most useful fall within the aesthetic domain and as Lang et al. (p. 44) point out: "Theory, practice, ethics and a form of consciousness are in a recursive relationship with each other". See Figures 14.2 and 14.3 for examples.

Reflecting activity: discussing domains of action

Firstly, introduce the concept of domains of action in supervision. Figure 14.1 can be used to support this. Then choose a recent conversation in supervision about a child or young person upon which to reflect. The following questions may be a useful prompt:

- In which domain/s have discussions in supervision about this child or young person been located?

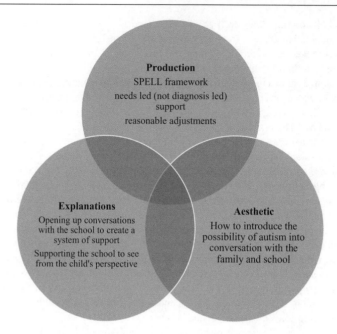

Figure 14.3 Domains of action in action: sharing a psychological formulation with the school to develop a shared understanding of a child's needs.

- How might this have influenced the discussions?
- Is there a domain where more discussion could usefully take place?

Try out discussions in a different domain and reflect on the impact of these.

This activity could be extended to consider how the domains of production could be applied to understanding the therapeutic process. For example, when working with a child or young person and/or the system around the child, in which domain/s do conversations take place? What is the impact of this? How could discussions in different domains impact the therapeutic process/ outcomes for this child or young person?

Illustrative example

Context: Amy and her ten-year-old daughter, Jessica, are attending an early intervention psychology service due to Amy's concerns about Jessica complaining of 'tummy aches' before school, feeling left out of her friendship group, and having increased numbers of 'outbursts' at home. Jessica's teacher has reported that there are no difficulties observed at school. Jessica is hard-working, doing well academically and is part of a friendship group although often chooses to 'do her own thing' at lunchtime. Through the process of assessment and formulation, the psychological practitioner and supervisor hypothesised that Jessica may be autistic.

Conversations in the domains of action: Discussion in the *aesthetic domain* supported the psychological practitioner to share worries about discussing the possibility of autism with the family and about sharing a formulation with the school. The practitioner and the supervisor were able to reflect upon the importance of transparency and a commitment to having potentially difficult conversations as part of being an ethical practitioner. In the *explanations domain*, consideration was given to questions such as 'Why are the family seeking help now?' and it was hypothesised that Jessica was beginning to struggle with friendships as the demands of a friendship group change over time, in line with the social and emotional development of her peer group. The practitioner was encouraged to seek to understand Jessica's own unique experience of school. Consideration was also given to the meaning that Amy and Jessica might make of the possibility of Jessica being autistic. In the *productive domain*, conversations took place in supervision about how to go about sharing a psychological formulation, how to encourage conversations in the explanations domain with the school, and how to link this to possible practical reasonable adjustments for Jessica in school.

Outcomes: There were positive outcomes for Amy and Jessica with both giving feedback that they had appreciated feeling listened to and having their concerns taken seriously. Jessica felt empowered by the opportunity to share her understanding of her difficulties with school and reported that the changes that were being put in place were already making a difference.

Supervisees as agents of change

It is hoped that the concepts and activities shared in this chapter demonstrate the way in which a systemic approach to supervision promotes the '3 Cs' – collaboration, curiosity, and openness to continued learning, in therapeutic practice. Thus, supervisors and supervisees embrace their roles as part of the systems of concern and support around autistic children, young people and their families, and support children, young people, and their families to be empowered to create positive, meaningful change in their lives. It is also hoped that supervisors will recognise the value of practitioners being supported to promote positive change in the system, for example, through advocating for practical changes and challenging deficit-based narratives about autism from a place of genuine understanding. Of course, it is hoped that over time, supervisors who are agents of change will support supervisees to also become agents of change (who will hopefully in time become supervisors themselves). There is space for many agents of change who practise with curiosity, collaboration, and openness to continued learning, appreciating the moral and ethical dimensions of this work, and recognising that: "Creativity involves making choices about how you enact your role in the context in which the task needs to be carried out" (Lang et al., 1990, p. 48).

With thanks to Rahul Balaji, Rebecca Chin, Megan Cork, and Meghan Hosch who reflected upon their personal and professional lived experience, academic and other learning, to support the development of 'Lanes of Learning'.

References

Andersen, T. (1987). The reflecting team: Dialogue and meta-dialogue in clinical work. *Family Process, 26*(4), 415–428. https://doi.org/10.1111/j.1545-5300.1987.00415.x

Anderson, H., & Goolishian, H. (1992). The client is the expert: A not-knowing approach to therapy. In S. McNamee & K. J. Gergen (Eds.), *Therapy as social construction* (pp. 25–39). New York: Sage Publications, Inc.

Bateson, G. (1972). *Steps to an ecology of mind: Mind and nature.* New York: Ballantine Books.

Bronfenbrenner, U. (1979). *The ecology of human development: Experiments by nature and design.* Cambridge, MA: Harvard University Press.

Burnham, J. (1992). Approach-method-technique: Making distinctions and creating connections. *Human Systems, 3*(1), 3–26.

Burnham, J. B. (1986). *Family therapy: First steps towards a systemic approach.* London: Tavistock.

Cecchin, G. (1987). Hypothesising, circularity, and neutrality revisited: An invitation to curiosity. *Family Process, 26*(4): 405–413.

Dwyer, P. (2022). The neurodiversity approach (es): What are they and what do they mean for researchers? *Human Development, 66*(2), 73–92. https://doi.org/10.1159/000523723

Edmondson, A. (1999). Psychological safety and learning behavior in work teams. *Administrative Science Quarterly, 44*(2), 350–383.

Fredman, G. (2014). Weaving net-works of hope with families, practitioners and communities: Inspirations from systemic and narrative approaches. *Australian and New Zealand Journal of Family Therapy, 35*(1), 54–71. https://doi.org/10.1002/anzf.1044

Fredman, G., & Rapaport, P. (2018). How do we begin? Working with older people and their significant systems. In *Being with older people* (pp. 31–59). London: Routledge.

Hawkins, P., & Shohet, R. (2012). *Supervision in the helping professions* (4th edition). Maidenhead: Open University Press.

Hoffman, L. (1985). Beyond power and control: Toward a "second order" family systems therapy. *Family Systems Medicine, 3*(4), 381–396. https://psycnet.apa.org/doi/10.1037/h0089674

Lang, P., Little, M., & Cronen, V. (1990). The systemic professional: Domains of action and the question of neutrality. *Human Systems, 1*(1), 34–49.

Lee, E. H., Pitts, S., Pignataro, S., Newman, L. R., & D'Angelo, E. J. (2022). Establishing psychological safety in clinical supervision: Multi-professional perspectives. *The Clinical Teacher, 19*(2), 71–78.

Maturana, H. (1985). *Oxford conversations*. In Conference jointly organised by the Kensington Consultation Centre, London, The Family Institute, Cardiff and the Charles Burns Clinic, Birmingham.

Milton, D. E. (2012). On the ontological status of autism: The 'double empathy problem'. *Disability & Society, 27*(6), 883–887.

NICE CG170. (2013). Autism: The management and support of children and young people on the autism spectrum. *BMJ, 100*(1), 20–23.

Pavlopoulou, G. (2021). A good night's sleep: Learning about sleep from autistic adolescents' personal accounts. *Frontiers in Psychology, 11*, 3597. https://doi.org/10.3389/fpsyg.2020.583868

Pavlopoulou, G., & Dimitriou, D. (2019). 'I don't live with autism; I live with my sister'. Sisters' accounts on growing up with their preverbal autistic siblings. *Research in Developmental Disabilities, 88*, 1–15. https://doi.org/10.1016/j.ridd.2019.01.013

Selvini, M. P., Boscolo, L., Cecchin, G., & Prata, G. (1980). Hypothesizing—circularity—neutrality: Three guidelines for the conductor of the session. *Family Process, 19*(1), 3–12. https://doi.org/10.1111/j.1545-5300.1980.00003.x

Stratton, P., & Lask, J. (2013). The development of systemic family therapy for changing times in the United Kingdom. *Contemporary Family Therapy, 35*(2), 257–274.

Todres, L., Galvin, K. T., & Holloway, I. (2009). The humanization of healthcare: A value framework for qualitative research. *International Journal of Qualitative Studies on Health and Well-Being, 4*(2), 68–77. https://doi.org/10.1007/s10591-013-9252-8

Tomm, K. (1984). One perspective on the Milan systemic approach: Part II. Description of session format, interviewing style and interventions. *Journal of Marital and Family Therapy, 10*(3), 253–271. https://doi.org/10.1111/j.1752-0606.1984.tb00016.x

Vetere, A., & Stratton, P. (Eds.). (2016). *Interacting selves: Systemic solutions for personal and professional development in counselling and psychotherapy*. New York: Routledge.

Chapter 15

Working towards a neurodiversity-informed service for CYP

Russell Hurn, Laura Crane, Maciej Matejko, Tiegan Boyens, Catherine Asta, Damian Milton, and Georgia Pavlopoulou

Learning from autistic CYP through curiosity, connection, and agency

Mental health services for children, young people (CYP) have, for many years, struggled with inadequate resources in terms of funding and staffing to meet rising referral rates, often relying on the development and expansion of social enterprises and charities in the voluntary sector to try to cater for the deficits of provision from statutory services. The UK Government has committed to reforming CYP mental health services with papers like Future in Mind (2015) and the Five Year Forward View of Mental Health (2016), which called for more integrated and collaborative multi-agency working to build a network of support around CYP and families.

Models like i-THRIVE (Wolpert et al., 2019) have challenged long-standing approaches to providing mental health care which focus on levels of intervention, leading up from primary (GP) care, through early intervention teams, to Child and Adolescent Mental Health Service (CAMHS) community teams and on to in-patient services, and instead to propose a shared approach for supporting CYP throughout communities. One could argue that such ideas challenge the individualistic 'I' culture of the Western world to adopt a more 'We'-centred approach that is often associated with more collectivist cultures. One may question, however, whether the move to 'we' is maybe more a cost-saving strategy than one that truly embraces the togetherness of all people; a debate that may be beyond the scope of this chapter, but is worth reflecting on, nonetheless.

In light of these driving papers, Workforce Development programmes have been commissioned to train new therapists to work directly with CYP (Ludlow et al., 2020). These programmes, originally commissioned to upskill CAMHS workers, have been developed to promote the recruitment and retention of new staff. They have tried to support the growth and transformation of existing services by promoting the five pillars of (i) Evidence-based

DOI: 10.4324/9781003352327-21

Practice, (ii) Collaborative Working, (iii) Accountability, (iv) Accessibility, and (v) Reducing Stigma/raising awareness around mental health problems. Yet this has been an uphill battle against engrained service cultures and historic practices. It is against this backdrop that we have turned our attention to the lost plight of autistic CYP.

Good neuro-affirming practice is everyone's business – not just the 'autism' expert in the service. In Chapter 3, Ann Memmott described the current status of services for CYP and suggested areas for improvement. These suggestions include professional development and training from autistic trainers for all staff members, considering the environment and accessibility of services, and working towards collaborative goals. Such suggestions seem basic and obvious and yet some CAMHS services fail, on a regular basis, to put these principles into practice for autistic people CYP. There appears to be a barrier holding current provision of mental health support back from reaching the ideal provision towards which we aspire. This barrier is fortified by historical deficit-based thinking embedded in organisational culture. A failure of clear direction from NICE and lack of training around neurodiversity (and/or training focused on deficit-based thinking and outdated resources), adds further layers of challenge. This barrier is not impenetrable but needs to be highlighted so we can overcome it.

We know that autistic CYP experience the world in a way that many professionals view as defective and in need of intervention. Current service provision is therefore problematic: it is deficit-focused and highly disrespectful to the many strengths the CYP may have, with CYP hiding their autistic characteristics in an attempt to fit into the neurotypical world. We have explored this tension throughout this book, starting with Amy Pearson's call to shift from prevailing deficit-focused narratives and consider individual experiences, through to Kieran Rose's reflections on the devastating impact of masking, and Jon Adams' passionate writings about his experience of trauma and the treatment he received.

It is important to emphasise that services have a duty not to change the person to fit what they offer but to mould their service and interventions around the shoulders of the CYP they are working with. As noted in Ros and Kieran's chapter, this change comes from a paradigm shift in the minds of professionals and subsequently the services they work in.

While we may not have all the answers, the important question to keep asking is: **without the right curiosity, how can we begin to learn what we do not know?** When we engage with clients to build a therapeutic relationship, we do so by meeting them where they are currently. The therapy then evolves into a relationship that is built on trust, acceptance, and a genuine positive regard for the CYP, whatever their presentation or back story may be. Yet this may not be the current experience of service for many autistic CYP.

Our curiosity as therapists can only serve the therapeutic process if we have established the right environment for meaningful conversations. This context is fundamental for the healing professions and the building of the therapeutic relationship is a common factor for successful psychotherapy. Many theories explore the support that arises from the actions of the therapist in forming a connection with a CYP in a session. These theories stem from the work of Anna Freud in the 1940s (Midgley, 2022) to Bordin (1979) identifying the concepts of tasks, bonds, and goals as components of the 'Working Alliance' between people. Subsequent papers identified the role of the relationship and its impact on therapeutic outcomes (e.g., Lambert et al., 1994), or how the inviting, open disposition of the therapist helps to build a mutually involved encounter that is caring, fun, and has a purpose for the CYP (e.g., Núñez et al., 2021). There are many ways to consider how to promote the best working alliance. Dan Hughes has adopted such an approach within Dyadic Developmental Psychotherapy (2017), emphasising the need for a playful, accepting, curious, and empathic (PACE) approach to therapy with the aim of promoting a sense of safety, affect regulation, and meaning for the client. Similarly, in terms of polyvagal theory, therapists can use the theory of neuroception to consider the safety of the encounter and to focus internally (on what is happening within, either themselves or their client) but also on what is happening externally, in the room (the environment and relationship). The therapists' awareness of these three areas is essential to support a strong working relationship, which will hold the emotional material brought by the client. These ideas may seem simple and fundamental, but for many the therapeutic relationship may still suffer due to issues with double empathy (see Chapter 1).

In 2018, Sweeney et al. developed a model of Trauma-Informed Practice. There were no groundbreaking revelations in this model, but a simple fundamental underlying principle: that we should be concerned with asking 'what happened to' our client (their story) rather than focusing on a medicalised view of 'what is wrong with them?'. Whilst answering questions about *what happened* may be nonspecific, the idea behind this – for a neurodiversity-informed approach – is to understand and appreciate how the individual *makes sense of their experiences*. This simple shift allows for professionals to stay curious and person-centred, to uncover the content and meaning of a client's story, and to act within this shared understanding. As such, clients are supported in the way they need, rather than offering a predetermined care package. This approach requires therapists to truly listen to their client's story: it is not a document or list of facts but something that has been lived and experienced.

For an autistic client who may have experienced a very unsafe world on their journey to the therapy room, this initial connection requires not only physical and emotional safety but also psychological safety in the person the CYP is communicating with. Trusting the person will come before trust in the therapeutic process. Crucially, therapists must invest time and effort to ensure understanding and steer away from the pitfalls of projecting professional biases onto the autistic person with quick interpretations or lack of thought for the intervention (Milton, 2016).

It is important to consider what makes autistic people feel 'more human' or 'less human' when engaged with systems and interactions. McGreevy et al. (2024), inspired by Todres (2009), propose an experience-sensitive approach to understanding autistic young people in clinical services. Every autistic person is different, and therefore any talking therapy will need to adapt around the individual to address social communication and sensory preferences and needs, information processing styles, and differences in describing internal states. It means working from the understanding that neurodiversity is part of our human diversity, and being accommodating and responsive to individual experiences and needs – adapting OUR way of working to create an environment that works for the autistic individual. There is no manual for adaptations and NICE guidance offers only a few suggestions. So how do we do it?

There are eight ways of relating to and understanding the autistic person in a dignified, sensitive personalised approach to care through exploring and understanding the uniqueness of the CYP, their story, and their role in working towards change. This is an adaptation of the articulation of eight bipolar dimensions that describe what constitutes health and social care processes and interactions that are 'humanising' or 'dehumanising' as summarised in Figure 15.1 below.

An autistic CYP may not really feel seen and understood by anyone. Teachers may be focusing on 'underachievement', low grades, 'laziness', or 'being distracted'. Peers may focus on their differences from others in a

Figure 15.1 Adopting an experience-sensitive approach to care (McGreevy et al., 2024).

negative way. Mental health professionals may see them mostly through the lens of deficit-oriented theories they had been taught at university and, for instance, assume they are to blame when misunderstandings happen or that they are unable to engage in relationships in different ways.

Really listening to the stories of autistic client means hearing, connecting, accepting, and trying to understand what has been said from their perspective. Most therapists would likely confirm this, but despite knowing this, it can be difficult to ensure this is always how we present in a room with a client. Excessive demands, work stress, family stress, and many other factors can contribute to the way we are in the room. Professionals must remember that it is an honour to be able to hear someone's story. It is a precious gift that a client bestows and if one is not truly present then important clinical material can be missed and professionals are being disrespectful to clients. It's crucial to first listen to what the CYP has to say about their struggles, to be understanding of their perspective and background. Diagnostic labels can be useful as long as they don't obscure the view of the human before you. Shifting practice from looking at autistic behaviour to understanding someone's experience of distress fits within a neuro-inclusive approach, by supporting well-being from a humanistic view and echos the critiques of the neurodiversity paradigm in current policy and practice as expressed in many behaviourally oriented clinical competencies, e.g., PBS Clinical Competence Framework (2015) as mentioned by McGreevy et al. (2024).

Sometimes autistic people meet therapists who have an idea about adaptations and are keen to offer them – they may use something that their service reinforces or something another autistic patient taught them. But does that work for your patient? Is the way you are conducting a session the best possible way for that person to engage? How would you know that without asking?

Do they need: – you to write things down? – to write things down themselves? – visual support?

Could they benefit from being able to engage in an activity of their choice at the same time (drawing, painting, walking)?

Could they benefit from recording the session? Finding ways of integrating their passions and focused interests into the session can also be very helpful. If a person has a particular passion or focused interest, work with them to integrate this into sessions. This can help build the relationship and support a person's engagement if done meaningfully and respectfully.

Ask what would help them verbalise (or express in alternative ways) what they want to say. Can they use voice devices? Type? Remember many autistic people are situationally mute or may simply find it easier to engage in authentic communication in alternative ways, e.g. they may prefer an agenda before each session made up of bullet points pulled together by them or they may express themselves through art, poetry, written word – consider how you can incorporate this in your session. Another example is that they may process things after the session – journaling and emailing thoughts might help too. Create a system that supports people to make the best use of sessions and be explicit about how and when they can share these with you. Additionally, they may be feeling overwhelmed and less able to talk or form a sentence. Create a sense of certainty and structure in your sessions. Other examples of an experience-sensitive approach may include providing clear, concise, and specific information about what to expect from your service and sessions before therapy starts and having regular check-ins to ensure things are working and remember that communication and sensory preferences may change over time.

Working towards a neuro-informed model for practice

The aforementioned Trauma-Informed Practice model (Sweeney et al., 2018) offers a framework for considering the key elements for service provision and design by bringing the language, understanding and commitment to trauma work into every aspect of mental health care (from supervision to peer support). As such, this model enables greater cross-agency working. Similarly, McGreevy et al. (2024) invite us to think of eight dimensions of a coherent 'humanising' framework that can be easily translated into everyday vocabularies and practices (see also Chapter 1). We can now consider developing something similar: to incorporate the key elements of the preceding chapters into a shared understanding, language, and commitment to providing wrap-around, accessible, and effective services for autistic CYPs when accessing mental health support. We therefore propose a model of Neuro-Informed Practice, with Figure 15.2 reflecting the many elements that may be integrated into service design and delivery to ensure a more neuro-affirmative approach to providing mental health care for autistic CYP.

The elements in Figure 15.2 below represent the lenses through which we see our provision of services, the *space* we provide, in which effective collaborative working relationships can be formed and developed as well as the *approaches* that define the underlying processes and driving beliefs of a system to support autistic CYP. All sections rely on each other to produce positive outcomes and the greater the overlaps that there are between these elements the more neuro-informed that services are likely to be (see Figure 15.3 below). Next, we explore each of the two lenses in more detail, aiming to bring them more into focus for our readers.

The space and the approaches

The space

Safety

Above everything, safety is the fundamental principle of therapy. Whether this is considered in terms of having safeguarding principles in mind to

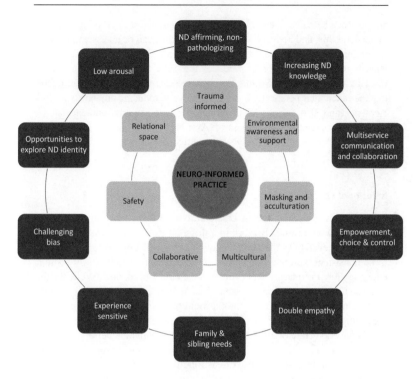

Figure 15.2 Neuro-informed practice.

protect the client or providing a low arousal state in which the client's autonomic nervous system is in a state of connection, safety is key. The client should feel welcomed and unjudged, able to feel a sense of ease to remain within their window of tolerance (Ogden et al., 2006), and securely anchored in the relationship space. Previous chapters have explored this topic from the perspectives of the CYP, family, and therapist, with the aim of recognising that therapy is the "intentional use of a safe and supportive relationship to foster clinical growth" (Kase, 2023, p. 46).

Environmental awareness

The development of safety within a therapy setting originates from an awareness of the importance of the environment. We all exist in an environment both physically and psychologically. We can create an internal sense of safety at times by imagining somewhere calming and evoking the same physiological reactions as if we are in that place physically. Our sense of safety is based on our neuroception and evaluation of our surroundings. Therapy will depend on the space being conducive to a calm and regulated state. Having someone understand this, and actively work to produce this, can be an essential part of determining the therapeutic relationship. We can therefore not assume that what is inherently safe for us produces the same felt sense for our clients. Instead, we must remain curious. As such, we can work alongside our clients to experience their perspective, to be proactive in reducing any harsh sensory elements, and also curious to ask about things in the environment that we may have no conscious awareness of. Ann Memmott's chapter gives a clear example of this issue from Carly's perspective, as she attended a care review meeting.

Relational space

This space is something that is created. Some of us worked in NHS teams where they would routinely work in a different room every session with clients. We believed back then that the therapist was the only factor that needed to be consistent, and that this person could moderate the change of room at every session. For many clients, this was the case, but for autistic clients, this was often not enough, and the space was as important as the person facing them. This relationship space is not a room but a microenvironment that we are asking someone to experience for an hour a week. A child entering a space in a heightened state of arousal is looking for potential danger around them, as well as between them and the therapist. A therapist has the role of providing this space and the responsibility of ensuring that it remains consistent across sessions. Chapter 4 by Ruth and Ellie asks us to consider how to best create safety in predictability and avoid last-minute changes. For example, changing the lighting to suit each client or ensuring certain toys or pictures is either available or removed. This does mean more effort on behalf of the therapist, but it also shows a willingness to value and respect the client with whom you are working. Ensuring that the environment around and between us is safe leads to a greater sense of safety within us.

Opportunities to explore identity

The CYP who are able to sit in a safe place with the therapist may still have to overcome the fear of exploring themselves. The expectations, biases, and negative responses of others may have shaped their identity, as described in Chapter 5 by Kieran Rose and Julia Avnon. Each child comes with a story or narrative about themselves and the world. Feeling safe within yourself and being able to express the uniqueness of your identity in a world that labels and is discriminatory is a major undertaking. We often talk about the importance of 'you be you' in the world. The authors here appreciate the simplicity of this statement and yet how hard is it to truly be yourself when the world sets limits and expectations around how you should behave to fit in with society. Amy Pearson's chapter expands further on this idea of reframing from the deficit contained in an identity label to an accepting affirming sense of self. The safety of the therapeutic relationship is fundamental to being able to get anywhere near a true sense of self-identity and for young people this may be a unique experience and one that should be taken with due consideration and respect. Exploration of identity also requires that the therapist adopts a multicultural, multigender, multicharacteristic, and Intersectional approach.

Multicultural stance

Venessa Bobb-Swaby in Chapter 7 describes the barriers and biases that she encountered for her and her family when trying to access support due to a lack of cultural awareness. A multicultural stance relies on respect and curiosity about difference. Whilst therapists cannot know every aspect of every culture nor fully understand the lived experience, there is the requirement to start from a stance of humility and curiosity to learn, in order to constantly reflect and facilitate conversations about cultural difference. Therapists should embrace the opportunities for these moments of discovery and be prepared to learn and feel uncomfortable as they face and challenge their own biases and assumptions which otherwise would have influenced or determined their interactions and intervention. There is a sense that therapists need to acquire cultural competency, which implies a standard of knowing where learning ceases when deemed competent. However, generating a safe place is about the opportunity to explore the client's perspective, and show interest and respect in the components of their identity throughout your work with them (Davis et al., 2018; Milton, 2014). Therapists will also be required to consider their own biases and the impact this may have on the space they are creating for the client (Pakes & Roy-Chowdhury, 2007).

Experience-sensitive

Life is more traumatic when the journey to becoming yourself is fraught. Attributing value to the individual, free from stereotypes and preconceived ideas, allows the client to truly feel safe and accepted within a therapeutic relationship. The interest we show in another individual indicates our acceptance and willingness to know and value their narrative. Just like a pot of marbles, every time we dip our hand into the glassy contents, we pull out a different marble. Each one reflects the light in a different way, each one contains its own unique pattern, and each one is part of the unified pot. With more and more evidence and research showing the link between autistic people being misperceived by the allistic (non-autistic) majority and being at risk of poor mental health and well-being as a result, your awareness and understanding of the role that double empathy plays in talking therapy is crucial. What assumptions do you make about a client if they prefer not to have eye contact? If they are echolalic (repeat others' words/sentences)? If they are situationally mute? If they like to hold a fidget toy? If they rock their body? Would you suggest they can wear a baseball cap or sunglasses when they meet you to adjust for sensory input? If not, why? Take time to reflect with your client, with supervision and in your reflective journals what may be the role and the impact of the double empathy problem – do you hold expectations and norms that are different from your patient's? What are these? Do you incorrectly assume they need to comply with neuro-normative rules? What rules do you model? Which ones may be helpful/harmful? How can you find out? An "experience-sensitive approach" (Pavlopoulou, 2021) promotes a sense of agency, and identifies strengths, barriers, and needs, to support well-being and to create opportunities for the person to flourish authentically, living their best life, according to their own norms. This is key in order to ensure that reasonable adjustments to access and getting involved in therapy are enabled.

Neurodiversity affirming

Shifting from a disorder to a neurocognitive difference or disability is necessary for the long-term well-being and empowerment of autistics (Walker, 2021), as explained in Chapter 1 by Amy. To affirm neurodiversity, we have to approach the individual not from a diagnostic, deficit-driven approach but from a non-pathologising position. We are affirming differences and celebrating the strengths of each person, involving them in self-exploration and supporting this process non-judgmentally. This factor is embedded into every other aspect of clinical practice discussed here and throughout this book and is starkly illustrated by many of the authors in the book.

Double empathy

Therapists tend to see themselves in a positive light. While we may struggle with feeling like an impostor at times, in that we feel we do not always feel confident that we know what we are doing, there can also be a sense that we know more than we think. As such, we therefore plod on with therapy regardless, not checking in with the client (Lambert, 2010). The therapist's training may look at the fundamentals of managing relationships, but every client produces a unique opportunity to build a relationship. With autistic CYP, this process of relationship building may be impacted by the double empathy problem (Milton, 2012). The double empathy problem is embedded in the lack of communication or recognition that there may be differences in views or perspectives with biases and experiences on both sides affecting the formation of the relationship. These issues are not addressed by avoiding them, but by acknowledging any mistakes and showing an acceptance to learn together. Ros Law writes very openly about her own learning in Chapter 12, which came from a genuine desire to develop and grow from a neurotypical to a neuro-informed therapist. This willingness to apply effort and to acknowledge the work that autistic people put into understanding and navigating the neurotypical world, and to make genuine attempts to meet this level of effort, is essential for therapist growth. CYP Improving Access to Psychological Therapies programmes emphasise the importance of collaboration, often with a focus on outcomes, but this collaboration should start with the formation of the relationship through openness and honesty, which should be modelled by the therapist. Talking therapy is designed around allistic thinking styles and doesn't consider that many autistic people struggle with sensory processing and alexithymia. An autistic person in talking therapy might not show or display the emotions that are socially expected of them in a session and may process, describe, and recognise their emotions differently from an allistic person.

With more and more evidence and research showing the link between autistic people being misperceived by the allistic majority and being at risk of poor mental health and well-being as a result, your awareness and understanding of the role that double empathy plays in talking therapy is crucial.

Collaborative

Taking a collaborative approach to the work means including the CYP at every point in the therapeutic journey. This collaboration empowers the CYP and values their unique view, beliefs, and wishes for the time they are investing in the work with the therapist. For many CYPs, coming to see a therapist may not have been high on their agenda of things to do each week; rather they may have been brought in by a well-intentioned adult keen for them to change. Collaboration then means tuning in to the needs and wishes of the client so they can be part of shaping the time together to meet their goals, which may just be not being made to come anymore. Collaboration, in such circumstances, might involve extending beyond the referred client to involve the family and community system that the YP exists in. It is not a one-off exercise but a continuing mutual system of support for the work, including regular review and evaluation each step of the way, identifying progress, or not, and planning the next steps.

Empowerment, choice, and control

The principle of collaboration ensures that clients are able to feel and exercise a sense of empowerment in their treatment, and this process comes through having the information they need and a sense of safety to make choices, backed by the belief that these will be respected. When empowerment, choice, and control do not exist in the relationship, it becomes unsafe and potentially traumatic. It's quite common for autistic people to feel like they only managed to flourish in adulthood, and a key element of this is more freedom – freedom to arrange your environment and daily routine to your needs. An autistic CYP has a limited capacity to change their schedule, escape overwhelming sensory environments, or pursue their authentic interests. They may be stuck with teachers who don't understand them or peers who bully them. This can lead them to feel like there is nothing to do to escape this situation or change it for the better. It's immensely helpful to have someone with whom it's possible to discuss possible alternatives or ways to implement adjustments in their present situation. Traumatic experiences can be alleviated by providing clients with appropriate choice and control in any therapeutic work where decisions are shared and the client's strengths and abilities are recognised, empowering them to make appropriate choices.

The approach

When we have found ways to integrate the factors above to create a safe, containing, and collaborative relational space, we rely on the support of the service to maintain this approach beyond the client with which we are working and to extend to all clients.

Multiservice

Services have a responsibility to work together. If we become a silo concentrating just on our work with no consideration or acknowledgement of other services that our CYP encounter, we stand to not only fail in our attempts to offer support or a clinically effective intervention, but also increase the chance of a relapse or deterioration in the client's well-being. As a community, we all play our part in the awareness, acceptance, and support of mental health services and Autistic CYP. When services are not connected, they are operating in a corporate survival state. The neuroception discussed above exists at this level, where managers and service cultures look to see how safe they feel in themselves, between themselves and other organisations, and in the economic and societal environment. What we need to create for CYP in our services is what our society also must create for caregivers and caregiving services. Promoting connectedness between social care, education, health care, and emergency services is essential to provide 'wrap around' mental health care (DOH, 2015).

Trauma-informed

For autistic CYP, the risk of exposure to adversity and potentially traumatic experiences is immense. Adopting trauma-informed practice within services is becoming the new trend, but with this comes the need to understand the autistic experience of trauma. Jon Adam's chapter graphically highlights his own traumatic experiences through life and through the subsequent care he was offered. Without a trauma-informed approach, we cannot be truly understanding of the experience of autistic CYP. At its essence is the simple switch from focusing on 'what is wrong with you' to a compassionate interest in 'what is your experience or your sense of what has happened to you'. This question, although trauma-informed, should be delivered thoughtfully as it may be perceived as overwhelming and nonspecific. What is needed is a more holistic approach that sees how experiences interweave, since being autistic cannot be separated out from that. Helen Minnis has researched for many years the overlap between trauma and neurodiversity to the point that she recommends that every CYP presenting with trauma is assessed for neurodivergence and every neurodivergent child is assessed for trauma (Minnis, 2013). Being trauma-informed is not simply one question, but a curious approach that transcends all we do.

Increasing knowledge of neurodiversity

Therapists have an ethical responsibility for continual professional development. Accrediting bodies and professional organisations expect that we will keep abreast of new research and developments in practice within the mental health field. It is equally important that we spend time learning about our clients. Taking an interest in the subject of neurodiversity beyond a therapeutic encounter is to honour those who will next visit you. This knowledge comes from every autistic person you meet or work with, as well as from others who work in the field. Indeed, earlier in this book Kieran Rose and Ros Law reflect on the process of learning that therapists go through and how important the commitment to deepening one's understanding of neurodiversity knowledge is for the benefit of clients and therapists alike. In 2022, NHS England funded the Anna Freud Centre to run the National Autism Trainer Programme (NATP), in partnership with AT-Autism. This is fully co-produced and co-delivered with autistic people, aiming to close the gap in professionals' skills, knowledge, and attitudes towards autistic people. NATP offers a humanising approach, differentiating it from many established or traditional courses where the major focus is on the clinical features of autism and how these are regarded and responded to. NHS expects members of staff to become NATP-qualified trainers in order to support their colleagues to inform practice through an examination of perceptions of autism. It offers insights and practical strategies drawn from autistic and trauma-informed experiences, whilst acknowledging the challenges faced by autistic people and staff working across different settings. It is important to support staff understanding of the value of modelling collaborative, relational, and person-centred values, with colleagues and with the autistic people they support, and to promote a balanced narrative about neurodiversity.

Masking and acculturation

We explored the difficulty in feeling safe enough to explore self-identity. Masking and acculturation are examples of when identity is hidden from sight either by pulling a veil across how you act and respond to events in the world or by changing your identity to assimilate into a different culture and therefore adopting behaviours that are not congruent with that innate sense of who you are or wish to be. While we all manage the way we present to the world depending on the social context, some people are forced to adopt this approach daily. As discussed by Kieran Rose and Julia Avnon, autistic masking is a trauma response to the environment rather than a choice of behaviour. In a sense, it is safer to conform. This behaviour, they point out, is a demanding process at a physical and mental level and can lead to burnout or mental health difficulties. No one thrives when they are perceived as broken, 'other', or disordered. It is likely that people come to therapy not to address their autistic identity but because they struggle with their mood, sleep, and stress levels. Allowing them to be unapologetically autistic in the session helps them to start unmasking their real self so that they can then work with you on mental health concerns and reflect on what works/what does not work.

Family and sibling needs

Every young person exists within a system, whether that be with parents, in what is considered a traditional family set-up, or living within the care system and sharing attachment figures with a group of children. As we have seen in earlier chapters (e.g., by Andrew McDonnell, and later by Nikita K. Hayden and Clare Kassa), the experience of the wider system (family and siblings) is important in understanding the needs of the individual CYP but also in supporting them. When a person is in distress, the ripples can be experienced throughout the system that the person resides in. These ripples will vary in intensity for each family member, but each one will feel the ripples in some way. Acknowledging and offering support to the system is therefore an essential component of the work. In a recent conference run by Sibs Charity, Heba Jayoosi explained 'I am hurt when my brother is hurt'. Services need to be able to include and recognise the needs of all family members and include supportive work to promote the best outcomes for all.

Challenging bias

As therapists, we should be able to be aware of, and reflect on, our work and interaction with autistic people. For many, this is part of routine clinical notes, for others maybe it is confined just to assignments when training. Embracing difference with compassion and recognising, naming, and challenging bias needs to become part of the new service culture as Richard Mills mentions in

Chapter 11. It is hoped that those reading these chapters will grab the flaming torch of change and instigate new ways of thinking within their services. This is no simple task and does require us to adopt an anti-deficit stance in our work, to identify where biases may exist (e.g., in its administration, its referral process, its recruitment) and challenge the appropriateness of these beliefs. This is not about pointing accusatory fingers in people's direction, but about questioning and being curious about the biases as they present to create an environment where a new approach is supported by all the staff who wish to grow, learn, and develop together.

Low arousal

One of the authors worked for a time in an old NHS community building. The upstairs where the CAMHS team were based was a long corridor flanked on both sides by inhospitable rooms with metal frame single-glazed windows that rattled when the wind blew. In the waiting room, the sound of the dentist drilling downstairs could be heard. Sirens from the police station a few hundred metres away were constant, the smell of old carpets, antiseptic, and traffic fumes permeated the brickwork. It was not a pleasant place to work and efforts to paint the waiting room using some leftover cans of paint bought from home one Sunday was frowned upon by senior management. It was a place of high arousal for many staff and patients. Adopting a low arousal approach (as discussed in Andrew McDonnell's chapter) is not solely about environmental conditions but rather taking the time to reflect on the conditions, events, or situations that for our individual clients may be highly arousing. Taking a low arousal approach means committing to working to gain an understanding of the child's perspective and helping them to stay within their window of arousal (Ogden et al., 2006). It is within this space of emotional safety that the executive functioning areas of the brain are online, where we can communicate, learn, and develop. This may require us to think about the length, frequency, and content of sessions, our administration processes, the way we use routine outcome measures, and the way we work together as a team.

The *Space* and the *Approach* provide two lenses through which to consider the role that you and your service play in the support of autistic CYP. The approach is not enough on its own without the therapist's and service's ability to create the space in which genuine connections can be made with the CYP requiring support, and this space is not enough on its own without the commitment of the service to adopt an approach that allows for an understanding of the uniqueness of the individual. Focus on the two can help to sharpen the overall picture so they produce an integrated whole neuro-informed approach (see Figure 15.3).

Whilst this does not provide all the answers, the hope is that in pulling together the key points, laid out so eloquently by the contributors to this book,

Figure 15.3 Bringing services into focus.

we can at least begin a united journey of discovery that promotes significant and lasting change to the experience of mental health services for autistic CYP and their families.

On a final note

In this final section, a young person reflects on her own apprenticeship, expressing concerns about the neuro-normative expectations of staff whom she had not previously questioned. She provides examples of young people feeling overwhelmed and questioning the perspectives adopted by staff. She hopes that many professionals will read the book to prompt them to consider their unconscious biases and deepen their understanding of autistic individuals.

I have spent six and a half years in therapy, with numerous therapists and therapies, a dozen medications, chemical treatment, hypnosis, and any other method you can think of under the sun to treat depression and anxiety. Who would have known that the best treatment I ever received was my autism diagnosis? I began to be able to help myself significantly now that I knew the real causes and solutions to my stress. Thanks to my diagnosis, therapy began working significantly better once I realised that phone call therapy proved the least mentally taxing since masking was second nature; even with a therapist. No wonder the past techniques of exposure therapy to anxiety triggers had made me even worse. Autism is not anxiety and being treated as such only led to masking. The label of autism was my saving grace, the answer to a lifelong question but because of the ignorance I had internalised, I felt like I was entering adulthood with a big red stamp on my head by society, labelling me 'redacted'.

In my experience as an autistic working with autistic and non-autistic people, I began to understand a neurotypical point of view. Some of my coworkers discussed a young boy who had low self-esteem. To them, they felt that the boy knowing his label of autism was what had caused him to have a negative view of himself and that autistic youth shouldn't be too aware and therefore limited by the label. As a fellow autistic, I understood far too well, that the lack of understanding about autism and the intolerance of difference by the people around him was what had truly limited him. If he had not been judged under neurotypical standards but instead accepted for his autism, he may have felt normal and understood, by his unique standards. I believe that autistic is what you are not something you happen to have like a sweater you can choose to wear when it's comfortable too. Autism is not inherently harmful, it's society's lack of acceptance and inclusivity that is. One of these same coworkers deemed me to be high functioning by the fact that no one had spotted I was autistic at work. This favoured others' experience of me over my own experience to define who I was and what I needed. Because I seemed like I didn't struggle (because I performed well with accommodations) they treated me like a non-autistic person without properly considering my needs. This later led to a massive meltdown which made me severely suicidal. This is the type of label that limits autistics as it stops them from being able to be seen as a person with a whole spectrum of experience. If I had been deemed as 'low functioning' and perceived as 'autistic enough', would they have made the same mistake?

It's important to remember that every person is unique and therefore has different needs according to their own, individual human experience. While diagnoses give you a good starting basis for how to specially cater the way to teach and communicate for each person, you need more than Knowledge. You need to listen to truly understand and not just respond. Do not under or overestimate anyone. I find that one of the biggest mistakes people make with supporting neurodivergent clients is that they base someone's support needs or level of 'struggle', on how 'uncomfortable' they make the worker feel. Just because a client verbally stims loudly or is non-verbal, does not mean they are 'more severe' than a client who seems 'socially better'. This can lead to the first type of client being underestimated and infantilised which can send a message to the client that are they not seen as capable or taken seriously which makes them limited. This puts the worker at a real disadvantage of being able to see just how many strengths, and talents, this person would show if they were regarded as the intelligent adult they are, and nurtured with an open mind and the patience to allow them to show who they are without harmful preconceptions. On the other hand, clients who are perceived to 'perform' better socially, may be doing exactly that, a performance. The ability to mask or even to be experienced as more socially palatable for neurotypicals does not mean a client doesn't need just as much support as the client harmfully labelled 'difficult'. Neurodivergency is a spectrum that affects all different parts of someone's life. By overestimating them and invalidating their 360 experience, you may miss other sides of their disability that they do need support with. By making them feel like they can't communicate this or that their needs are less important, you teach them to mask which means they may struggle alone and even experience mental health problems. So don't be ignorant and make quick judgements, everyone deserves to be supported so that they can lead a life which makes them feel seen for all parts of who they truly are.

References

Bordin, E. S. (1979). The generalizability of the psychoanalytic concept of the working alliance. *Psychotherapy: Theory, Research & Practice, 16*(3), 252–260.

Davis, D. E., DeBlaere, C., Owen, J., Hook, J. N., Rivera, D. P., Choe, E., ... Placeres, V. (2018). The multicultural orientation framework: A narrative review. *Psychotherapy, 55*(1), 89. https://psycnet.apa.org/doi/10.1037/pst0000160

England, N. H. S. (2015). *Future in mind: Promoting, protecting and improving our children and young people's mental health and wellbeing.* London: Department of Health.

Hughes, D. (2017). Dyadic developmental psychotherapy (DDP): an attachment-focused family treatment for developmental trauma. *Australian and New Zealand Journal of Family Therapy, 38*(4), 595–605. https://doi.org/10.1002/anzf.1273

Kase, R. (2023). *Polyvagal-informed EMDR. A neuro-informed approach to healing.* New York: Norton.

Lambert, M. J. (2010). Prevention of treatment failure: The use of measuring, monitoring, and feedback in clinical practice. *American Psychological Association.* https://doi.org/10.1037/12141-000

Lambert, M. J., Bergin, A. E., & Garfield, S. L. (1994). The effectiveness of psychotherapy. *Encyclopedia of Psychotherapy, 1*, 709–714.

Ludlow, C., Hurn, R., & Lansdell, S. (2020). A current review of the children and young people's improving access to psychological therapies (CYP IAPT) program: Perspectives on developing an accessible workforce. *Adolescent Health, Medicine and Therapeutics*, 21–28. https://doi.org/10.2147/AHMT.S196492

McGreevy, E., Quinn, A., Law, R., Botha, M., Evans, M., Rose, K., ... & Pavlopoulou, G. (2024). An experience sensitive approach to care with and for autistic children and young people in clinical services. *Journal of Humanistic Psychology, 1,* 27. https://doi.org/10.1177/00221678241232442

Mental Health Taskforce. (2016). *The five year forward view for mental health.* London: Department of Health and Social Care.

Midgley, N. (2022). Anna Freud – advocate of the Child. *The Psychologist.* British Psychological Society. Retrieved from: https://www.bps.org.uk/psychologist/anna-freud-advocate-child

Milton, D. E. (2012). On the ontological status of autism: The 'double empathy problem'. *Disability & Society, 27*(6), 883–887. https://doi.org/10.1080/09687599.2012.710008

Milton, D. E. (2014). Autistic expertise: A critical reflection on the production of knowledge in autism studies. *Autism, 18*(7), 794–802. https://doi.org/10.1177/1362361314525281

Milton, D. E. (2016). Disposable dispositions: Reflections upon the work of Iris Marion Young in relation to the social oppression of autistic people. *Disability & Society, 31*(10), 1403–1407. https://doi.org/10.1080/09687599.2016.1263468

Minnis, H. (2013). Maltreatment-associated psychiatric problems: An example of environmentally triggered ESSENCE? *The Scientific World Journal, 2013.* https://doi.org/10.1155/2013/148468

Núñez, L., Midgley, N., Capella, C., Alamo, N., Mortimer, R., & Krause, M. (2021). The therapeutic relationship in child psychotherapy: Integrating the perspectives of children, parents and therapists. *Psychotherapy Research, 31*(8), 988–1000. https://doi.org/10.1080/10503307.2021.1876946

Ogden, P., Minton, K., & Pain, C. (2006). *Trauma and the body: A sensorimotor approach to psychotherapy* (Norton series on interpersonal neurobiology). New York: WW Norton & Company.

Pakes, K., & Roy-Chowdhury, S. (2007). Culturally sensitive therapy? Examining the practice of cross-cultural family therapy. *Journal of Family Therapy, 29*(3), 267–283.

Todres, L., Galvin, K. T., & Holloway, I. (2009). The humanization of healthcare: A value framework for qualitative research. *International Journal of Qualitative Studies on Health and Well-being, 4*(2), 68–77.

Wolpert, M., Harris, R., Hodges, S., Fuggle, P., James, R., Wiener, A., ... Munk, S. (2019). THRIVE framework for system change.

Index